AMERICA AND THE AMERICANS—IN 1833–4.

AMERICA AND THE AMERICANS—IN 1833–4.

BY AN EMIGRANT

RICHARD GOOCH

Edited, with an Introduction and Notes, by
RICHARD TOBY WIDDICOMBE

Fordham University Press
New York
1994

LC 94–25157
ISBN 0–8232–1594–6 (hardcover)

Library of Congress Cataloging-in-Publication Data

Gooch, Richard, 1791–1849.
America and the Americans in 1833–4, by an emigrant / Richard Gooch ; edited, with an introduction and notes, by Richard Toby Widdicombe.
p. cm.
Includes bibliographical references.
ISBN 0–8232–1594–6.
1. United States—Social life and customs—1783–1865. 2. New York (N.Y.)—Social life and customs. 3. United States—Description and travel. 4. New York (N.Y.)—Description and travel. 5. Gooch, Richard, 1791–1849—Journeys—United States. I. Widdicombe, Richard Toby, 1955– . II. Title.
E165.G63 1994 917.304'56—dc20

94–25157
CIP

Printed in the United States of America

To Jill
with gratitude and love

CONTENTS

LIST OF ILLUSTRATIONS

PREFACE

The author of "America and the Americans," Richard Gooch, remarks in *Facetiae Cantabrigiensis* that he is "a mortal enemy to *long prefaces*" (ii). I cannot but agree, and yet it is important that I tell the story of how I came to edit *America and the Americans*.

A little over ten years ago I was planning a research trip to Britain to investigate what British libraries possessed by way of little-known texts about American culture. Crick, Alman, and Raimo mentioned Gooch's manuscript, so I decided to take a look at it. I fondly hoped that it would talk about the New England Transcendentalists. It didn't, but it did say some scurrilous things in an original, abrasive way about a culture in formation. I made some photocopies of representative pages—text and illustrations—and moved on to other, better-known archival material: letters by Theodore Parker, essays by Ralph Waldo Emerson, and so on.

Eight years passed, and I spent much of my time doing what was demanded of me by myself and others: getting my doctorate, building my career, moving around the country with the frequency of an Army brat, publishing as often as was good for me. Nevertheless, I took a look at the Gooch manuscript occasionally and delved around a little to find out who Richard Gooch was. The truth is, however, that I probably wouldn't have done much more than this desultory puttering around had I not audited a class taught by Beth Witherell, the Editor-in-Chief of the Thoreau Project. She showed me the fascinations and complexities of textual editing, showed me that there are serious but little-understood intellectual issues involved in putting out an edition of a text. I read Jerome McGann's *Critique of Modern Textual Criticism* and found it unimpressive: illogical, poorly argued, slight. I read Tanselle and Bowers and enjoyed the rigor of their arguments and the exactness of their scholarship. I examined Henry Binder's edition of Crane's *Red Badge of Courage*, found weaknesses in it, and felt—probably wrongly, possibly arrogantly—that I could do better.

It was at about that time, too, that I became seriously interested for the second time in my "career" in deconstruction and the idea of canon formation and the marginalizing of discourse. I admired the rebelliousness of poststructuralism, and—coming as I do from a generation of scholars marginalized by demographics and academe itself—had some fellow feeling for those who had been marginalized. Suddenly, I realized that an edition of "America and the Americans" was what I really wanted to do. It would challenge me, teach me much about the byways of American and British culture (the sorts of artefacts and issues that New Historicism valorizes and New Criticism, in its many guises, neglects), and restore something that did not deserve to be forgotten—or, better, completely ignored—even by the experts on travel literature and Anglo-American relations: Gooch's account of the United States at the dawn of the American Renaissance. I've tried to incorporate these realizations in the way I've presented the text, and in the detail provided in the textual and historical notes. I've tried to share my enthusiasm with the reader. I hope I've succeeded.

I have had more fun with this project than with anything else I've done in academic life—more fun than was decent, perhaps. It matters little that Gooch seems from everything I've found out to have been unpleasant and pedantic, aristocratic in the worst possible way. It matters only that I have come to know him well, and, so, to know myself a little more.

ACKNOWLEDGMENTS

This book would not have been possible in anything like its present form without the help of numerous people and institutions. The list of those who helped me by responding to my inquiries, by finding abstruse texts for me, and by guiding me away from numerous pitfalls is a long one indeed.

I'd like to thank W. W. S. Breem, Librarian and Keeper of the Manuscripts at the Honourable Society of the Inner Temple in London; Tod J. Butler, Chief of the General Reference Branch of the Textual Reference Division of the National Archives in Washington, D.C.; G. D. Bye, Head of the Photography Department at Cambridge University Library; Kathleen Cann of the Department of Manuscripts at Cambridge University Library; R. G. A. Chesterman, Assistant Archivist at the Chester Record Office; R. N. Chrystal, Assistant Service Manager of the Life and Pensions Division of the Scottish Equitable in Edinburgh; Phillip Clayton-Gore at the Public Record Office on Chancery Lane in London; Christopher Date, Assistant Museum Archivist at the British Museum; Jeff Feinsilver at the Wisser Library of New York Institute of Technology on Long Island; Lilian Gibbens, Westminster Heritage Researcher for the City of Westminster; Victor Gray, County Archivist at the Essex Record Office in Chelmsford; Jim Green, Curator of Printed Books for the Library Company of Philadelphia; M. Halford, County Archivist at the Shropshire Record Office in Shrewsbury; D. J. Hall, Under-Librarian at Cambridge University Library; K. Hall, County Archivist for the Lancashire Record Office in Preston; Jeannette Harkin, Librarian at the Supreme Court Library of the Royal Courts of Justice in London; R. J. H. Hill, Senior Librarian at the Hereford City Library; Guy Holborn, Librarian at Lincoln's Inn Library in London; Gillian C. Howarth of the Public Information Office at the House of Commons; Sue Hubbard, Assistant County Archivist for the Hereford Record Office; Brian Hughes, Director of Education and Arts of the Metropolitan Borough of Bolton; Sue James of the Bodleian Library at Oxford; Kathryn Johnson, Curator of the Manuscript Collections at the British Library; Annette M. Kennett, City Archivist for Chester City Council; I. H. Kenrick, Research Assistant at the Royal Commission on Historical Manuscripts in London; A. J. McDonald of the Search Department at the Public Record Office in Kew; E. McNeill, Librarian and Keeper of the Records at the Honourable Society of the Middle Temple in

London; Barry Mills, Local Studies Librarian for the Department of Education and Arts of the Metropolitan Borough of Bolton.

Then, from the lower half of the alphabet, there's A. E. B. Owen, until recently Keeper of Manuscripts at Cambridge University Library; Dorothy Owen, Keeper of the University Archives at Cambridge; Malcolm B. Pratt, Sub-Librarian of St. John's College Library in Cambridge; Diane Raper of the Law Society's Library in London; D. B. Robinson, County Archivist at the Surrey Record Office in Kingston upon Thames; J. A. V. Rose of the Search Department of the Public Record Office on Chancery Lane in London; E. Shenton of the Search Department of the Public Record Office at Kew; Ellen Slack, Manuscripts and Archives Librarian for the Historical Society of Pennsylvania; Nicola Smith, Librarian at the Local Studies Library in Southwark; T. G. Smith, Librarian and Archivist of H.M. Customs and Excise Library in London; Kitty Uthe, Head of the Interlibrary Loan Office at the University of California at Santa Barbara; A. M. Wherry, Head of Record Services for the County Council of Hereford and Worcester; C. Wilkins-Jones, Local Studies Librarian at the Central Library in Norwich; and Roberta Zonghi, Curator of Rare Books at Boston Public Library in Massachusetts.

I'd also like to thank the librarians at the New-York Historical Society, where I did much of my research, and at the New York Public Library. Without those two resources, my research would have been much more difficult. I'm also grateful to the Syndics of Cambridge University Library for permission to publish the manuscript and the accompanying illustrations, and to the AAUP and New York Institute of Technology for providing me with a research grant by means of which to complete a substantial part of this book. I owe a great deal to Beth Witherell, Editor-in-Chief of the Thoreau Project, for showing me how fascinating textual editing could be. The greatest debt is to my wife, Jill, who has—at least figuratively—sat down to dinner for three for nearly a decade, save the mark!: myself; herself; and RG.

INTRODUCTION

GOOCH'S VISIT TO THE UNITED STATES: FACT OR FICTION?

I don't think I'm particularly suspicious by nature, so when I began to investigate the details of Gooch's visit to the United States I did so not from any sense that Gooch's account may have been invented, but rather, in the spirit of archival accuracy: I owed it to other scholars to be as accurate and thorough as time and resources would permit. It was only as my investigations continued that the possibility really began to take shape that Gooch had written an imaginary, highly satirical, impressively sustained portrait of America in the early 1830s instead of a travelogue based on firsthand experience.

My research enables me to present a significant amount of evidence both for and against Gooch's having visited the United States.

Evidence for Gooch's Visit

1. In the first chapter of *America and the Americans*, Gooch says that he embarked for the the United States "early in 1833" (7) and even specifies the packet on which he sailed, *The President*. He is similarly specific about when he left the United States: Volume I, Chapter X (50) mentions the date: late-May 1834. The word of a Tory high churchman of the period should, one assumes, be worth something.

2. Gooch gives many specific and vivid details about New York life that imply that he was an eyewitness to events. He spells some words phonetically ("enjoins" for "engines") in an effort to characterize the local New York dialect, an effort that suggests oral transmission and his presence in the United States. He includes, too, several newspaper clippings in the manuscript, some of which (such as a lengthy extract from *The Crisis*) were ephemeral enough to have been difficult to obtain except by his being there.

To such evidence, one can add some speculation:

3. Why would Gooch have lied? He was certainly rich enough and leisured enough to afford the trip; his eyewitness presence would be valuable in drawing his satirical portraits of Americans; he risked embarrassment or worse by perpetrating a hoax on his readers and publisher.

Evidence against Gooch's Visit

1. We know from the opening chapter of *America and the Americans* that Gooch says he arrived in the United States at the Port of New York. "The Index to New York Arrivals 1820–1846" (in the General Reference Branch of the National Archives and Records Administration in Washington, D.C.), which lists all those entering the United States via the Port of New York, contains only one reference to a Richard Gooch, and this reference fails to match the details of our author in all respects but one: gender! There are no indications that the "Index" is incomplete, and I have, moreover, checked the Index against that in the National Archives–Northeast Region to ensure accuracy. The government, then, has no record of Gooch's having visited the United States.

2. Gooch's comment that he left for the United States "early in 1833" on board *The President* must refer to that packet's sailing on February 22, 1833, from London, for the ship did not sail again from London to New York until after the middle of the year. *The New-York Commercial Advertiser* for April 1, 1833, notes its arrival at the Port of New York and fortuitously gives details of the voyage because it was an unusually arduous and lengthy one. After leaving London *The President* arrived at Portsmouth on February 27 "to repair damages, and land the crew of the brig Hannah, of Newry, for London, which came in contact with the P. in the Channel, on the night of the 22d, and immediately sunk—crew saved." On March 15, *The President* "exchanged signals with ship Charles Warton" and shortly thereafter "fell in with large fields of ice and several large icebergs" ("Arrived Since Our Last" [1 (col. 4)]). Gooch in his brief description of the voyage mentions none of these details, but mentions others that are much less noteworthy. It is true that he talks in Volume I, Chapter I of the trip being a "tedious" one, "during which the passengers were more than once on their knees, every moment expecting to 'go down,' as they phrase it" (8), but such a description sounds more conventional and hyperbolic than it does accurate and specific.

3. The passenger list for this voyage of *The President*, which has been archived among the "Ship Passenger Arrival Records" at the General Reference Branch of the National Archives, shows no record of Gooch in either first class or steerage. One name has been erased, but it would appear to be a false start for one of the first-class passengers, whose name is subsequently

written down again three lines below.[1] The passenger list indicates that there were 118 passengers in steerage. This figure hardly agrees with Gooch's comment in Volume II Chapter XVII that the packet contained "nearly 200 poor creatures" (166).[2]

4. The New-York Historical Society, a treasure trove of ephemeral information about New York City, has no references to Gooch whatsoever. If he did visit the city, he kept a lower profile than the text of *America and the Americans* suggests.

5. Gooch was supposedly in or on his way to or from the United States between early 1833 and July 1834. Yet, the Register of Readers in the British Museum's Central Archives indicates that Gooch was in England on July 18, 1833, renewing his six-monthly ticket (Letter to the author from Christopher Date).

6. The Gooch Collectanea at Cambridge University Library contains a marginal note to a story written by Gooch entitled "Peter Soames: or Bachelors All. A Tale of To-morrow, Yesterday, & Today." The marginal note reads: "Begun at the British Museum, the 14th day of March, 1834" (Add. Ms. Pt. 5 fol. 33). Gooch was supposedly in the United States until the summer of that year, probably July.

7. During 1833 and 1834 while he was supposedly in the United States, Gooch had three books published: *The Book of the Reformed Parliament*; *The Georgian Era* (the four volumes of which Gooch was—according to Gooch himself—the main editor); and the first edition of *Nuts to Crack*.[3] It is difficult to see how Gooch could have accomplished all this from across the Atlantic.

To such solid evidence, one can add some speculation:

8. Since almost all of Gooch's discussion is centered on New York during the months of March-May 1834, one has to wonder what he did in the United States from April 1833 until March of the following year. Some time could have been spent arranging for the 1835 American reprinting of his *Nuts to Crack* by E. L. Carey and A. Hart in Philadelphia, but such arrangements would surely not have been so time-consuming as to occupy him for a year.

To the question: Did Gooch visit the United States? there are some rather involved answers which square with *some* of the facts and speculations I've mentioned here. It is possible that Gooch visited the United States for a much shorter period than he claims in *America and the Americans* and that his arrival at the Port of New York went unrecorded because of a bureaucratic error or because Gooch for some reason traveled incognito. It is possible that *America and the Americans* is not by Gooch at all but was simply put in amongst the Gooch Collectanea by mistake, although it is surely impossible to explain away the fact that the handwriting in the other manuscripts grouped under Add. Ms. 2616 is the same as that in *America and the Americans* and, from irrefutable evidence, Gooch's.[4] It is possible to develop a scenario whereby Gooch produces *America and the Americans* as an amanuensis for, say, a relative or friend, but such a theory is highly implausible on commonsense grounds alone, even if we forget for a moment the weight of internal evidence against it.

The question of whether Gooch visited the United States as he claims he did is ultimately unanswerable. On the one hand, there is the archival material, which militates against Gooch's work being an eyewitness account. On the other, there are his numerous references to being in New York, a parody of Whitman's claim in "Song of Myself": "I am the man, I suffer'd, I was there" (l. 832). There is a remarkable narrative quality to *America and the Americans*. The standard practice of travelers such as Mrs. Trollope, Thomas Hamilton, or James Stuart was to write from experience; the operating method of those constructing guides for visitors—S. H. Collins, for example—was to inundate the reader with information. Data was a substitute for eyewitness description. Gooch adopted a different approach in creating his dystopia. He relied upon his skills as a raconteur and collector of anecdotes to gather together the observations and complaints of others (both published and unpublished) as well as his own. To this he added reportage from the accounts of newspapers such as *The Sun*, *The Man*, and *The Crisis*.[5]

The power behind *America and the Americans*, a power most evident in the many vivid descriptions of New York life, derives from Gooch's need to be convincing in order to persuade would-be emigrants from Britain of the error of their ways. He was moved, I think, to write *America and the Americans* for two reasons. First, he was increasingly unhappy with the decline in Tory fortunes during the 1830s; his account, then, is a contribution to the propaganda effort. Second, he was frustrated by the accounts of British travelers sympathetic to the United States. For him, such accounts were grossly misleading, and fundamentally unpatriotic because they encouraged emigration. Gooch may, indeed, have intended his account as a direct refutation of one text in particular: James Boardman's *America and the Americans*. Boardman's work was published in 1833; it portrayed the people of the United States sympathetically; it would have infuriated Gooch if he read it. Some structural similarities and verbal echoes between the opening sections of the two suggest that he may have. Indeed, one can view the coincidence of title as Gooch's pointed attempt to set the record straight as he saw it. If his purpose was to stem the tide of emigration, it scarcely mattered to him whether he visited the United States (why be distracted by firsthand information?). From any perspective, the question of whether Gooch's visit was fact or fiction is an intriguing one, one which adds a *frisson* to everything in *America and the Americans*. As a work of fact, Gooch's text is useful but predictable As a work of fiction, it is impressive, clever, even (in places) inspired.

Gooch's Viewpoint in *America and the Americans*

In *America and the Americans*, Richard Gooch tells a vitriolic tale of the United States and its citizens. His tale has a circular form: it begins with his voyage out to New York "early in 1833" (7); it ends with his return to England in late May 1834. His tale has substance: it discusses every important aspect of American society at that time. And it has a consistent viewpoint, too: that of the disappointed enthusiast. Gooch insists, disingenuously, at the beginning of his account that he voyaged out to the United States after being converted to an affection for the country by William Cobbett's *Emigrants' Guide* and its favorable report on American life. Indeed, he insists that he dislikes English society and English politics enough to consider America "the only land where all the Cardinal Virtues [are] to be found" (7).

Gooch's insistence is merely a narrative device intended to highlight by contrast his criticisms of the United States in the 1830s. Rather than a disappointed enthusiast, Gooch is actually a Tory apologist determined to slow the mass emigration to the United States from Britain by concocting an early nineteenth-century version of Dante's *Inferno* set in the New World. With topic after topic and issue after issue, Gooch lambastes American culture. Some of his charges are fair in substance if not tone, for American life was rude at this time in comparison to the sophistication of upper-class life in Europe; most are, however, highly satirical confections spun from the accounts of other travelers, from a selective reading of contemporary

American newspapers, and perhaps from his own eyewitness observations. Their primary value lies in what they reveal about Anglo-American relations a generation after the War of 1812. Gooch's account is, in the last analysis, so interesting because an English gentleman thought it necessary to defend English culture by writing a sustained polemic against a nation less than three generations old. Rather than respond to the criticisms of English life implicit in the mass emigration of members of the British working class, Gooch chose to vilify the country to which they traveled, hoping, presumably, to persuade those undecided would-be emigrants to reconsider. "Better the devil you know" is a phrase that comes to mind.

The late–twentieth-century reader will find some of what Gooch writes objectionable. His anti-Semitism, for example, is offensive. It is, however, typical of his time. Like all prejudice, some of this anti-Semitism is founded on the fear of difference. Some comes from another, more particular source: the misguided notion that the banking system was under Jewish control both in the United States and in Britain. In making his charges Gooch is careful—as he nearly always is—to quote chapter and verse from *American* newspaper stories. His inflammatory editorial remarks are, however, his own. He goes to no source but his own vicious prejudice when he offers the following analogy: "It is as natural for a multitude of Jews to be found where there is room for plunder, as it is for a multitude of birds of prey to scent carrion" (107). It says much about American society in the 1830s that Gooch was able to find overtly anti-Semitic stories from American newspapers with apparent ease; it says more that he felt such anti-Semitism might dissuade would-be emigrants from hazarding the voyage to the New World.

The late–twentieth-century reader will find something paradoxical, too, in Gooch's viewpoint. On the one hand, he is manifestly anti-Semitic, as even a glance at Volume II, Chapter VI will show. On the other, he is consistently harsh in his attacks on both the institution of slavery and American policy toward the Indians. He sustains such a perspective through three chapters (Vol. I, Chapters XIII, XV, and XVI). With regard to slavery, he criticizes Thomas Jefferson for fathering slaves, terms then-President Jackson "one of the largest slave-owners in America" (73), and comments in a highly emphatic way that George Washington may have been the "*father*" of the country but he also "died a Slave-Owner!" (82). More generally, he terms slavery obscene and savage and avers that "every American who upholds Slavery, and the barbarous policy they now pursue towards the poor negroes in the United States ought to have 'Traitor' branded on his forehead" (77). In relation to the treatment of Indians, Gooch excoriates the American government for its treatment of Blackhawk, among others. He calls American policy toward the Indian "selfish & barbarous" and "a stain on their [Americans'] character, as a civilized nation, of the blackest dye, Slavery excepted. . ." (63). He astutely comments: "They who were the original possessors of the soil are treated as outcasts & intruders" (67).

The paradox in Gooch's attitude to minorities is reasonably easy to resolve: Gooch is keen to exploit for his own purpose any evidence of American inconsistency. He constantly reminds his reader that slavery and the mistreatment of Indians goes on in a country whose constitution espouses equality. He hopes, I suspect, to sow some seeds of doubt in an emigrant's mind, to make him or her think: "If the American government fails to live up to its own ideal of equality, how can I be sure that *I* won't be mistreated?" He does not, however, believe that equality is morally or ethically right. That is very clear from his discussion of racial prejudice in American society. He may complain that the American constitution is "*infamous*" because it "bears *a lie* upon the face of it" (76). Yet, two chapters earlier he considered ideas of equality mere "*vapourings*" (63). In fact, Gooch disingenously uses prejudice as it suits him best. He appeals to anti-Semitism knowing that his reader may well believe such nonsense; he castigates slavery and the mistreatment of the Indian to score rhetorical points.

Gooch's strategy in *America and the Americans* is the very opposite of evenhanded reportage since he wants above all to assert the validity of the Tory dislike of the young republic. He gives a tiny amount with one hand; he takes vast swaths with the other. In this way he hopes to make his criticisms more convincing. He may not be disinterested, so his strategy suggests, but he is not entirely biased either. The first chapter effectively demonstrates his method. He begins by praising the Bay of New York as a "very fine one, spacious and deep." He finds "its general appearance . . . imposing," and he is clearly impressed that it is "capable of containing the largest fleet in the world" (8). Once he has landed in New York, he takes the time to comment that the hotels in Manhattan are "commodious & handsome" (9). This is the extent of what he likes about New York from his first impressions.

Ranged against these examples of measured praise for New

York are a litany of complaints. All the islands in the New York area (most obviously Staten Island and Long Island) present "a sorry picture to an eye accustomed to English Scenery" (8). The custom-house officials display "the characteristic surliness natural to their countrymen" and have the temerity to confiscate a parcel Gooch is carrying (9). The accommodations in the New York lodging houses are "disgusting" (9). Shoplifting is common. Half of the inhabitants of New York go to bed drunk (among them, women!). And, just in case the reader doesn't understand Gooch's viewpoint, he makes some harsh generalizations to drive the details home. His criticisms are "but a drop in the ocean of ills which every emigrant has to guard against" (10), for the American character is "malignant" (11). Indeed, Gooch concludes that "there never was a more sensitive or more revengeful character than that of an American" (12).

Gooch's perspective of the disappointed enthusiast yields some moments of marvelous detail and broad comedy. They have the heightened color of fiction, for they rise above their initial intention of dissuading would-be English emigrants from trying the voyage across the Atlantic. They stand on their own as brilliant set pieces. If these episodes were based on his own observations, then they were acutely done; if they were founded on the recollections of friends and acquaintances who visited the United States, he has made them convincingly real and immediate. Three in particular come to mind: May Day in New York (Vol. I, Ch. IV); New Year's courtship customs (Vol. II, Ch. I); and American food (Vol. II, Ch. V). The first of these contrasts the pastoral idyll of an English May Day with its urban equivalent in New York; the second satirizes the behavior of drunken young men determined to woo eligible young women; the third recounts the experience of dealing with some food that wouldn't go away. The last of these is the funniest and the most characteristic of Gooch's narrative strategy. It moves from the general to the particular; it uses telling details; it links recollections casually. Gooch comments:

> And here I am reminded that should you chance, at a boarding-house to begin the week with dining off a tough old American settler, in the shape of a goose, it is 10 to one but a portion of the same will, in some shape or other, be served up for Saturday night's supper. For your Americans are very clever at re-dishing up all sorts of things, much longer than they are *sweet*, and a peep into their kitchens, where there is

a want of order and economy, and a continual messing, hissing, frying, phizzing, stewing, and chopping, would, I fancy, satisfy any fastidious stomach for a week.

I recollect one day sitting down to a gander of the first water, on the first day of the week, felicitating myself on the treat which awaited me, mistaking it for an American roast goose. But upon trying my masticating powers, I gave up eating in despair, it was so tough. Of course I concluded I should see it no more. Supper came and there again was the gander. Gander again for the next day, dinner & supper. Well, I thought, there must be an end of it now. Alas! how deceitful are our anticipations. Our gander was the 3rd day served up for dinner in a pie, the remains of which graced the supper table. I was resolved to see no more of it, and to that end contrived to pocket a leg. But who shall say what to-morrow may bring forth—I had scarcely sat down to breakfast the following morning, when forth came the giblets of our gander, cooked I know not how, and they kept possession of the table for another day. I resolved there should, however, be an end of my tormentor, and between tearing & gulping, I spoiled the dish—nor did warrior ever triumph with greater glee over a fallen enemy, than I did in the final destruction of our American gander (101–102).

America and the Americans in Its Historical Milieu

It is hard for a reader at the end of the twentieth century to imagine what Richard Gooch's world was like. Now the United States is the most powerful country on earth; Great Britain is a minor island nation with the last few remnants of an empire in the guise of a commonwealth. Then the United States was a democratic experiment barely two generations old (the last surviving signer of the Declaration of Independence, Charles Carroll, didn't die until 1832); Great Britain was the most powerful country in the world, poised for sixty years of imperial consolidation and already the possessor of an empire the like of which has never been seen before or since.

If the two countries were on either end of a see-saw of historical rise and fall, they were at least together in ways that make them equally alien to us. Now both countries are urban; then they were rural. Now both countries have metropolises that are bursting at the seams; then New York and London were little more than messy agglomerations of villages. New York had barely been laid out past midtown Manhattan, and Central Park wasn't even a dream; London had few of the monuments for which it is famous. Trafalgar Square hadn't been completed; Buckingham Palace was being built from the former Buckingham House; the Tate Gallery site was occupied by Millbank Penitentiary.

More important, however, than the change in the urban skyline, more significant even than the radical change in global status for the two countries, are those social and cultural differences between historical periods which the modern reader easily passes over because it is so hard to question the "givens" of a particular historical epoch. On the one hand, there are the differences in everyday living that rarely make it into the history books but which matter so much to individual human experience, the sort that Daniel Pool (in *What Jane Austen Ate and Charles Dickens Knew* [1993]) and Christina Hardyment (in *Home Comfort* [1992]) so brilliantly analyze. On the other, there is the infrastructure we take for granted in the developed countries. It simply didn't exist 160 years ago, even though the populations of the two countries were much smaller then. Sanitation was inadequate and the water supply unregulated; as a result, cholera epidemics in both New York and London were depressingly frequent. The railways were in their infancy, and public transport as we think of it today almost nonexistent. Roads were at best macadamized with pulverized stone; as a result, they were dusty when dry and hopelessly muddy when wet. Industry was insufficiently regulated so that working conditions were, by modern standards, always arduous and sometimes dangerous. Medicine was primitive; indeed, it was not until the 1840s that anesthetics were used and not until decades later that the importance of antiseptics was understood. The result of all these differences? Life expectancy (which stands today at over 70 years for both sexes) stood in the late 1830s in Britain at 39.9 for men and 41.9 for women. In some industrial areas it was as low as *15* (McCord 212). The figures for the United States were little better.

These large–scale differences between the historical milieu of late Georgian England and that of the last decade of the twentieth century are important to an understanding of Gooch's *America and the Americans* because they lie behind the assumptions he unconsciously makes about what he sees and says. But a more pointed question about the historical context for Gooch's account needs to be asked. Was there anything about Jacksonian America that might explain the virulence of Gooch's anti-American sentiments, the intensity of his satire? The answer is resoundingly "yes."

By the time Gooch visited (or claims that he visited) the United States, Andrew Jackson was at the beginning of his second term in office, having in 1832 defeated the anti–Masonic nominee, William Wirt, and the National Republican ticket of Clay and Sergeant in "one of the most decisive 'victories' in the annals of American politics" (Van Deusen 68). Jacksonian democracy was a powerful force in American politics, and in 1833–1834 it was at its height. It is not hard to see what Gooch, as an Anglican Tory and a country gentleman, would have found offensive about it. The political philosophy associated with the ideas of Andrew Jackson has a few central tenets: freedom and equality of opportunity for white males; devotion to the needs of the common man; the construction of a society allowing for the accumulation of wealth; and anti-intellectualism. With regard to the last of these tenets, it is worth remembering Jackson's comment about someone whom he wished to replace in his administration: "'he is only fit to write a book and scarcely that'" (quoted in Morison 424). None of these characteristics would have made the United States an appealing place for Gooch or, from his perspective, a worthwhile destination for emigrants. The discussion of equality and the common man would have offended his country-gentleman ways; the idea that wealth should be available to anyone single-minded enough to acquire it would have appalled him because it struck at the class system. Most of all, Gooch, who followed politics closely enough to write books about it and edit partisan newspapers, would have been worried at what the opening of the franchise might do. He had already seen the Great Reform Act pass in Britain in 1832, an Act which increased the ratio of qualified male voters from 1 in 8 to 1 in 5 (Robbins 98–99). As a representative of agricultural interests, he would have been unhappy with the greater voice given to the emerging middle class in Britain. What was happening in the United States would have horrified him: between 1824 and 1840 the votes cast in the presidential election increased sevenfold, from 356,000 to 2,400,000 (Nevins and Commager 170). That horror comes out clearly in his discussion of the mayoral race in New York City in 1834 (see Vol. II, Ch. VIII).

And there were less savory aspects to Jacksonian democracy that Gooch would have found, after taking a stiff dose of humbug, equally unappetizing. As Kenneth Davis has remarked with only a modicum of exaggeration, Jacksonian democracy had a "flip side": "a new level of militant, land-frenzied, slavery-condoning, Indian-killing greed" (120). Gooch, whose single-minded intent with *America and the Americans* seems to have been to discourage British emigration to the United States, skewers Americans for their immorality over the slavery issue and the question of Indian removal, their hypocrisy over the idea of the common man being the common *white* male. Americans' treatment of minorities was a prominent issue when Gooch was writing his account of the United States. The movement to nullify the tariffs was dividing the North from the South in a way that presaged the Civil War; the Indian Removal Act of 1830 probably saved the Indians from extermination, but it was an extraordinarily callous, self-serving, and immoral Act. Gooch, in publicizing the treatment of Blackhawk and other Indian chiefs, capitalizes on the issue. His detestation of slavery, which *may* have been heartfelt, certainly benefited from the fact that Britain through the Slavery Abolition Act of 1833 had outlawed slavery in the British Empire.

Given Gooch's dislike of the tenets of Jacksonian democracy, it may at first seem odd that he likes Andrew Jackson so much as a President. Here personality may be as important as the historical context. He probably liked President Jackson's promotion of the spoils system, for Gooch himself certainly held on to the coattails of the Tory Party for more than a decade; indeed, as he complained once to Sir Robert Peel, he lost a fortune in so doing. He clearly liked Jackson's opposition to the Second United States Bank because Jackson was, he felt, opposing the moneyed interests and the intrusion of monopolistic business. More than this, he may have been able to see ahead the economic chaos that would result. He just as obviously admired Jackson's forthright, autocratic style of government, the style that earned him the unflattering nickname "King Andrew." He may, finally, have liked President Jackson because, from his (Gooch's) perspective, the result of his policies would, surely, discourage British immigration if only the British would understand what the United States was *really* like. As Samuel Eliot Morison has put it: Jacksonian democracy "catered to mediocrity, diluted politics with the incompetent and the corrupt, and made conditions increasingly unpleasant for gentlemen in public life" (424).

Jacksonian democracy was not the only cause for Gooch's detestation of most things American. Two other characteristics of American life at this time would have offended him greatly: the ubiquity of religion, and the idea of "manifest destiny." As a Church of England patriot of the first water, Gooch finds the evangelical strain in America distasteful, and he pokes fun at such manifestations of that spirit as camp meetings. It is in no way accidental that the longest chapter in *America and the Americans* (Vol. II, Ch. IX) is devoted to Church and State and, in particular, to the sensational trial of Rev. E. K. Avery for the murder of Sarah Maria Cornell. As a believer in the Established Church and the idea of religion as a buttress of government, Gooch finds it a "hopeless task to attempt to enumerate the tenets of the 365 sects of Fanatics that abound in America"(125). It is not so much, however, that the task is hopeless as that the sheer number of different religious groups suggests that religion means something different, perhaps disturbing, in American life from what it means in England. Robert Riegel in *Young America 1830–1840* has commented that for Americans at this time "Religion was not vague and remote, but of immediate an dvital importance, for men felt that God watched them every second with a searching eye, rewarding and punishing, advising and interfering. Man searched his conscience and pored over the words of Holy Writ to make sure that he was not offending a God who not only was loving but also could be terrible in His justice" (17). Gooch sees an opportunity here, I think, for dissuading would-be British emigrants from trying the passage to America: "Would you want to settle in a country that treats religion in this way?"

"Manifest destiny" dates as a phrase from 1845, but it was current as an idea much earlier.[6] And at this time, as Arthur Ekirch points out in *The Idea of Progress in America, 1815–1860*, the right of Americans to populate the continent and, by extension, to be a power in the world was not mere words but a dynamic, felt reality (37). This belief would have disturbed Gooch considerably for one very simple reason: it put the United States in direct competition with the British Empire as the major power on earth. It amplified the warning evident in the Monroe Doctine of 1823. As a patriot, Gooch would not brook such a challenge. His irritation fuels his discussion of the American government's attitude to both the Indian and the slavery issues. Gooch surely felt this hegemonic threat, for even in the 1830s the United States was "a bustling and kaleidescopic [*sic*] community, giving evidence of the nature and greatness of its future" (Riegel 22).

Gooch's focus is not, however, on all things American. He

manages to cover a great deal of ground in his polemic, but almost everything is viewed through the prism of New York, then as now the most populous city in the United States. The use of such a prism raises another question, one related to the discussion of Jacksonian democracy: Was there anything about New York in the 1830s that might explain the virulence of Gooch's anti-American sentiments, the intensity of his satire? The answer, once again, is "yes."

Some facts about New York may show why Gooch chose to expend so much energy on criticizing it in the harshest terms. Between 1815 and 1840, the city's population grew almost 300 per cent, and much of that was due to the one thing that Gooch wanted most to stop: immigration (Spann 2). In 1830, New York absorbed 14,000 immigrants; five years later that figure was 32,715; at the beginning of the next decade, 60,609 (a 20 per cent addition to the city's population in one year) (Patterson 109). Conversely, 60,000 Britons *emigrated* in 1830; 100,000 in 1832; and 130,000 in 1842. Of these, three-fifths were Irish (over whom Gooch would have lost little sleep) and two-fifths were English, Welsh, or Scots (McCord 213). The greatest wave of this tide of emigrants came to the United States, many of them to New York. Gooch didn't need to be a mathematician to know that the United States was for some reason more attractive to many Britons than the home country. It was this knowledge that led him to write *America and the Americans*.

New York would have worried Gooch too because of its commercial power. It was in no way the equal of London, for that city saw a sizable portion of the world's trade come through its port, and in 1830 two-thirds of Europe's merchant fleet was British (McCord 216). Nonetheless, Gooch could, I think, extrapolate, and he has to have been concerned at the growth in New York's commerce. In 1835, for example, New York City saw more than 1,000 ships from 150 foreign ports dock in lower Manhattan (Spann 2). Domestically it was well situated to control trade to New England and, via the Erie Canal, to the West. By 1840, the Port of New York dealt with more than half the nation's imports and almost one-third of its exports. It was, as Edward Spann has remarked, "the wonder of the commercial world and the chief American focus of North Atlantic trade" (2). In light of such statistics it is surely no surprise, given Gooch's purpose in his travel account, that he should at every opportunity berate the city for any fault he could substantiate and some that he couldn't.

This question about a causal connection between the historical milieu and Gooch's intense dislike for the United States may, however, be asked in another equally informative way: Was there anything going on at this time in Great Britain and, more particularly, London that might help to explain the peculiar tone of *America and the Americans*? Once more, the response is "yes."

Keith Robbins, in *Nineteenth-Century Britain: Integration and Diversity*, has pointed out that the English identity appeared "self-confident" at this time; after all, the English could point to "a national continuity within the same political frontiers over a longer period than any other contemporary European state" (8). Yet, Robbins continues, that self-confidence hid the fact of cultural difference. London since Cobbett's time and before had been resented by the rest of Britain; it was called the "the Great Wen" (quoted in Hibbert 177), a blight upon the land. There was a major division between the industrial North of England and the commercial South that only increased as the Industrial Revolution picked up speed. Most important, England was not Britain, although then as now the two terms were frequently conflated; indeed, England, Scotland, and Wales had only finally been unified as a political entity in 1801 by an Act of Union. Each country within the Union was separated by language and by custom, and even within England people from one part of the country were sometimes unintelligible by reason of accent to people from another region. In the particular as much as in the general, England was not a united country and neither was Britain: it was not until 1858 that the English counties were integrated into a common railway system (Robbins 25); it was not until 1880 that the country's myriad local, idiosyncratic time zones were standardized by Act of Parliament (Robbins 27). It is against this background of ethnic rivalry and division that Gooch's anxiety over English emigration to the United States needs to be read. Further English emigration threatened national identity; American linguistic innovations threatened the English language even as they ensured its globalization.

The fact that neither English nor British identity was set in the nineteenth century fueled Gooch's anti-American jingoism, and there were other events in England that must have troubled him, too. Indeed, his editorship in the 1830s of several provincial newspapers friendly to the gentleman farmer's cause indicates as much. In 1830, rural riots led to 2,000 men being arrested and no fewer than 19 being executed. In 1831, riots in Bristol led to 12 deaths and more than 100 injuries. In 1833, the Tolpuddle Martyrs tried to gain—via the Friendly Society of Agricultural Labourers—a just reward for their labor: they got only imprisonment and, for six of them, transportation to the penal colony in Botany Bay. In 1833, too, the Factory Act tried to address some of the workers' concerns by reducing the maximum work week for children to 69 hours. And in that same year, the National Political Union rioted at Cold Bath Fields in London. Finally, from 1834 to 1836, Robert Owen organized the Grand National Consolidated Trades Union to fight for workers' rights.

It was not, however, in labor relations alone that Gooch found cause for alarm. Increased urbanization and its attendant problems led, in 1829, to Robert Peel's Metropolitan Police Act and London's first organized police force and, in 1831–1832, to the first serious cholera epidemic in Britain. In 1833 the Coercion Act was passed to combat Irish unrest. In 1834 four Cabinet members resigned over the political handling of religious issues (McCord passim). In 1834, too, the symbol of British government, the Palace of Westminster, burned down (Hibbert 192). Gooch may be forgiven for feeling perhaps that the difficulties of life in Britain in the early 1830s when combined with the rosy misestimates of life in the United States by English propagandists demanded a response. *America and the Americans* is that response, an effort single-handedly to turn back emigration by pointing out—or, rather, pointing up—the hardships of life in America for the hordes of would-be emigrants.

One cannot help but be impressed by the single-minded intent of Gooch's jeremiad against the United States, and the tone of it should not obscure the fact that much of what he says is fundamentally accurate, albeit seriously exaggerated. Life in New York City was as gritty as he depicts it as being: from the pigs in the street to the rubbish everywhere; from the fires to the violent crime. New York was unpleasant for all but the richest few for one simple reason: it was growing too fast for the comfort of its inhabitants. And Gooch was right about the United States in general: its culture was not *at this time* the equal of England's or, for that matter, much of Europe's. What Samuel Eliot Morison said about the United States of 1850 applies even more to that country two decades before: it was "a pretty crude country . . . by present standards, or European standards of that era" (475). It was, as Robert Riegel remarks, "exhibiting the traits of adolescence" (22).

Nevertheless, one cannot help but feel also that Gooch might have taken the "glass houses" admonition seriously, might have looked more carefully at the historical milieu of contemporary England. New York was everything he said it was, but then London (where Gooch lived and from where he says he sailed in 1833) was just as bad. If one looks at only two of Gooch's favorite brickbats that he lobs at New York—rampant crime and inadequate sanitation—it is obvious how hypocritical he is.

In 1800—that is, a generation before Gooch wrote *America and the Americans*—more than 100,000 inhabitants of London supported themselves through crime and more than £2 million was lost each year to theft. According to Patrick Colquhoun, from whose work *A Treatise on the Police of the Metropolis* these figures are taken, it is "much to be feared that no existing power will be able to keep them [the criminals] at bay" (quoted in Hibbert 226). As to sanitation, it is worth remembering some facts about London's water supply at this time. First, it was in private hands and was turned on for only a few hours each week. Second, it was dependent on old elm pipes (some of which dated from the Elizabethan age) which frequently ruptured. Third, the major source of water, the Thames, was polluted (at mid century at least) by 278,000 tons of raw sewage per day (Hibbert 187; Pool 202, 31). Christopher Hibbert's description of the Thames gives the lie to Gooch's claims about New York's sanitation. According to Hibbert, the river was "greeny black" and "its consistency so thick that each time the tide went down a greasy, foul-smelling scum was deposited over the mud" (187). In a supreme irony, it was the Thames, the river that Gooch implies is cleaner than the East River and cleaner than the Hudson, that killed Gooch. On September 4, 1849, he died of cholera while living in a boarding house in Southwark; in all likelihood, he caught the disease from untreated drinking water drawn directly from the Thames.

America and the Americans in the Context of Anglo-American Travel Literature

It would be singularly redundant of me to sketch in the background to Gooch's account of the United States in the 1830s, for the story of Anglo-American travels in the nineteenth century has been well told many times. Cultural studies owes a significant debt to Henry Tuckerman, Jane Mesick, Max Berger, Allan Nevins, Peter Conrad, and Christopher Mulvey; each has in his or her own way described aspects of a transatlantic relation between two countries divided by a common language and joined by a divisive history.[7]

What I do need to do, however, is to assess the place of this previously unknown account of America in the 1830s within the established tradition. And it is an extraordinarily rich tradition. Mulvey numbers the nineteenth-century Anglo-American accounts alone in the "some hundreds" (3). A little more helpfully, Mesick, Berger, and Nevins provide extensive (although probably not exhaustive) bibliographies that list almost 300 British accounts of the United States between 1785 and 1860. Much more precisely, no less than twenty-six accounts of Britain's former colony were being written or were published while Gooch was, perhaps, in the United States; one of these even sported a title *almost identical* to Gooch's ms.[8] In the context of publishing in the late Georgian era, such prolixity represents a veritable boom. The details of those twenty-six are listed in the Bibliographies section in the back of this edition.

Sometimes, indeed, I can almost visualize a nightmarish scene in the Bay of New York on a day in 1833 or 1834: British travelers crowding on the dock, pen and paper in hand, observing the scene and writing about—among other things—their fellow Britons writing about each other . . . a sort of closed interpretive circle. In light of such competition, an obvious question arises: What does Gooch offer that the other travelers do not? My response is that *America and the Americans* constitutes a deliberate, sustained (albeit unsuccessful), and—in some particular regards—unique effort to reorient the British attitude to the United States at the dawn of the Victorian Age. It is certainly not the best account of American life during the 1830s (Martineau's *Society in America* is more thorough and authoritative), yet it is equally clearly more entertaining, substantial, and informative than many.

Gooch's account is more entertaining and useful than some

other British travelers' accounts of the early 1830s for a number of reasons. Because Gooch's text is organized topically, he avoids the awkward commingling of narration and exposition which detracts from the value of Power's *Impressions of America; During the Years 1833, 1834, and 1835* (1836) and Hamilton's *Men and Manners in America* (1833). Because Gooch adopts a polemical stance, he sidesteps both the awkwardness of Murray's balancing act in *Travels in North America During the Years 1834, 1835, & 1836* (1839) and the vapidity of Collins's *The Emigrant's Guide to . . . the United States* (1829, 1830). Because of his concentration on detail, he avoids the easy generalizations of Abdy's *Journal of a Residence and Tour in the United States of North America* (1835) and Henry Tudor's *Narrative of a Tour in North America* (1834). Because of the ubiquity of his focus, he avoids the narrowness of Shirreff's agricultural monograph *A Tour Through North America* (1835) and the partisan vitriol of Fidler's *Observations on Professions, Literature, Manners, and Emigration in the United States* (1833), a work that Allan Nevins has dismissed as containing "the jeremiads of . . . an ass" (*America Through British Eyes* 94).

In the Preface to *America and the Americans*, Gooch alludes to two contemporary works in the subgenre of British commentaries on American life which he feels his discussion supersedes: Basil Hall's *Travels in North America in the Years 1827 and 1828* (1830) and Mrs. Trollope's *Domestic Manners of the Americans* (1832). His feeling has some validity, for Hall's *Travels* is marked by political naïveté and prejudice, and Trollope's *Domestic Manners* by superficiality and cant. Even though Gooch's Tory sympathies put him in the same camp as Hall and Mrs. Trollope, his criticisms—many of them more extreme—are founded on more careful observation and on more extensive use of primary sources.

The discussions of early–nineteenth-century British travelers' accounts of American life broadly agree that the major British accounts of American life during the first half of the nineteenth century are those of William Cobbett (1818), Frances Anne Butler (Fanny Kemble) (1835), and Charles Dickens (1842). Each is demonstrably more significant than Gooch's account, yet Gooch's work does compare favorably with them in that his broad perspective, assertiveness, and attention to statistical detail counterbalance the weaknesses of the three: the narrow geographical and agricultural viewpoint of Cobbett's *A Year's Residence in the United States of America*; the hesitant, self-reflexive quality of Butler's *Journal*; and the impressionistic tendency of Dickens's *American Notes*.

Gooch's commentary presents a previously unknown interpretation of American culture. It helps in an understanding of the English view of the United States and, as a consequence, this country's view of itself. As Jane Mesick concludes in *The English Traveller in America, 1785–1835*: ". . . the detailed analysis of [the] English attitude toward the United States in the critical fifty-year period after the founding of the nation, cannot fail to make some contribution to our knowledge of American conditions at the time, and to present in a new and interesting light many of the institutions which we Americans have come to take more or less for granted" (345).

LIFE OF RICHARD GOOCH

The principal published sources of information about Gooch's life are three in number: Frederic Boase's biographical entry for Gooch's son, Richard Stephen St. George Heathcote Gooch in *Modern English Biography*; John and J. A. Venn's biographical note on Gooch in *Alumni Cantabrigiensis*; and Ralph Thomas's sketch of Gooch's life in *Notes and Queries*. Manuscript sources are also three: Gooch's letter of March 9, 1846, with memorial and testimonials to Sir Robert Peel (British Library Add. Ms.); Gooch's last will and testament, dated September 3, 1849 (Public Record Office); and the manuscript notes of Sir Robert Forsyth Scott, Master of St. John's College, Cambridge (1908–1933).

From these sources and from several others of lesser value, it is possible to construct a chronology of his life in some detail:

1791 or 1792	RG born in Norwich. He was the second son of Thomas G., Esq. of that city.
ca. 1809	RG publishes a rhymed arithmetic primer for young people entitled "Introduction to Arithmetic."[9]
1819	
November 16	RG admitted as a sizar at St. John's College, Cambridge.
1820	

October 7	RG's first day of residence.
November 13	RG matriculates.
1821	RG unsuccessfully submits a poem entitled "Evening" for the Chancellor's Medal, Cambridge University.
1822	
April	RG's "Letters from Cambridge. Letter I.—Water Parties" published under the pseudonym T– — in *The Brighton Magazine.*
August	RG's "Letters from Cambridge. Letter II. Breakfast Parties" published under the pseudonym T– — in *The Brighton Magazine*.
1823	RG's *The Cambridge Tart* published under the pseudonym Socius.
June	Unflattering reviews of *The Cambridge Tart* printed in *British Critic and Quarterly Theological Review* and *Blackwood's Edinburgh Magazine*.
1824	
October	RG's "The Confessions of a Cantab" published anonymously in *Blackwood's Edinburgh Magazine*
November	RG's "The Confessions of a Cantab. No. II" published anonymously in *Blackwood's Edinburgh Magazine*.
1825	RG's *Facetiae Cantabrigiensis* published under the pseudonym Socius.
October 19	RG leaves Cambridge University ("name off" as Sir Robert Forsyth Scott puts it in his ms. notes).
1827 March 15	RG readmitted to St. John's College, Cambridge as a pensioner.[10] Kept the Lent Term only.
November 12	RG admitted to the Middle Temple.[11] Pays customary £4.00 fine upon admission.
1829	RG's first son born: Richard Stephen St. George Heathcote Gooch.[12]
1830	RG's "Charity. A Sonnet" published in *Juvenile Forget-Me-Not*.
	RG's "The Tears of Virgil" published in

	Amulet.
1832	RG's *Redemption; the Song of the Spirit of Hiram; and Other Poems* published.
1832–1834	RG is main editor of *The Georgian Era*.
1833	
July 18	RG renews his six-monthly Reader's Ticket to the British Museum. At this time he is living at Pump Court, Temple.
1833–1834	RG in USA (he Claims) from April 1833 to late May 1834.[13]
1834	RG's *Nuts to Crack; or Quips, Quirks, Anecdotes and Facete of Oxford and Cambridge Scholars* is published. RG's *The Book of the Reformed Parliament* is published.
March 14	RG begins, while at the British Museum, a story entitled "Peter Soames: or Bachelors All. A Tale of to-morrow, yesterday, & today."[14]
1835	RG becomes editor of the *Bolton Chronicle*, and a friend of the Mayor of Bolton at that time, Stephen Blair.[15]
	RG's *Nuts to Crack* published in Philadelphia.
	RG's *Oxford and Cambridge Nuts to Crack* (the second ed. of *Nuts to Crack*) published.
March	RG's *Key to the Pledges of the New Parliament of 1835* published.[16]
March 21	RG renews his six-monthly Reader's Ticket to the British Museum. At this time he is living at 4 Brick Court, Temple.[17]
1836	RG's *The Masonic Melodist* published.[18] RG's *Facetiae Cantabrigiensis*, third edition, published.[19]
March 3	RG admitted to the Anchor and Hope Lodge of Freemasons in Bolton.[20]
1837	RG becomes editor of the *Chester Courant*.
	RG proposes the Honourable F. Dudley Ryder as the Conservative candidate for Chester at the General Election.[21]
1838	RG publishes in Hereford a series of twenty

	Letters in favor of the New Poor Laws.[22]
1840	RG becomes editor/publisher of the *Hereford County Press*.
1841	RG becomes editor/publisher of the *Ludlow Standard*.
April 3	RG founds the *Norwich and Norfolk Times and the General Advertiser*. At this time, he is living at 8 Exchange Street.
1842	
April 21	RG publishes the last issue of the *Norwich and Norfolk Times and the General Advertiser*.[23]
1843	
February 25	RG presents a memorial to the Lord Chancellor, Lord Lyndhurst, in an unsuccessful effort to receive a government appointment under the provisions of the New Bankruptcy Act. He applies too late. He is still attempting to secure the same position or a similar one as late as December 28, 1843.
June 21	RG presents a memorial to the Lords of Her Majesty's Treasury in an unsuccessful effort to be appointed to a lucrative position in the Customs. He is too old.
November 30 (?)	RG appointed by Sir Thomas Fremantle (First Secretary of the Treasury) to a lowly position of Treasury Extra Clerk in the Office of Receiver of Fines in the Customs.[24]
1844	
May 20	RG requests J. Bailey Junr., Esq., MP and W. L. W. Chute, Esq., MP to support his efforts to be appointed "official Assignee" (Letter, with Memorial and Testimonials, to Sir Robert Peel fol. 242). They do so, but the effort fails. RG is living at this time at 28 Stamford St. (presumably in Southwark, London).
1845	

March 18	RG presents to Lord Brougham & Vaux the draft of a bill entitled "A General Registration of All Charitable Bequests," for which he receives "some credit" (Letter . . . to Sir Robert Peel fol. 232).
March 27	RG's third and fourth children are born: Percy Blair, and Ruth. At this time he is living at 3 Southampton Court in Middlesex (in what is now a part of London): Registration Sub-district, St. George Bloomsbury; Registration District, St. Giles and C.[25]
1846	
March 9	RG presents a memorial to Sir Robert Peel requesting "promotion to some appointment where my abilities may be better appreciated" (Letter fol. 234). RG receives a reply on March 12. At this time (and certainly until June 25 [?]), RG is able to receive cards at 29 St. James Street, Piccadilly.[26]
June 15	RG unsuccessfully tries to be appointed Store-Keeper in the Chatham Dockyards.
June 25 (?)	RG writes again to Sir Robert Peel (who was soon to leave office) requesting that he "may not be overlooked in the filling up of any vacant offices" (Letter fol. 225). His request is unsuccessful.
1847	
February 5–10	RG's library is sold by Puttick and Simpson, 191 Piccadilly, London. Number of items, 1,405; total value of sale, £391.14s.[27]
1848	RG's *Confessions of the Faculty* published under the pseudonym Socius.
1849	
September 3	RG makes his last will and testament.
September 4	RG dies, of cholera. He was living at this time at 22 Blackfriars Road in the county of Surrey (now the Borough of Southwark in London).[28]
1850	

March 5	RG's last will and testament is duly witnessed by Sarah Gerard, who lived at the same address as RG.
March 8	Ann (or Anna) Gooch, RG's wife, appointed curatrix of the will's executor, RG's son Frederick Mackellar, since he is a minor.
1887	
July 12	RG's mss. presented to the Cambridge University Library by Dr. H. R. Luard of Trinity College, University Registrary from 1862–1891. The provenance of the Gooch mss. is unknown; the mss. presented by Luard form Add. Ms. 2616: RG's Collectanea.[29]

NOTES

1. The apparent reason for the deletion and re-entry of the passenger's name (Sherman Converse) offers an interesting sidelight into customs of the age (with regard to first-class passengers at least). The shipping clerk began by listing the name of a gentleman; he had to erase it because good manners demanded that the names of the ladies (in this case Maria H. Bankhead and Lydia E. Kelley) be listed before those of the gentlemen.

2. It is possible, of course, that the captain took on some illegal passengers, so that the discrepancy in numbers is illusory. Gooch remarks in Volume II, Chapter XVIII: "And at Portsmouth the Captain [of *The President*], as these *Packet-Bashaws* are called, took in more passengers, mostly the poorer sort of Irish, upon the most mercenary principles" (170). It's not clear from the term "mercenary" whether the profit went to the shipping line (in which case they would presumably have been legal, declared passengers) or straight into the captain's pocket (in which case they would presumably not have been declared on the passenger list).

3. Gooch remarks in his letter, with memorial and testimonials, to Sir Robert Peel that he was "a principal compiler of 'The Georgian Era'" (fols. 232, 234).

4. The handwriting in Add. Ms. 2616 is also the same as that in Gooch's letter, with memorial and testimonials, to Sir Robert Peel, a manuscript that is signed by Gooch and that presents a synopsis of his life history that fits in all respects what is known about him from independent secondary sources.

5. RG may have been in New York and have bought the newspapers from which he quotes and from which he clipped out stories; they were available, however, in the British Museum and elsewhere as well

as through the mail carried on the packets. In Volume II, Chapter VIII, Gooch refers to "files of American papers" as if such things were a well-known resource.

6. The phrase "manifest destiny" was first used by John L. O'Sullivan in *The United States Magazine and Democratic Review*. For a discussion of the phrase and the concept, see Kenneth Davis 131.

7. The authors cited produced the following texts: Tuckerman, *America and Her Commentators. With a Critical Sketch of Travel in the United States* (1864; rpt. New York: Antiquarian P, 1961); Mesick, *The English Traveller in America 1785–1835* (New York: Columbia UP, 1922; rpt Westport, CT: Greenwood P, 1970); Berger, *The British Traveller in America, 1836–1860* (New York: Columbia UP, 1943); Nevins (comp. and ed.), *American Social History As Recorded by British Travellers* (New York: Henry Holt, 1923) and a revised and enlarged edition of the same: *America through British Eyes* (New York: Oxford UP, 1948); Conrad, *Imagining America* (New York: Oxford UP, 1980); and Mulvey, *Anglo-American Landscapes: A Study of Nineteenth-Century Anglo-American Travel Literature* (Cambridge: Cambridge UP, 1983).

8. The appearance of Boardman's text (*America and the Americans, by a Citizen of the World*) may explain why Gooch's wasn't published: two accounts almost identically titled would point unerringly for any publisher to the market in travelers' tales being oversold.

9. Ralph Thomas—in *Notes and Queries*—mentions that his father was a friend of RG's and that RG told him in 1832 that he had published "a small work on arithmetic in verse when he was about seventeen" (4 [col. 1]). The Cambridge University Library's collection of RG's mss. contains an "Introduction to Arithmetic." I have, however, been unable to ascertain where and when it was published; it may be that the text is the one with that title mentioned in *The Nineteenth Century Short Title Catalogue* as published in Edinburgh in 1804 (2: 304 [col. 1]). The date is not right, but it is the closest one to the required date of 1807 or 1808 cited by standard bibliographical sources.

10. As the Chronology mentions, RG was first admitted to St. John's as a sizar and later as a pensioner. For the distinctions between the two classifications (and a third, also: The Fellow Commoners), see Scott's *St. John's College Cambridge* 96–97. It is clear that between 1819 and 1827, RG had gone up in the world.

11. Both Boase and the Venns incorrectly state that he was admitted to the Inner Temple.

12. I have been unable to discover when RG married, and whether, indeed, he married more than once. In 1845 RG's wife was Ann or Anna Gooch (née Hitchon); she may have been his only wife. It is possible, however, that RG was married at the time of his first son's birth to Georgiana Jemima Heathcote. The Cambridge University

Library Add. Ms. 2616 Pt. 8 ("Miscellaneous Mss.): fol. 183 is a love poem to her; and the names chosen for RG's first son may be significant. In addition, RG's treatment of his eldest son is rather odd. He failed in his last will and testament to make him his executor (the duty fell on his second son, Frederick Mackellar), and remarked there only that his eldest was "already well provided for." At present this line of reasoning is all speculation; I have been unable to trace any such first marriage in either the *Gentleman's Magazine* or the *Edinburgh Magazine* for the 1820s.

13. The dates for RG's stay in the United States are based on internal evidence in the ms. They are in clear conflict with other evidence that places RG in England during that time. For a discussion of the nature of RG's visit to the United States, see the first section of this introduction.

14. I am indebted for this detail to a marginal note in RG's handwriting next to this story. The note reads: "Begun at the British Museum, the 14th day of March, 1834"; for the story and the note, see Add. Ms. 2616 Pt. 5 ("Cantabrigia"): fol. 33.

15. The source for this detail is Ralph Thomas in *Notes and Queries*. *The Bolton Chronicle* itself was edited anonymously. It is worth noting, perhaps, that Puttick and Simpson's sale catalogue of RG's library lists under item no. 383 Clarke's *Lancashire Gazetteer* of 1830. My source for the information about RG's friendship with the Mayor of Bolton is one of the testimonials to Sir Robert Peel (Letter [Letter B] fols. 237– 238).

16. No copy of this work is catalogued in the British Library's holdings. My bibliographical source is *The English Catalogue . . . January, 1835, to January 1863* 299, and *The English Catalogue . . . 1801–1836* 236 (col. 1).

17. My source for this information as well as for the earlier citation in this Chronology (July 18, 1833) is Christopher Date, the Assistant Archivist at the British Museum (Letter to the editor).

18. No copy of this work is catalogued in the British Library's holdings. My bibliographical source is Sparke's *Bibliographia Boltoniensis* 70. RG is described in the entry as "an attorney's clerk and a musician." RG was, of course, admitted to the Middle Temple in 1827, and was living on Temple in London in 1833 and 1835; however, he was never called to the Bar (Letter to the editor from E. McNeill). The publisher of *The Masonic Melodist* was W. Holcroft; according to Scholes's *Bolton Bibliography* 81, William Holcroft "and his assignees" printed and published the *Bolton Chronicle* from September 1836 until 1841. It was, of course, this newspaper that RG had edited in 1835 and, perhaps, 1836.

19. I have been unable to trace a second edition of *Facetiae Cantabrigiensis*. It's quite possible there never was one; the publisher may simply have labeled the 1836 edition as the "Third" in order to imply that the book was popular.

20. My source for this detail is Sparke's *Bibliographia* 70.

21. My source for the information about the Honourable F. Dudley Ryder is one of the testimonials to Sir Robert Peel (Letter [Letter A] fols. 235–236).

22. My source for the information about the Letters in favor of the New Poor Laws is RG's memorial to Sir Robert Peel (Letter fol. 232). The twenty Letters may have been among the items in RG's library, sold at auction by Puttick and Simpson, February 5–10, 1847. Lot no. 1095 is described as "Broadsides, Election Squibs, Curious Tracts, &c. *a parcel*."

23. My source for the information about the *Norwich and Norfolk Times* is Steadman's 1971 FLA thesis. Steadman offers the following description of the newspaper: it "carried a prospect of Norwich Castle in his [*sic*] banner, was published every Saturday at 4d and consisted of 4 pages of six columns each. It accommodated few advertisements, and claimed to be independent of politics. It was a very well-produced paper, although the first issue contained a paucity of local news. It supported the Established Church and the State, and was particularly concerned with the interests of the farmer and landowner. It could not meet the challenge of other local newspapers with similar ideals. . ." (169).

24. RG was definitely appointed a Treasury Extra Clerk in the Office of the Receiver of Fines by Sir Thomas Fremantle, probably in 1843. His memorial to Sir Robert Peel (fol. 230) makes that clear. The Public Record Office at Kew in London contains corroborating evidence and points strongly at November 30 as the date of his appointment. *Treasury—Treasury Board Papers 1843, Alphabetical, No. 1: Public Offices A–M* (T2/182) includes a citation on fol. 111 which reads: "Nov. 29, 1843 Number 24643 1852 Extra Clerk recomm$^{\underline{d}}$ to be employed in the Rec$^{\underline{r}}$ Generals [*sic*] Office at this port." *Treasury—Treasury Board Papers 1843 Numerical* (T2/185) includes a citation under the date Thursday 30 Nov, 1843 which reads: "Customs 1852 24643 disposed of Sir G. Clerk Sir T. F." Unfortunately, it is impossible to know if the person appointed was RG because the actual documents referred to in the above indexes were destroyed (as inessential paperwork) during the last half of the nineteenth century at the recommendation of Mr. Cotton, Assistant Superintendent of the Registry at the Treasury.

Just how lowly a position Treasury Extra Clerk was is suggested by the position coming below Established Clerks, Classes 1–3 and above Temporary Clerks in the December 1847 "List of the Clerks Employed in the Department of the Storekeeper General" (Public Record Office, ADM 7/807: *Naval Stores Diary 1822–1880*); by the fact that nowhere in the public record associated with the Customs from 1843 to 1849 does RG's name appear; and by the fact that RG complains bitterly in his memorial to Sir Robert Peel about how servile the position is. He accepted the position, he says, "with an implied hope of promotion, &

not being aware that no matter my ability, education, or integrity, I never could rise above *five shillings* per day, and even that witheld [*sic*] should sickness visit me for four successive days. . ." (fol. 230).

25. I have been unable to discover when RG's second child, Frederick Mackellar, was born. A national register of births, marriages, and deaths in the United Kingdom was not established until July 1, 1837, and no Frederick Mackellar Gooch is listed as having been born between that date and RG's death. In his last will and testament (dated September 3, 1849), RG refers to Frederick Mackellar as a "boy," and a codicil makes clear that on March 8, 1850 he was still a minor (that is, less than twenty-one years of age). It is probable, then, that Frederick Mackellar Gooch was born between 1829 (the year of the birth of RG's eldest son, Richard Stephen St. George Heathcote Gooch) and July 1, 1837.

26. It is likely that RG gave this address as one at which cards could be left because of its snob value. St. James Street was known for its clubs. No. 29 had been famous a generation earlier as the house at which the caricaturist Gillray lived, worked, and died. Right next door at No. 28 was (and still is) Boodle's Club, one of the most famous clubs in London. In 1846, No. 29 housed two commercial enterprises: William Card, Flute Manufacturer, and E. Hummel & Co., Hosiers. It may be that RG boarded (as had Gillray) above the shop; it may even be that he owned the premises. It is most likely that he had some arrangement with one of the shopkeepers to collect any cards and letters left for him. For the history of Nos. 28 and 29 St. James, see *The Dictionary of National Biography* 7: 1253–1256 (col. 1), and Timbs' *Clubs and Club Life in London* 104. For the specific information on No. 29 as it was in 1846, I am indebted to Lilian Gibbens (Letter to the editor).

27. Almost all of the items were books, and the total number of those books was significantly greater than the number of items since many were multiple lots. In addition to books, there were several items of furniture (desks, cabinets, and bookcases), some busts, and some engravings. Coincidentally, one of the desks (a mahogany writing desk) was sold to a Mrs. Gooch.

RG's library reveals his tastes to be those of a well-read gentleman. Sermons, theology (in foreign languages as well as English), travel, parliamentary procedure, literature, medical reference, railways, fencing, history, gems, Greek and Latin texts, and genealogy are only some of the categories represented. RG presumably sold his library in order to supplement his income as an Extra Clerk supporting four children and a wife. The total sum realized by the sale was the equivalent of about six years of income as an Extra Clerk. Some of the money, of course, would have gone to the auction house.

28. RG had clearly come down in the world in the last half-dozen years of his life. In 1843 he had begun petitioning powerful political acquaintances for lucrative preferment after having sacrificed a for-

tune in the 1830s on supporting the Conservative cause (see his Letter . . . to Sir Robert Peel fol. 225). In 1845, he was living in what is now Bloomsbury in Central London, a rich and fashionable area then as now. In 1847, he sold his library. At the time of his death, he was living on Blackfriars Road quite close to the Blackfriars Bridge. In the 1840s, that address fell within the parish of Christ-Church in the union of St. Saviour's, and as Samuel Lewis's *Topographical Dictionary* makes clear it was not an entirely salubrious area: "It consists of several ranges of good houses on both sides of Great Surrey-street, including Nelson-square on the east, and a portion of Stamford-street on the West. There are manufactories for hats and glass, and for various articles of statuary in Roman cement, besides extensive saw-mills, a large cooperage, and works for refining antimony and making albata" (1: 549). It contained a workhouse (enlarged in the 1830s), two almshouses, and three charities. RG (and his family, too, presumably) seemed to be living at the time of his death with at least two other people, George Allingham and Sarah Gerard. No. 22 Blackfriars Road, where he died, may have been a boarding house.

29. I am indebted for this information about the provenance of the Gooch Collectanea to Kathleen Cann of the Department of Manuscripts at Cambridge University Library.

STATEMENT OF EDITORIAL PRINCIPLES

In "A Daughter's Story: I Knew Her Best," Linda Gray Sexton remarks that the purpose of a literary executor is "to keep the work both viable and alive after the author dies" (20 [col. 2]). The purpose of any textual editor seems to me the same. With that in mind and guided by Thomas Tanselle's masterly essays "Some Principles for Editorial Apparatus," "The Editing of Historical Documents," and "External Fact as an Editorial Problem," I have edited Gooch's *America and the Americans* according to the following eight principles:

1. The text would be "clear," free from the distractions of supralinear numbers or symbols. Notes would, then, be keyed to the text by page. My concern here was to make the text as readable as possible.

2. Notes about the text would cover emendations made by me, alterations made by Gooch, and any noteworthy features (such as marginal or verso additions) of the manuscript itself. All significant changes to the manuscript—except those governed by principles 7 and 8—would be cited or discussed in the notes. My concern here was to allow the reader to reconstruct the text in its various phases, and to indicate Gooch's process of composition, which was rapid and, at times, careless.

3. Notes of an historical sort would comprehensively cover the text's allusiveness and describe the cultural background which Gooch, of course, took for granted. My concern here was to enable a reader to understand Gooch's attitudes as fully as possible in order to be able to judge their value.

4. Gooch's spelling would be corrected and regularized, but neither standardized nor modernized. Gooch's rather idiosyncratic habits of capitalization would be retained on the assumption that his habits were generally intended to provide emphasis in a way that was fashionable at that time. I have altered his use of capitals and lower-case letters only where such use is clearly distracting to the modern reader, or is manifestly wrong. Here I wanted to reproduce the text as far as possible as it might have appeared had it been published in the waning years of the Georgian era.

5. Grammatical errors would be corrected when their presence would be distracting or when, in my judgment, a late-Georgian publisher or Gooch himself would have done so once the manuscript reached the production stage.

6. Factual errors in the manuscript would be corrected, my

thinking here being that Gooch would have expected as much from any publishing house of the period. Significant changes by Gooch in quotations from secondary sources would, however, be retained since they might be purposive rather than accidental. The notes would make clear the nature and extent of Gooch's changes to the primary source.

7. Gooch's punctuation would be changed only in order to correct obvious errors by him or in order to make his meaning clearer. I would adopt a very conservative approach to such changes and resist throughout the temptation to modernize.

8. The titles of books and newspapers mentioned by Gooch would be italicized as per modern usage. Authenticity here—in other words, the inconsistent use by Gooch of quotation marks—would be a disservice to the modern reader. Similarly, the use of quotation marks to indicate dialogue would be made consistent and reflect modern American usage. Finally, paragraph indentions would be added since the text was written almost entirely flush left.

Throughout I have tried to balance two conflicting needs: ease of reading, and historical authenticity. As these eight principles suggest, I have fulfilled the ease-of-reading requirement by modernizing those features of the text which are inconsequential, and the concern for historical accuracy by reproducing any significant features of the text as they would have appeared to Gooch's contemporaries.

A NOTE ON THE TEXT

"America and the Americans—in 1833–4. By an Emigrant" is catalogued as Add. Ms. 2616 Pt. 4 in Cambridge University Library. The manuscript forms part of the Gooch Collectanea, a collection consisting of six boxes of material divided into eight parts. The contents of the collection and the provenance of the manuscript are discussed in the Introduction to this work.

The manuscript is a unique whole draft of Gooch's account, although a later version of the first two chapters of Volume II was prepared by Gooch, possibly for periodical publication, possibly for distribution to would-be publishers of the entire text. The manuscript consists of 189 folios and fifteen loose-leaf cartoons in watercolors painted over pencil sketches. Each folio is approximately 21 cm x 29 cm, and each cartoon (affixed by sealing wax to paper of the same size as that used for the text) 14 cm x 11 cm. It is loosely bound into signatures of inconsistent size and stitched at eight anchor points with thread. The paper is coarse and slightly discolored with age.

A close examination of Add. Ms. 2616 Pt. 4 reveals that Gooch wrote the chapter subheadings after the text for each chapter, leaving sufficient—sometimes *barely* sufficient—space for them at the top of each folio that begins a chapter. Gooch read through and corrected the manuscript at least once and possibly twice. Corrections made at two different times can be discerned. One set of corrections is in ink, is definitely Gooch's, and occurs extensively throughout the text; another is in pencil, is probably Gooch's, and occurs very infrequently.

The one physical oddity to the manuscript is that the two volumes have been transposed. As a result, the correct sequence should be the title page to Volume I (an unnumbered folio), fols. 1-6 (the continuation of the title page, and the preface), fols. 100-189 (the text of Volume I), fol. 99 (the title page to Volume II), and fols. 7-98 (the text of Volume II). It is this sequence that I have followed, and it is one that Gooch clearly intended. There is substantial internal evidence supporting my decision to re-order the manuscript folios in the sequence outlined above. The continuation of the title page, which lists the topics discussed, follows this sequence and not the sequence imposed by the folio-numbering. The placement instructions for the cartoons, instructions which are clearly in Gooch's hand, assume that Volume I according to the folio-numbering is actually Volume II and vice versa. The text itself refers to one illustration (the medical dandy's cloak and rosette) in such a way as to make it clear that Gooch knows he is writing text for Volume I even though the folios' sequence indicates otherwise. Finally, the sequence of volumes in the manuscript as it has been bound makes no sense; when the two volumes are transposed, however, there is an obvious organization: from Gooch's arrival in New York to his return to England a wiser man.

It is surprisingly simple for such a major mistake to occur. Since Gooch numbers the chapters anew for each volume (I-XVI and I-XVIII) and gives no indication of volume number in his chapter headings, it required the transposition of only *two* folios for the error to happen: the volumes' title pages. It is even possible to see how the two folios might have been swapped, since the opening folio of Chapter I of what is properly Volume I begins with a subheading *America and the Americans, Etc: Etc: Etc:* that could be misconstrued as a brief recapitulation of the work's title page and, so, intended as an opening reminder for Volume II. Once such a transposition occurred, it took only the binding of the manuscript and the numbering of the folios to make the error permanent. Since the binding and the pagination appear to have been done by the Cambridge University Library itself and were certainly not Gooch's work, no one is likely to have noticed the error. It *is* a fairly subtle one, although its consequences were considerable.

is to be some puppet-exhibition, or such a song as "Jim
Crow" to be sung, then it is the American play-goers are
on the qui vive. The best friends of the New York Theatres
are foreigners of all sorts, but especially
the English & Irish Emigrants. One evening when I
happened to be at the Park Theatre, during Mrs Wood's
engagement in New York, that Queen of Song performed
to nearly an empty house. I confess the dreary effect
given me such a chill, that, disgusted with American
indifference, I made my escape as soon as she had
ended her part; and my disgust was far
from being diminished, when an American gentleman that I knew near me, on seeing
me rise to depart, cried out, 'don't go yet. They are going to
sing "Jim Crow!"' Cruel brute — thought I. The Sun American
paper of March, 1834, speaking of Theatricals in
America, says, "The 'big bugs' of Boston have an odd
way of doing business. Whenever a rare actor is announced
at the Tremont, a general rush is made for the box
tickets; and in order to secure a select audience, (and a
pocket full of money into the bargain,) the sagacious manager
puts up the seats (room for 5 or 6) in the first & 2nd
rows of boxes at auction. During the late engagement of the
Kembles at the Tremont Theatre, the seats in the aforesaid
rows brought from 15 to 21 dollars each; and one gentleman
actually paid 50 dollars for a seat, out of pure spite to a
less wealthy (or perchance less genteel) neighbor who had bid against
him. When Master Burke's first engagement was announced in
the Literary Emporium, the single tickets were sold at
auction for from 5 to 7 dollars each!" One thing struck
me particularly — that whereas nearly
all Church-goers in America were females,
very few were ever to be seen at the Theatres.
At the play-houses, as everywhere else, chewing
and spitting is the universal

Plate 1. Folio from the ms. of *America and the Americans*. By permission of the Syndics of Cambridge University Library.

EDITOR'S TABLE OF CONTENTS TO *AMERICA AND THE AMERICANS*

AMERICA AND THE AMERICANS—IN 1833–4.

A traveler has a right to relate and embellish his adventures as he pleases, and it is very impolite to refuse that deference and applause they deserve.

—Rudolf Erich Raspe, *Travels of Baron Munchausen* (1785)

To Be Published Dec^{r}., 1834. In 2 Vols. 12mo, 12/0.

HAVE AT THE AMERICANS:

OR,

THE UNITED STATES IN 1833-4.

(Embellished with 15 Engravings.)

Descriptive

=of=

THEIR MANNERS, CUSTOMS, HABITS, CLIMATE, FASHIONS, AMUSEMENTS, MATRIMONY, & COURTSHIPS. NOTIONS OF GENTILITY. STATE OF THEIR YOUTH, MORALS, & EDUCATION. PATRIOTISM. POLICY TOWARDS INDIANS. TREATMENT OF FREE BLACKS. SLAVES & SLAVE TRADE. DISEASES, DOCTORS, QUACK-DOCTORS, & PATIENTS. PROVISIONS, QUALITY & PRICES. BANKING SYSTEM, GOVERNMENT, CORPORATION PATRONAGE & EXPENCES. BALLOT, LATE ELECTIONS. RELIGION, LAW, DIVINES, JUDGES & MAGISTRATES. LABOUR, LOW PAID, & WHAT KIND IN DEMAND. PACKETS, CAPTAINS, & VOYAGERS. HINTS FOR SETTLERS. PRESENT STATE OF EMIGRANTS & FUTURE PROSPECTS FROM EMIGRATION. ETC. ETC. ETC. ETC.

By An Emigrant.

PREFACE

WHEN Messrs Trollope & Hall made their tour of the United States, they, like the gallants of old, took care to forwarn or poursuivant to announce their coming, and the consequence was, Jonathan sat to them pretty particularly on his guard. Not so did your humble Servant. He fell plump amongst them, like Jupiter's boy amongst the fabled Frogs, and being esteemed nearly as harmless, they jumped, smoked, croaked, and joked about him "as naturally as pigs squeak," little dreaming the said log contained "a child taking notes" and "faith he'll print 'em." Though in honestly depicting America and the Americans, a writer may as soon expect to be applauded by them for his pains, as look for "Thank You," from old maid or Bachelor, when walking rough-shod over the gouty toes of the one, or the shoe-pinched corns of the other.

Everybody knows that the writings of the above travellers have not only been universally abused in America, as unjust, but many English look upon The *Domestic Manners of the Americans* as no better than caricature. Notwithstanding, even Mrs. Trollope has not come up to the original, and she might fairly be censured for not giving the truth, the whole truth, and nothing but the truth, especially for the manner in which she dismissed that degrading blot upon the people in the United States, *Slavery*! But your high-minded Americans are so far from feeling grateful for her forbearance, that they have seized upon the paltry advantage the lady's name afforded them, and have naturally shewn her up in character & caricature, throughout the States, in their Shops & at their Theatres, in true Covent Garden or Billinsgate costume, with a short pipe in her mouth, a red jacket, and her arms akimbo. Nor have they stopped here. When I first found myself in New York, I had never read the works of either Mrs. Trollope or Captn Basil Hall, but having their "*showing injustice to America & the Americans*" constantly dinned in my ears (and, by the by, I found that not one American out of 50 had seen their writings) I was curious to see, read, and judge for myself, and entered a shop with the intention of purchasing these condemned books. "Sir," was the bookseller's answer, "I durst not keep them by me. To be known to have sold them would ruin me!"

What will become of my bantling *nous verrons*. I mean, however, without fear of consequences, whether my book be sent to Coventry or not, to speak of *America as it is and The Americans, as they are,* ***Civilly, Politically,*** & ***Religiously***—in short, to set the world, and Englishmen in particular, right on a very important subject, as intimately connected with the progress of Civil and religious Liberty, that the true interest of unsuspecting thousands may not be sacrificed to *American cupidity, & the false theories of self-sufficient cold-blooded Political Economists:* that the term **Republican**, as applied to the people of the United States, may be *no longer misunderstood*. And this is the more necessary, when the *republican mania* is as widely spreading; when even some of the legislators of this country are associating themselves with or giving countenance to those employed in *wickedness* tempting our able artisans, our husbandmen & our yeomen, the very sinews of the country, to abandon English homes & English comforts (humble though they be) for a land where neither the climate, the soil, the people, their institutions, or their habits, have one congenial characteristic wherewith to reward them for their sacrifice of kindred, nativity, & the loss of famed institutions; where judicial fraud has no check, and the poor no protection.

If it be said that I have been more *satirical than just*, I answer, *that I have in no instance departed from the truth. I am prepared to defend what I have written.* I could even now heighten the picture. But, say some "the truth is not always to be spoken." Most true—but your American is not a character to be improved by ordinary means—he is a selfish, jealous, vain, touchy being—*a slave to his prejudices & a Slave-master*—and as such I treat him. Let the republican of liberality & justice but once stir his soul, and no one will sooner hail its presence and applaud him for having achieved that greatest of conquests involved in the saying of the Grecian Sage, *Γνῶθι σεαυτόν* than ***An Emigrant***.

VOLUME I

Plate 2. New York Medical Dandy. By permission of the Syndics of Cambridge University Library.

AMERICA AND THE AMERICANS
ETC: ETC: ETC.

CHAPTER I

Cobbett and His Guide—Bay of New York—Long Island Not Healthy—General Appearance of the Bay & Country—Emigrants Should Seek a Lodging—Dangers from Sleeping Several in a Room—Robberies & Murders Frequent in America—Banditti in New York—Robbery of Booth the Tragedian—Shameful Treatment of Anderson the Vocalist

When Cobbett took his final leave of the United States it was in a spirit of such bitterness for what he had there experienced, that he jumped on board the packet about to convey him to England, took the shoes off his feet, rubbed them together over the side of the vessel, and declared he would not carry with him so much as the dust of the soil of America. This Anecdote was told me by several in New York, and by one of the family of his next-door neighbour. Yet in the very teeth of this *leave-taking* did he write his *Emigrants' Guide*, by which he has allured many to the very country he so heartily despised, to linger out their days, as do the Emigrants in a great majority of instances, in penury & misery.

With my *political prejudices* against English Government & English Institutions strengthened by such writings as his, I was at length led to turn my thoughts towards America, as the only land where all the Cardinal Virtues were to be found, the very *Palestine* of plenty and political honesty; where only the Genius of Liberty and Independence had planted her Shrine; where, indeed, there was no such thing as *religious persecution*, no party clap-traps practiced, no misrule, no injustice, no pinching poor poverty, no pauperism, no rags, no aristocracy, no purse-proud citizens; but liberty of conscience, labour well-paid, justice—pure unadulterated justice, unblushing honesty, and universal love and sympathy.

With these notions I took my passage for America early in 1833; and after a tedious voyage, during which the passengers were more than once on their knees, every moment expecting to "go down," as they phrase it, I entered the Bay of New York, not much prejudiced in favour of our Yankey Captain. It is customary for persons to describe the general appearance of strange shores on approaching them. I shall only say that the Bay of New York is a very fine one, spacious and deep, and is capable of containing the largest fleet in the world. It is generally pretty well lined with Shipping, and its sides, one of which is a complete flat and the other a rising ground, are here and there studded with pretty houses. In short, its general appearance is imposing. You have Staten Island on your left, and Long Island to the right. The latter is described as the most desirable spot in America. I can only say I did not take it to be an Eden from its appearance, and I knew a family of 6 who left it in May 1834, on account of continual bad health.

Indeed, this & all the islands in the neighbourhood present but a sorry picture to an eye accustomed to English Scenery— The soil is generally poor and overspread with stones and rocks—I saw a cultivated field here & there, but trees are so few that one would fancy the first to be seen had, as the celebrated Robert Hall, said of the Willows in Cambridgeshire, been put up by Nature as signals of distress—the effect is dreary in the extreme. In vain you search for variety, or the undulating hill & dale which in England fades so sweetly away into the distance, never tiring never ceasing to delight. Every scene in America wears a wide wearisome appearance to the sight. The trees run tall, but they are wanting in foliage and are meagre & feathery in their appearance. In vain you look for the bold wide-spreading forest oak, the rich chesnut, or the balmy lime, the bold clump, or the o'er-arching avenue—such as adorn our English parks, public walks, and pleasure grounds. No subdued sunbeams dart across the rich corn or bean-fields, no shadows stretch forth their mantles to relieve the eye—full blazing burning sol is everywhere, parched plains and heated atmosphere, bright, dazzling, overpowering to all. Should you reach New York after the rain, as I did, you will have to wade up to your middle in mud to reach their wharfs.

I have no doubt but your English liberals fancy there are no such things as custom-house officers & dues to encounter on reaching the republic of America. They are, however, under a mistake—I found no difference between those of England and America, except that the latter partook of the characteristic surliness natural to their countrymen, and though I had been told I might take any thing ashore with me, I was refused a small parcel of little or no value.

No sooner does an Emigrant set his foot in New York, the great commercial city of republican America, than he discovers the truth of Shenstone's Verse—

> Whoe'er has travell'd life's dull round,
> Where'er his stages may have been,
> Must sigh to think he still has found
> The warmest welcome at an Inn.

The Hotels in New York, to which an Emigrant, however, will not do well to hasten, are large red-brick buildings, commodious & handsome, but are a very *barrack*! and their habits of sleeping six or more in a room is by no means after the most approved models. There is, however, no alternative, unless you choose to pay at the rate of 5 dollars a week, £1 English, for the privilege of sleeping by yourself but your American Landlord would not hesitate to break such a contract at midnight, should a traveller arrive and he be in want of half a bed for his accommodation. The only way to deal with them is to be resolute, lock your door & keep the key yourself. Nor is there any such thing as eating a quiet dinner. You must share the loaves & fishes with the multitudes of men, women & children generally found at the New York Hotels, including Emigrants of all sorts, characters, & classes.

The best & cheapest thing for an emigrant to do, on landing, is to seek a lodging-house without loss of time, to which at once to remove his luggage, and he will easily procure a decent one, board & bed, for 2 1/2 or 3 dollars per week—But here again you must be subject to the disagreeable necessity of having as many sleepers in your room as your landlord choose to stow away. This is a most disgusting, and, it appears, dangerous thing to submit to: especially as I may fearlessly assert, that nearly half the inhabitants of New York go to bed *drunk* nightly. Some persons have *queried* this assertion: but I say that they do so only from ignorance. It refers to nearly all classes, and I have seen even *ladies* but indifferently *on their guard* ere sol has set—I say *ladies*, in the haut ton sense of the word; and I have further known instances—I might add I have seen instances—of ladies declining to see company ere noon from *indisposition* of course.

One case of danger, from having fellow-lodgers in the same room, occurred in the neighbourhood where I at one period lived: it was that of a wretch who, for some fancied injury or insult, rose from his bed after the other persons were asleep, and endeavoured to *gouge out* the eye of a man whom he supposed asleep, but luckily did not succeed. Another atrocious case, two streets from my lodgings, proved more fatal. A lodger rose from his bed in the night, and with a knife stabbed his bedfellow through the heart; and to shew the species of companion one may encounter in New York, I had but just taken possession of a room in one lodging-house, when I luckily became master of the fact, that one of the inmates was suspected to have fled from Yorkshire, after committing a murder. Of course it was not long before I decamped. Another fellow, I was told, had in a fit of madness, or *drunkenness*, killed & wounded nearly a dozen persons, somewhere in the neighbourhood.

But such things are not confined to that city. The *Sun* paper of April, 1834, states, as a *warning*, that on the previous 3rd of March "a young man by the name of Worthington, a transient lodger at a public-house in Natcitoches, arose from his bed at about 3 o'clock in the morning, and, with a large knife, killed one person, & wounded several others, who lodged in the *same room with him*. It is supposed that he was wholly unconscious of the act, and that he committed it while in a state of temporary delirium, occasioned by an habitual, though *moderate* use of ardent spirits." Such things need no comment. They are but a drop in the ocean of ills which every emigrant has to guard against.

Murders are common all over America, and some atrocious acts of parricide have been lately perpetrated up the country. One son, in a trifling dispute, stabbed his father to the heart. And though it has been said that you might sleep in New York with your doors open, robberies occurred beyond number during my residence, and once an advertisement appeared from a police Magistrate, stating that a *depôt* for stolen goods had been discovered, wherein were found nearly 3 score hats, cloaks, &c. which the owners were desired to call & claim, & I never found but housekeepers were universally provided with the best means for securing their doors. Nor are robberies by Americans less frequent than in other parts of the world, by more civilized nations, though they have a habit of shaking off the odium by attributing them nearly always to Emigrants.

Shop-lifting I found, upon inquiry, to be a very common crime, as well as that of breaking into & robbing stores. Besides it is a notorious fact, that there is a species of *Banditti* in the outskirts of New York, rather in the suburbs, called, I believe, *Hiders*, who make it unsafe for persons to appear abroad after dark. Several persons were robbed & barbarously treated by them during the time I was there. Mr. Booth, the tragedian, was robbed of 500 dollars on the highway, near New Orleans, and was treated so barbarously also, that his life was despaired of. The head clerk of a Bank in New York on leaving his office for the day, was attacked, robbed, & found nearly dead, covered with blood, in Wall Street shortly before I left; another case was that of 4 men breaking into a house in Prince Street, I believe, in broad day, who plundered it and stabbed the owner to the heart; and a sailor belonging to the Packet in which I took my departure, was robbed of 18 dollars and nearly murdered in the city. Crime is very prevalent, and this may be attributed in a great degree, I have no doubt, to the fact of almost every other house being a grog-shop, where neat ardent spirits are consumed to a Scandalous extent, morning, noon, and night; and, as may be imagined, scenes of Vice & debauchery are perpetrated in proportion.

One instance of the malignant character of the nationality and revenge of which the American is capable, was manifested in the treatment experienced by the English vocalist, Mr. Anderson. In a moment of levity, he had been imprudent enough to make some allusions to the Americans, in the hearing of an American (it is said the Captain) on board the packet in which he went over. This was reported by the American in question, and the consequence was, the New Yorkers would not permit Mr. A. to appear at the Park Theatre, where he was to make his *debut*. Nor would they receive the English man's apology, that he was in liquor when the remarks escaped him! But after committing various depredations upon the Theatre, they would no doubt have murdered Mr. A, had he not taken shelter on board a vessel, in the Bay of New York, and seized the first opportunity to sail for England. There never was a more sensitive or more revengeful character than that of an American. If you by accident interrupt him in a tale, he will instantly stop and a week after you will be sure to be told of having insulted him at such a time—perhaps be treated with a *cowhide licking*! of which anon.

CHAPTER II

General Appearance of New York—Counsellor Emmet's Monument—Streets Long & Straight—Shops or Stores Dirty—Shopmen Unshaven—Churches—No Ringing of Bells as It Savours of Loyalty—Theatres & Museums—New York a Huge Dunghill—Crowded with Hogs Often Smeared in Blood—High Rents—Houses in the Hands of Speculating Jews—No Chance for Industrious Men to Acquire Wealth as in England—Americans Insensible to This Fact

THE city of New York is by no means imposing in its effect at first sight, standing, as it does, on a complete flat. It has one general appearance fatiguing to the eye. To name it with the British metropolis is ridiculous. But several of its streets are long, wide, & straight. Some call the latter a beauty. I confess I prefer the curve, & therefore didn't admire it. The pavements are like the Americans themselves, rough & unhewn, and you are ever & anon in danger of dislocating the ancle, from the large deep holes which occur in the flags. Its principal public buildings are the City Hall, the Masonic Lodge, the City Hotel, and the Roman Catholic Cathedral in Broadway, which is no more than a moderate sized Church, with a wooden steeple, in which there is a peal of bells the mayor of New York will not suffer to be rung, because it savoured of *loyalty*. In a church in the same street stands the monument to the memory of Counsellor Emmet, who was obliged to fly from Ireland for treasonable practices & was brother of the Irish Barrister of the same name, executed for high treason, whose fate our poet Moore has so pathetically lamented in one of his Irish melodies.

At the bottom of Broadway is their principal promenade, by the Battery, certainly the finest in or about New York, & from which is a grand view of the bay. In this, the chief street in the city, the shops, or *stores*, as the Americans call them, are very mean in appearance, and the windows are kept so dirty, that I was often obliged to rub off the filth to see any object that dimly appeared from the interior; & it is a most disgusting sight to an Englishman to see the slovenly unshaven fellows that present themselves at the doors in the characters of shopmen, not only

Plate 3. American Civilization: Or an Everyday Scene in the Streets of New York. By permission of the Syndics of Cambridge University Library.

in Broadway, but in every part of the city, and in many streets the filthy state of the Shops & shopwindows are still worse than in Broadway.

Chapels of all denominations are dignified with the title of Churches; and they are likewise appropriated to the purposes of schools, upon the Lancastrian System. Next to the Churches, the most interesting objects are the theatres—the two deserving of notice are the Park & Bowery. The latter has a portico supported by a handsome row of fluted pillars, not unlike that of the Haymarket Theatre, in London. The street in which it stands is here & there studded with clumps of trees and very much resembles one of our large old-fashioned English villages. The Bowery, though smaller than the Park Theatre, is decidedly the prettiest structure, both front & interior. There are two Museums, private property, containing some objects worthy of notice, the charge for seeing either of which is 25 cents, a shilling English. There is an annual exhibition of pictures which is held in Clinton Hall; I saw nothing above mediocre talent. In Clinton Hall also, public lectures are occasionally given on various subjects.

The streets of New York, with the exception of one or two, are generally kept in the most beastly condition. Filth of all sorts is hourly shot out of every house into them, and, in plain English, New York is one *huge dunghill*! The filth is left to accumulate months together, for the hordes of Boars, Sows, and hogs to revel in, that constantly range at large. It would naturally be supposed that care would be taken to do everything that could protect the inhabitants against the stench & effluvium that must arise, to the danger of the lives of all, in so hot a climate. This is not the case, and on one occasion, the inhabitants of Pearl Street, wherein is situated the house that Washington occupied as his Head-quarters, swept up the whole into one large mass and had a board painted & stuck in the midst, upon a pole, inscribed "*To the memory of the Corporation of New York*."

But this has moved them to no extra exertion, in New York. In the neighbouring city of Brooklyn, but lately a village, a better spirit is abroad. "The Common Council," says the *New York Advertiser* of the 31st of May, 1834, ordered the nuisance of one of their beastly Slaughter-houses to be abated in 5 days under a penalty of 100 dollars—also a pool of stagnant water to be filled up under a similar penalty. "And our corporation," says the Editor, "will do well to initiate their brethren on the other side of the water."

One of the greatest nuisances to be met with, in New York, which indeed recurs in all the large towns & cities in the United States, is the hordes of beastly swine that you meet at almost every turn you take, often smeared from the pools of blood in which they have been feasting & wallowing; and I have not only been obliged to run to get out of their way, but I have seen the legs of well-dressed females smeared by them as they pass along, in the most disgusting manner. These pools of blood arise from hogs & other beasts there being slaughtered in sheds by the side of the streets to the number of 50 at a time, when blood & refuse is all poured forth & left to take its chance in the public ways, with other noxious matter. I was one day walking in the Bowery, when a chemist I knew threw out the contents of a bowl, mostly nitric acid, where some 20 pigs were collected. One of them *Swilled* it up without ceremony, & a most delicious draught he found it. For a moment he stood astonished, but as the nitre began to operate, he gave a fearful grunt & scampered off as if he had swallowed Old Nick himself.

I have seen a score calves' & sheep's heads lying about a single street, thrown there by the butchers. These dainties are not less admired in America, when they are served up, than they are in England; but the truth is, your American *helps* are too lazy and *independent*, to give themselves the trouble of preparing them for the cook. They are cast forth with the hair on, and are seldom larger than the head of an English wether.

But worse yet remains to be told. I have seen dead pigs & cats lying in the outskirts of the city, which live pigs were devouring; but worse than this, I one day told 5 dead horses (horses are not allowed to be killed & are therefore suffered to wander & die of starvation) lying near the same spot, which a herd of pigs were busy feasting upon—no wonder they boast of New York pork—in fact I was told by the Americans, that no person had an idea of fine pork till they had tasted that of New York. It is understood the Corporation of New York had the power of correcting the pig nuisance as well as others, and once a year the police, under their orders, were in the habit of going forth with covered carts to what is called scour the streets for the pigs—that is, of capturing all abroad. But so little is their authority regarded, or so little inclined are they to effect any healthful reformation, that the butchers invariably make a successful attack on the carts & police, and liberate their captives, who are suffered to have another year's revel, boars, sows, litters and all, violating by their presences every sense of decency.

Fancy yourself, in the midst of all this, after nearly a week's rain (to carry off which there are no common sewers & it is often, therefore, collected in floods), under a burning sun such as England never experiences, and some idea may be found of the horrible stench that arises from the *living* mass. In fact I have seen Vapours rising from it, under such circumstances, nearly as overpowering as a moderate English fog. Is it therefore wonderful that the cholera raged in this neglected city to a frightful extent, & the melancholy recital of the heart-rending scenes that occurred, would form an episode too fearful to dwell upon? It is even suspected that a great number were entombed alive, from the brutal haste with which the bodies were collected & shot in waggon loads into holes in a spot situated in the outskirts of the city, which is now called *Potter's Field*; and notwithstanding dreadful stenches have arisen from it in consequence, will it be believed, that the money-loving speculators in New York are at this moment occupied in laying out new streets, which are to be forthwith raised over the scarcely cold remains of those who were so fearfully cut off.

The buildings recently erected in New York are undoubtedly on a handsome scale, but they have the great inconvenience of being too expensive for the means of the people. The consequence is, that respectable families are obliged to content themselves with two small rooms, in one of which they cook, eat, and sleep—and the real tenant generally is driven to the necessity of letting off so much, to be able to raise the enormous rents, which far exceed any in England, that they generally occupy the cellars. And this is the case in almost every part of the city. In fact nearly half of the population of New York live in cellars, & they will tell you it is the pleasantest part of the house! I have seen mechanics with a family of 10 in one cellar, living in such a state of filth & wretchedness as should scarcely be paralleled in the worst parts of London—Saffron Hill included. The house in which I lodged had a family in the cellar, the matron of which was near dying from the suffocating state in which she constantly lived, and indeed the effluvium from this portion of the building had all the effect of bad air from an ill-ventilated hospital.

But this is the universal state of the houses in New York, especially in the Spring & Summer months, as may well be supposed from the fact, that the rent of a small house is 500 dollars a year, whilst the larger sort in the best parts of the city, are charged at the rate of 2000 dollars per annum, and 145 dollars a year is commonly paid for two small unfurnished rooms in the business part of the city, where a house of 4 or 5 rooms lists for about 300 dollars a year. The consequence is that though a young man may obtain a single lodging for a dollar or a dollar & a half per week, he must sleep in the same room with 5 or 6 other persons, sometimes more. (Up the country 40 have occupied the same room.) So that in fact an apartment in New York lets for nearly 6 times as much as one may be procured for in almost any part of London, 4 or 5 shillings being the average price of a small furnished room in the British metropolis, which the occupier has likewise the inestimable advantage of enjoying by himself.

The truth is, every thing in New York and all the large towns & cities in America is in the hands of speculators, mostly wealthy Jews, who are furnished with unlimited means from the monied English Jews, & are thereby enabled to grind the poorer & middling classes to the very dust. No plain-dealing, honest, industrious man, whether foreign or American, has a chance of amassing wealth under such circumstances. I have often pointed out these facts to the Americans with whom I associated, but they are so stubborn in their prejudices, so determined not to be *taught by strangers*, that I got more abuse than thanks for my honest endeavours to rouse them to a sense of their true situation.

CHAPTER III

SUDDEN TRANSITION FROM DAY TO NIGHT—DANGER IN CONSEQUENCE—WATER SCARCE—NO MEAT BUT PORK ALLOWED TO BE SOLD IN THE CITY—NO DINNER IN CONSEQUENCE IN BAD WEATHER—FIRES VERY COMMON—OUGHT TO SLEEP WITH ONE EYE OPEN IN CONSEQUENCE—AMERICANS BOAST THEIR FIREMEN ARE THE BEST IN THE WORLD—WILFUL FIRES FREQUENT

ONE thing to be guarded against, in America, is that of being too far from your home at the close of day. There is no twilight and the transition from day to night, in New York in particular, I can compare to nothing more characteristic, than the sudden extinction of the only candle in the room. And should you be taking a country walk at the time, you will have to grope your way home to the danger of your life & property, by falling, either into the hands of the *Hiders*, or the loch; or you will risk breaking your legs over the huge stones suffered to lay in the road, perhaps get a fall or two, as I have done, by coming in contact with their beastly hogs.

Another inconvenience, springing from that prolific source of evil, *monopoly*, is the high price charged by the proprietors of the waterworks, in New York, for supplying private houses. The consequence is, very few of the middling & none of the lower classes enjoy its benefit, and there are probably not 6 private pumps in all New York. So that, should any one forget to supply-himself with water for the purposes of cleanliness and cooking before night comes on, he would probably be under the necessity of walking a quarter of a mile, in the winter up to his knees in Snow, in the Summer drenched with rain, to procure a supply at a public pump, at which he would, most likely, have to wait till a horse has had his turn, and break his neck over a pig in going or coming.

And a person who cannot relish New York pork at all times, will frequently, in inclement weather, be obliged to live on bread & vegetables—as no other meat, not even a steak, is allowed to be sold out of the public markets, which in some situations are at a distance of 2 miles from your dwelling. This shameful monopoly I understand to be allowed as a privilege in the hands of the Corporation of New York, and through that & the coarseness of the weather, I was obliged to go without my dinner 3 times in one week. A butcher in the neighbourhood where I was living, was not only, to my knowledge, twice heavily fined for selling steaks in the city, but he was at last ruined & obliged to shut up his shop or store, in consequence. Such things would not be borne in Aristocratic England: but I can assure my readers, that not only are they passively suffered in republican America, but much worse is suffered without a murmur.

I have seen 50 houses blazing away during the same night, and the people run laughing to witness their destruction with a levity I never before saw, except at a fair. "There's another fire, ha, ha, ha"—and away they run, helter-skelter, followed by the firemen dragging their *enjoins*, as they call them, with a spirit of enthusiasm I never before witnessed. The latter stop for nothing, frequently cutting each other's traces amidst vollies of oaths, the bellowing & swearing of the fellow who precedes each engine with a speaking trumpet, and the uproarious clamour of thousands of men & boys. They boast that their firemen are the best in the world—at a row I confess it—and the scene at a Yankee fire is truly animating. You will see 10 or a dozen engines at the same fire, their several trumpeters bellowing, "play away, number one," "stop number two," "pull away number 3"—"play away number 4," and so on, each engine being known by its number only. All this time the swearing & shouts of the people & boys are terrific. It is by no means an uncommon thing to see a fireman with 3 or 4 of his fingers off, cut away by pumping. But this never damps their ardour.

Plenty of work is cut out from them by incendiaries & others, and they are constantly on the alert. They have regular houses, called the "Fireman's Retreats," where they refresh themselves, and to such a ridiculous extent is their enthusiasm carried, that it is impossible sometimes to sleep from the noise they create in dragging their engines about, for mere *sport*—I should call it wantonness. The boys will frequently give false alarms, by lighting a little straw behind a shed to deceive them, and thus they are sometimes kept crossing & recrossing the streets, swearing & bellowing, till it is impossible to rest in your bed for the noise, & the terror they create. Several times did I see between 40 & 50 families burnt out of house & home the same night, during my stay in New York, and when I mentioned it with a humane *allusion*, I was invariably laughed at for my pains—"That is a mere nothing," was the general reply.

I have elsewhere noticed the fact that every American citizen must serve as a militiaman, or fireman, for a period of 7 years, without fee or reward, and if any fireman is absent from his post he is fined 20 dollars. It is a common practice in America to insure houses & property for double their worth, and then to burn them down to get the insurance money. I knew of several cases in New York, being commonly talked of, and persons named as incendiaries, and it is only surprising the companies are not more on the alert. One young man told me that one old fellow, a carpenter, who had become possessed of some hundreds of dollars by burning his workshop down, advised him to adopt the same course; and upon inquiring I found it was a fact that his shop had been destroyed by fire more than once. I have seen letters from Emigrants since my arrival in England mentioning similar facts, and I can assure my readers, that in New York, it is quite necessary to sleep with one eye open, as I endeavoured to do, to escape being burnt alive.

The American firemen, like their brethren generally, are determined not to be behind the English, and the *Sun* American paper of the 16th of May, 1834, after rehearsing the deeds of the London Fireman's Dogs, *Tyke and Chance*, of whom some marvellous tales are told, says "Two or 3 years since a dog belonging to a member of the Resolution Hose Company, in America, manifested a similar partiality for firemen, and usually accompanied his master to fires. We have also heard of a dog (adds this one writer) whose attachment to the Niagara Hose Company, is not a little extraordinary. It is said that on hearing an alarm of fire, he immediately hastens to the Hose house, and barks furiously until the arrival of a member. He has been known to seize the rope with his mouth, & attempt to assist in dragging the carriage to a fire."

Plate 4. A Scene in the Merry Month of May. By permission of the Syndics of Cambridge University Library.

CHAPTER IV

May Day at New York—Landlords and Tenants—Cry o' the Street—Multitudes on the Move—Departure of the Israelites a Farce to it—New York in a Blaze—Juno in her Element—Bugs & Mosquitos—And Other Vermin in Great Plenty

MAY Day in England either reminds us of the sheets of white odoriferous bloom that line the hedge-rows, or of rustic beauties with bright eyes & glowing faces, rich with the healthful effects of a fresh breeze, rambling before sunrise, in search of some token of their true-love. With what a different face is the "merry month of May" ushered in, in America, more especially in New York. In vain you rise with a joyous recollection of Old English doings—the poetic charm is quickly dispelled by the mob & bustle that universally prevails, as if the population were flying at one outlet of the city, whilst an enemy were careering in at the other. Let the reader fancy ten thousand families on the move, bag & baggage; every street lined with men, women, & children, cars, handbarrows, and other vehicles, in one continuous moving mass, and he will have some faint idea of the First of May, the true Stirring-time in New York.

"*Do you want a help*?" is the cry of cart and barrowmen, as nearly every house pours forth its contents into the streets. The family scenes are truly ridiculous as they trudge along. Hundreds of beds having been emptied into the middle of the street (for it is considered unlucky to carry them to a fresh residence), the car is loaded and off it goes, followed by a handbarrow; next comes little Bobby shouldering a pair of bellows with a brush in one hand, followed by Susan with a long brush and sundry other utensils; & black Moll in the rear shouldering the warming-pan. Thus they advance, followed by a long train of other families similarly accoutred. "Twang twang," go the frying-pans, saucepans, & boilers dangling by the cart side—now & then an avalanche slips from above with a thundering crash, followed by a volley of round oaths. Down comes a basket of earthen ware—"my god!—There's a tea-pot broken," cries one. "Take care of the china, Susan, we shall have that down next, I guess."

Crash it comes—"I thought so"—followed by another volley of oaths from the cartman, who is probably an American Captain of horse, but an Englishman by birth: for I knew one fellow who had been a serjeant of dragoons in England who held that rank in the American service, when I was in New York and was by trade a cartman, and a more vulgar specimen of "we Americans," I never met with.

At last some of the Cavalcade stop at their new domiciles, from which it is probable the occupants have not yet departed, but out they must go, and, unless some one will give them shelter—perhaps lie abroad all night. I was told that 5 families were obliged to do so in one street, and I have every reason to believe such things general in New York, upon these *moving occasions*. Indeed few people are aware of the shameful inconvenience to which persons in New York are put by the mercenary Landlords, on the First of May, from the arbitrary law that regulates the having and letting of houses. The custom is for the owner to call upon the occupier a short time previously to May Day, to inquire if he intends to remain in his house for another year, intimating at the same time his determination to *raise the rent* a few dollars, already too exorbitant for any industrious artisan to pay. Should you demur, he says nothing but claps a note on the door-post stating that the house is to be let, and from that instant you are continuously annoyed by persons coming to see the interior, whom you are obliged by Law to admit, and there is a penalty if you wilfully take down the note. At one house where I happened to lodge, I have known 10 inquiries during dinner, and should it be a rainy day, they are sure to come in throngs, much to the consternation of a decent housewife, with many of which class America does not abound.

One day I was so much annoyed by persons coming in, that, *vi et armis*, I tore down our landlord's note, spite of the Chief Justice and Andrew Jackson, neither of whom called me to account. Should any person hire the house, no intimation is given you of the fact, except that the note is removed, and in consequence you are surprised on the 1st of the "merry Month of May," by the stopping of a motley group, composed of Carts, hand-barrows, and all the household heavily laden, as already described, and an intimation that you must forthwith turn out to make room for a fresh tenant, who has closed with your Jew-landlord at his advanced demand.

On the approach of night commences another scene that might defy the world for a parallel. A vast accumulation of all sorts of filth has been made in the middle of every street; but chiefly from the contents of the thousands of beds turned out. This is fired in every direction, and in every direction the blazing mass is seen most imposing. Such a *bon-feu* is no where else to be seen. Swarms of firemen & engines are rushing in all directions, some drawn to one spot by roguish boys with a false alarm, others by real necessity, and a stranger would imagine that the whole of New York was actually blazing. At length you retire to rest (should you be so fortunate as not to be obliged, like Shakespeare's ghost, to walk the night), tired with assisting your host to remove his goods, and with hopes that the turmoil is over. In this you are wofully mistaken. With the dawn of day begins a 2nd remove to which the Departure of the Israelites must have been a farce. You would think all the people of America were now about to disperse themselves, for the 1st time, over the United States.

In the meantime the blazing & burning continue, and is kept up for a period of a week, during which the boys are jumping, shouting, laughing, & tossing the fragments in all directions—and at the close of the whole you see the streets of New York, for a long time, covered with old shoes, hats, frills, petticoats, pattens, tin-boilers, saucepans, broken bottles, pans, iron pots, and every other description of filth that the new comers have raked up from the holes & corners of a whole city, the population of which is none of the *tidiest*.

Now you hug yourself with a certainty that all is over—alas! there is worse behind. All married ladies in America bargain for the privilege of white-washing and thoroughly cleaning, alias *swamping*, their house once a year—you will find it fully set forth in the marriage articles of both gentle & simple, and in this particular an American fair does for once rule absolute. No soothing, no compromise the husband may attempt can save him from this yearly dilemma. Like the stirring hum of a hive of bees before swarming, the half impertinent & altered tones of the voices of both mistress & maids, the manner in which they will whisk by you in the hall or passage, will give you sufficient intimation that Juno is about to take the reins, and happy is the man who knows where to hide his head till the storm is "blown over."

A most woful plight would a new comer find himself in, should he remain ensconced in his lodging on the first day of her rule. All the household helps are summoned to her aid, white & black—and topsy-turvy goes the furniture, pictures, books, papers, &c; none are spared a tumble, unless you secure them with lock & key, and before you can say "Jack Robinson," you will find yourself up to your ancles in water, running in well-supplied pailsful from every room in the house. Should a stranger in his simplicity be so unlucky as to call during the operation, it is 10 to 1, but a pail of dirty water is dashed in his face as he mounts the steps with intent to knock at the door, before he recovers from which, a black wench in the act of washing the windows at the top of the house, nearly drowns him with another. I was myself unfortunate enough to make one visit before the work was complete, and had actually a large jug of water dashed in my face by the lady of the house, who opened the door to cast it forth just as I was in the act of mounting the steps—for all the houses in New York are graced with a flight at the entrance. Husbands generally retire patiently from the scene, and experience tells them when to return.

This practice of burning & washing no doubt has its origin in a desire to render their dwellings more healthy and it is also a conspiracy to destroy the live stock, with which the best houses are terribly furnished. There is, however, enough left, & to spare—for in the summer you will find your beds lined with bugs so thick you might mistake it for beading, by the hand of some cunning artificer; as for mosquitos, there is no want of them either. They will generally be found pretty thick on the ceiling of your bed-room at night, and one remedy I found for them was, carefully destroying as many as I could by holding the blazing candle close to the ceiling and burning them as English people will sometimes see the poor harmless gnat destroy itself.

I have heard much of the painful nature of these pests of the winged tribes in the West Indies & other warm climates, but in America they seemed to me to "out Herod Herod." You seldom feel their bite at the time, but a slight irritation follows after a few days, when persons rubbing their legs in an agony of excitement, they become so swollen, that they find it impossible to get on either stockings or shoes, and you will not infrequently find your American friend lying *tandem*, like your helpless flannel-wrapped gouty Old Englishman, in which situation he will probably be confined for 2 or 3 weeks. There is no deficiency of other Vermin, and in the outskirts of New York the bellowing of the Bull-frogs may be heard for miles.

CHAPTER V

Domestic Manners of the Americans—The Female Character in No Esteem—Dollars the Idols of the American—Morals at a Low Ebb—American Ladies Sheepish—Husbands Absolute Hogs—All Americans Early Risers—Seldom Wash Their Hands—A Breakfast Table—No Civility Practiced by either Ladies or Gentlemen—Dinner Table a Perfect Babel of Eatables—First Plate Crowded with Something off Every Dish—Elbows Poked in Your Face—Knives & Forks Rarely Clean—Both Men & Women Chew & Smoke Tobacco—Men Always Spitting—Women Sucking Sweets—Good Teeth Scarce—Americans Not Hospitable—American Wives in a State of Utter Subjection—Their Parties Stupid Things

IT is a fact might be as confidently admitted as any of Euclid's axioms, that there is an utter absence of all social communion and fireside-enjoyment in America—indeed, their habits, looks, actions, and words (though speaking the same language and springing from the same stock) are as unlike English as they can well be. But one of the most remarkable features in American Society is, notwithstanding their affectation of gallantry, the low estimation in which the females are held by the men.—Had the Americans caught their idea of women from the creed of Mahomet, they could not have held their intellectual powers cheaper than they do. An Englishman loves them for their social qualities, a Frenchman for the charm they give to the living-picture, as the idols to which he constantly sacrifices his constitutional gallantry; but an American looks upon women as the mere animal. If he believes they have a soul, he never suffers them to discover it by either word, look, or action.

His idol is his dollars. He lives upon dollars, talks of nothing else but dollars, & sleeps & dreams of dollars. The consequence is, as might naturally be expected, that morals are at a very low ebb, and are but little studied or understood by the American ladies. And this is remarkably apparent in their intercourse with the male part of society. There is a saying in England, that if a man does not look you in the face whilst addressing you, he is not to be trusted: no American lady looks a gentleman in the face either when speaking to him, or when she accidentally meets him, or he addresses her, either in a room or elsewhere. The head is half averted with an *affected bashful*, or what might more properly be designated a *sheepish* look—*mauvaise honte*. There is none of the liveliness of the French woman, nor of the virtuous confident manner of the English woman. Both the latter have their rank in society assigned them, and they assume their proper stations. An American lady does not know her place, and she constantly seems doubtful if she has any business in Society at all—She is constantly left to cater for herself.

This is an evil in the Domestic circles of America, which hangs like a dead weight upon their progress in civilization, & continually checks moral improvement—nor can they ever hope to approach, much less enjoy, the charms of polished life, till it is removed. An American husband is an absolute hog in his own house. The little time he does spare from the pursuit of his beloved dollars, is spent in eating, smoking & spitting, or in phlegmatic silence, with his heels on the dinner, tea, or supper table. Perchance he throws himself on a Sofa, and mostly falls asleep after dinner—and if he has company, he does not fail to amuse them *à la drone*. Conversation is out of the question.

One thing must be admitted, the Americans waste none of their time in unnecessary night-rest. They are up by 6 o'clock, winter & Summer, and after a general yawn, the family assemble at the breakfast-table (which is sure to be crowded with fried, baked, & boiled) most probably with unwashed hands: for it is no libel to say of them, especially the poorer sort, that they rarely condescend to use soap or water during the winter season. Buckwheat cakes, fried potatoes (the latter is an eternal dish with them), beefsteaks, bread, butter, & coffee are the general display at boarding-houses: nor do the tables of private families differ sufficiently from the foregoing, to make it necessary to notice it. Should you unfortunately oversleep yourself, you must be content with the coffee-dregs and scraps—no additions will an American housewife make. Each one rises and retires at pleasure. The men will take their hats and leave the home without uttering a word to their dearest friend on earth; and the ladies practice the same *independent* habit. Nor is there any conversation or friendly interchange of sentiment during the progress of the meal.

In lodging-houses you are summoned to dinner, which begins & ends in the same manner as their breakfasts. Their tables are crowded with a perfect *babel* of eatables; and it is a custom, at both public & private establishments, for each one to be helped to their *first* plate. The host begins by placing upon it a slice of meat, and it is then handed to the lady, who heaps upon it vegetables of all sorts, tarts, pie, and, probably, seasons the whole with a piece of cheese in the centre. You afterwards help yourself, and it is no uncommon thing for your neighbour's elbow to be poked in your face, whilst he is reaching across the table to carve himself a morsel from a favourite dish. They have carving knives & forks on the table, but they seldom use them. Nay, they will rather take the trouble of wiping their own wherewith to assist you. "But help yourself, Sir," is eternally in their mouths. I have often dined with a leading Physician in New York, at whose table I never saw either a clean knife or fork, & they commonly feed themselves with the former, to the great danger of their mouths & throats. The knives are made of such bad materials, that it is painful to cut or carve with them. In fact I have preferred taking my beefsteak in my hand & eating it *à la nature*. I once heard an emigrant offered 15 dollars, American money, for a dozen English-made knives & forks.

All their habits, in fact, partake of a want of cleanliness & the decencies of life. I have often seen what are called ladies in New York, open their doors & blow the contents of a certain feature into the streets. But this exceeds in cleanliness the habits of their husbands, who are continually spitting their tobacco chewings about the house. The richest Turkey carpet is not spared by them. This habit is universal in America. Both men & boys (from the Chancellor to the chimney-sweep) are infected with it. Their spitting-pans are the ordinary supporters of the chimney-piece, in dining-room, parlour, or drawing-room: but they are not always put in requisition. A miniature painter with whom I was intimately acquainted, an Englishman, told me, that an American *gentleman*, literally a gentleman in every other respect, actually spit a handful of tobacco upon the carpet, under the table, during one morning's sitting. I one day stepped into a house of entertainment but had not sat down long when another American gentleman, in the heat of argument, spit a mouthful over my dress, nor did he offer any apology for so doing. But so careless are they in the indulgence of this filthy habit, that I saw a man spit several times into the lap of a female, without noticing what he was about; and upon her discovering it, she exclaimed, "I'll be hanged if the fellow has not made a spitting-pan of my lap!" My readers may imagine with what pathos this exclamation was delivered, when I tell them she was an English Emigrant who had not laid aside her native love of cleanliness.

But it is not uncommon for females in America both to smoke & chew tobacco. Indeed, the American ladies are not much behind their lords in habits of a tendency far from pleasing. Ladies of fortune and some pretension to breeding, may be seen in the streets & at home, with a *huge piece of Sugar Candy Sucking & enjoying it* with all the *goût* of a spoiled *Slobbering* child. I have seen them lift their veils & take a bite, and even bite off a piece & present it to a friend or companion as a condescending schoolboy would do, and when the stock is exhausted, they coolly walk into a store, or shop, for a fresh supply. This love of sweets infects the American females of all ranks—and accounts in some degree for the universal benefit they might derive by employing a dentist—I saw but few Americans with sound or white teeth.

Hospitality is but little understood and practiced less by the Americans, and should you call upon them about the dinner hour, they will often rather spoil whatever is in preparation by a delay of 2 or 3 hours, than ask you to partake of it. I speak of those in towns & cities. The same miniature painter I before named was on one occasion employed to take the likeness of the wife of an American Captain, a man of some property & *no little consequence*, in his own opinion. His wife, however, is an amiable woman, and in the kindness of her heart asked the miniature painter, a young man of retired & gentlemanly manners, to stay to dinner. The Captain was rather late in making his appearance, and his lady had just taken his place, with the artist on the opposite side, when he entered, and seeing the stranger seated, actually attacked the young Englishman with a volley of oaths and the grossest abuse, adding, that he had never made himself so familiar with him, that he should presume to sit down at his table. The young man retired in disgust, & the poor woman stood trembling & in tears, at the brutal scene she witnessed. The man who boasted his citizenship where *all men are born equal*, knew the value of his dollar-reputation too well to suffer a poorer man than himself to dine at his expense, setting aside the indignity which a republican must *naturally* feel at the liberty the young man had taken by accepting the invitation of his wife.

Ladies in America have no such privileges. They live in a state of utter subjection, and are never consulted by their "lords & masters." Their duty is obedience, and it is exacted in full. I have often seen the husband return home at night, commonly a little the worse for liquor, and retire to his bed-room without so much as speaking to his wife, or noticing his guest, who has, perhaps, expected to pass the evening with him.

Their parties are the stupidest things possible, either at home or abroad. I joined in several Gypsy excursions to Long Island & elsewhere. Instead of that joyous freedom of heart & tongue which characterize the English on such occasions, or the *gaieté de coeur* of the French, whom they affect to copy so much, they did little else but eat & drink, and seemed quite out of their natural element. An American married lady seldom joins a party of pleasure abroad. It is a notorious fact that you seldom or never see an American & his wife walking in the streets arm-in-arm. They leave their wives to walk out by themselves, and find their way back how & when they please. There are some exceptions. This neglect forms a striking contrast to the English emigrants, whom you may see walking together in that comfortable cleanly guise, which so eminently characterizes the married people of all classes in Britain.

CHAPTER VI

American Fashions—Dresses of Females—Bonnet Compared to a Smashed Lobster—Naked Legs & Feet—Indecent Display of Their Persons at All Times—Why Not Corrected—Mottoes for Seals—Blackhawk's Compliment—Fashions of the Males Have a Tendency to the Foppish—Black-stocks—A Sign of Cleanliness—A Medical Dandy's Cloak—Rosette Compared to an English Warming-pan

IT was once doubtful, it is said, from the decent length of an American female's garment, whether she had any feet at all. That doubt, however, is now completely removed. For they wear their garments so short, as to exhibit the whole of the calf of the leg to the gaze of their Beaux—in fact, in the display of their persons, both at home & abroad, they exceed the most coquettish Parisian Belle, though in their manners they want that naïvetée which in the latter makes it palatable, in a degree. During the cooler season they generally wear tightish frilled trousers, by which their legs are decently kept in the shade; but in the hot weather, they not only dispense with them, but appear in the streets with naked legs, feet, & bosom, with a parasol to shield their faces from the Sun, and simply a muslin cap to cover the head. I am now speaking of New York; higher up the country the excessive display of their persons is still greater.

The style of their fashions are the most tasteless & outré imaginable. The preposterous length of their bonnets exceed any thing I ever saw in England, even at the time when the lady's hat was made a subject of ridicule in our English Pantomimes. One writer in an American paper, in the Spring of 1834, with great truth said of the bonnet of an American lady, who came under his observation, that it "resembled in color & shape a *smashed lobster*!" & was "here & there ornamented with knots, or bows, like peeled Onions!" This latter observation I had myself often made to a friend, as I passed by them in the Streets of New York. Indeed no woman in England could appear publicly in the British Metropolis dressed as the American married ladies generally are, and hope to preserve her

Plate 5. American Belles. By permission of the Syndics of Cambridge University Library.

character—"Egad! Sirs," as I once heard Abernethy say during one of his amusing lectures, "the very boys would run after her."

Perhaps one reason for American ladies wearing such short garments is that they are generally admired for small and pretty feet. Nevertheless, it is impossible for an English eye not to be shocked at the display they make of their persons, both at home & abroad; and it is surprising that amongst their divines some second Tillotson or Rowland Hill has not sprung up to censure & correct such dangerous incentives to vice, as the female habits & fashions in America really are. But in Republican America, where very many of their *spiritual teachers* are taken from the very *outcasts* of European society, who, it is well known, rule the female devotees with as iron a hand as ever did the priesthood of any Roman Catholic community; when it is also well known that at their American Camp-meetings, their love-feasts, etcetera, these same pastors assist in scenes of debauchery that would shock a practiced libertine; it is not surprising that the ladies of America are wanting in that greatest charm of their sex, a cultivation of the delicate, ladylike, adornment and concealment of their persons, which indicates purity of mind & sentiment, and the presence of moral sense; nor that American husbands are not gifted with a very savage sense of propriety.

One disagreeable fashion, to my eye at least, is that of American females almost universally dressing themselves in a glaring red, when at home, the effect of which is almost as offensive to the sight as are their painted edifices. And never did I see the female form so distorted by those tasteless things, modern corsets & stays, as it is in America. It is a fashion for the gentlemen to carry their admiration of small waists to an excess and the ladies have, in consequence, carried their cultivation of it to such a pitch, that I feel no hesitation in saying, many girls never live to be women in consequence. In a room the most respectable married females take a pride in exhibiting the whole of the bust bare. In the streets females of *character* will be seen in the most gaudy trappings with their stockings full of holes.

And here I must record an anecdote of an American Lady & the celebrated Indian chief, Blackhawk. The latter was one day presented with a plume of feathers, a tomahawk, & a *Scalping-knife*, by an American lady, upon some public occasion, & she is said at the same time to have put her arm round his neck & to have kissed him. Upon this, he patted her on the head, exclaiming, "My God, Madam, what a *brave scalp* you would make."

I one day saw a letter addressed to a lady, the motto on the seal of which ran—"*Where the devil do you come from*?"—and mentioned the fact to the wife of a physician. "Oh," was the remark, "that is a very common expression." Words for ears polite, thought I. But what is to be expected from a people whose *Matrons* recently countenanced the notorious Fanny Wright & publicly attended upon her whilst delivering lectures, in New York, against persons living in the *connubial* state.

In fact America is centuries behind most of Europe in every thing that indicates mental superiority, unless it is in the application of those scientific discoveries that have a tendency to increase their store of dollars. A man worth a million of dollars is a thing to be worshipped in the eyes of an American. The fashions of the male population of America are scarcely less preposterous than those of the females, and have a decided tendency to *foppishness*, which is the more ridiculous in them, as they have not the cleanly habits which usually characterize a fop. The best drest amongst them will be constantly seen with a dirty beard of 2 or 3 days growth, not infrequently on a Sunday. And it is a curious fact, that the young American *Belles* of Long Island have formed a Society, binding themselves not to accept an offer of marriage from any gentleman who does not wear a *black-stock*, as conducive to cleanliness. But what may we not live to hear & see.

It is the custom of the majority of the medical men, both practitioners & students, apothecaries included, in the State of New York, to wear the outré cloak which is exhibited in the frontispiece of this volume. It is generally blue cloth, with a velvet collar, and made so large as to wrap round the person in folds, and so long that a kind of train sweeps the Street as they amble along, leaning over to the left side, the body forming a curve, that the rosette, dangling from a silk cord, may be fully exhibited to view. This rosette forms a striking part of the costume, as it is never smaller than a full-sized English *warming-pan*, such as may be seen shining, redolent of comfort, in the hands of the smirking well-favoured chambermaids at our English Inns.

CHAPTER VII

Theatricals in America—The Bowery the Prettiest Theatre but Not So Fashionable as the Park—Saw Both the Kembles & Mrs Wood Play to Empty Benches—Americans Have Made No Progress in the Histrionic Art—Their Tragedian, Forrest, a Mere Imitator of Kean—Mrs Drake Very Clever—Americans Fond of Low Comedy—Best Friends of Theatres Emigrants of All Sorts—Jim Crow Preferred to Mrs Wood's Divine Singing—Theatricals at Boston—Play-goers Mostly Men—Spitting Tobacco Universal at Play-houses—Whites Not Permitted to Sit with Blacks—Man Carried to Prison for So Doing—No Hissing Allowed—Parties Subject to Imprisonment for It—Actors Might Recover Damages if Hissed

I have already stated that the two principal Theatres in New York are *The Park* & *The Bowery*. The latter is by far the prettiest though not the most fashionable. I saw the Kembles play at both, as I did also Mr. and Mrs Wood, and from the thinness of the audiences, I confess I was puzzled to imagine how the former could have realized the sum report said they had, in America. It is no reflection on the Americans to say that they have as yet made no progress in the histrionic art. The worst provincial company in England equals the best America can boast. Their principal tragedian, Forrest, about whom they affect to be so proud, is but a brawling imitator of Kean, with scarcely a spark of either taste, feeling, or genius, and no discrimination. Their Mrs Drake, on the contrary (who is said to be either English born or born of English parents) has no popularity, save with the American *Sun* paper & one or two others, of discrimination. Yet she possesses all the genialities of which Forrest is deficient, and frequently plays with a simplicity and natural pathos not unworthy of our Miss O'Neill—Notwithstanding, I have frequently seen Mrs Drake perform her best characters to empty boxes.

The truth is the Americans are no judges of good acting, and are only won by novelty, or the lowest species of the comic school, in which they delight. Whenever there is to be some puppet-exhibition, or such a song as "*Jim Crow*" to be sung, then it is the American play-goers are on the *qui vive*. And in the American paper, the best friends of the New York Theatres are foreigners of all sorts, but especially the English and Irish Emigrants. One evening when I happened to be at the Park Theatre, during M[rs] Wood's engagement in New York, that Queen of Song performed to nearly an empty house. I confess the dreary effect gave me such a *chill*, that, disgusted with American indifference, I made my escape as soon as she had ended her part; and my disgust was far from being diminished, when an American gentleman near me whom I knew, on seeing me rise to depart, cried out, "Don't go yet. They are going to sing '*Jim Crow*'!" *Quel brute*—thought I.

The *Sun* American paper of April 15, 1834, speaking of Theatricals in America, says, "The 'big bugs' of Boston have an odd way of doing business. Whenever a rare actor is announced at the Tremont, a general rush is made for the box tickets; and in order to secure a *select audience* (and a pocketful of money into the bargain), the sagacious manager puts up the seats (room for 5 or 6) in the first & 2nd rows of boxes at auction. During the late engagement of the Kembles at the Tremont Theatre, the seats in the aforesaid rows brought from 15 to 21 dollars each; and one gentleman actually paid 50 dollars for a seat, out of pure spite to a less worthy (or perchance less genteel) neighbor who had bid over him. When Master Burke's first engagement was announced in the *Literary Emporium*, the single tickets were sold at auction for from 5 to 7 dollars each!"

An English actress & vocalist with whom I lately dined, told me that when she was passing through Boston, she was persuaded to take a benefit concert at the Tremont Theatre, and had a very crowded house in consequence. But notwithstanding, she was charged so high for the use of the house and the lighting of it, that she had not 20 dollars left for her pains, and when she had settled her bill at the Hotel, she was *minus* a like sum—mine host keeping pace with the rest. Whilst there the day of her departure, the judge honoured her with a call & conversation *tête à tête* in the midst of which our landlord entered the room & drawing a chair towards where they were talking coolly seated himself between her & the master of law. One thing struck me particularly—that whereas nearly all Church-goers in

America were females, very few were ever to be seen at the Theatres.

At the play-house, as everywhere else, chewing tobacco and spitting is the universal practice, and should you quit your seat for a few minutes, it is ten to one but you find it covered with filth on your return.—No person of color, whether free-black or not, is allowed to sit in any part of the house but the gallery, one half of which is appropriated to their use, and no White is allowed to sit amongst them. I was one night at the theatre when a White man, a stranger, had taken his seat with the *despised* blacks. A constable desired him to come out & take a seat on the other side. He declined doing so, as he said he was "*very comfortable*." Upon this the constable collared him and took him off to prison. Would this have been endured in England?

But still more tyrannical is the fact that no person is permitted to hiss an actor, or in any way to express their disapprobation, without subjecting themselves to be collared and hauled off by an officer. I recollect being once at the Haymarket, in London, when our admirable Liston played so indifferently in one of his favourite characters, whether he was under the influence of the grape I know not, that he was both *hissed & hooted* with impunity. Had your free-born American attempted so to express his choler & disapprobation, he or they would not only have been hauled off to durance vile, but I feel no hesitation in saying, that a performer bringing an action against persons who had so *defamed* him, in any court of Law in America, would obtain handsome damages for the assault. It is probable, however, that both Judges & Jurors would make an exception in favour of *born* Americans. These are refinements to which aristocratic England has not yet arrived.

CHAPTER VIII

Amusements of the Americans—Balls & Sleighing—The Former Not Respectable—But Are Fully Attended—Ladies Sometimes Mistake a Gentleman's Lap for a Seat—Dancing So-so—Sleighing a Favourite Winter Sport—Will Rise from Their Warm Beds at Midnight to Pursue It—Boys Break Their Necks down Declivities—Accident on Lake Erie—Stages Travel as Sleighs—Skating & Sliding Also Popular—Numbers Lose Their Lives by Drowning—Bathing Used in Hot Weather by Both Men & Women—The Latter Expert Swimmers—And Use the Ordinary Rivers—No Public Baths

Amongst the Amusements of the Americans are *Balls & Sleighing*. The first has long been *blackballed* by the genteeler classes, the latter is passionately pursued, when the frosts & snow permit, by all grades. A female attending an American Ball would be at once suspected of being no better than she ought to be, and certainly I have seen most extraordinary exhibitions at this class of public amusements in New York. A Lady will not infrequently, for instance, mistake the lap of a gentleman for a seat—I scarcely need add that the dancing is not after the style of the most approved Parisian *artistes*—I was not infrequently reminded of an English country wake as the couples footed it up & down, the gentlemen mostly with their arms round the ladies' waists. But although it is not considered respectable to go, and the charge is a dollar, they are generally crowded by well-dressed persons, and are held at the principal Hotels every night.

Sleighing is decidedly the favourite amusement with Americans during the winter Season. The Sleighing machine is very like an English Phaeton off its wheels, and you will sometimes see them drawn by 2, and even by 4 horses, every one of which has a string of bells round its belly or collar, the object of them being to warn persons of their approach, as in passing over the snow or ice in the rapid manner they do, accidents must otherwise be of frequent occurrence. And such is the passion of the Americans for this, I confess I thought childish amusement, that should a fall of snow happen in the middle of the coldest winter night, and they are bitter enough, God knows, numbers will turn out of their warm beds, &, cloaked till they look more like Russian bears than anything mortal, be seen flying (as you may call their driving, there being no clatter of either horses' hoofs or wheels) in all directions.

Boys, mere children, have their sleighs to themselves, which they carry about with them & watch the coming of any gig or other carriage, to which they will dextrously seize an opportunity of attaching it with a long rope they carry for the purpose, to the hinder part of the passing vehicle. I one day saw a boy so attach his sleigh, but after a ride of no great distance, the gig suddenly turning the corner of a street, he was thrown against the abutting house, which upset both him & his sleigh with a force that nearly killed him. It is a common thing to see 2 or 300 boys with their little sleighs shooting one after the other down a declivity with a fearful velocity. The method is to approach the top & placing the sleigh on the edge, to throw themselves upon them, giving them all the impetus they can with their feet, which are held up in the air the moment the machine begins to shoot along, the body being at the instant thrown upon the chest, & supported by the hands grasping the Sleigh on each side. Thus they will follow each other down the declivity in scores, in rapid succession, and they may be frequently seen to come in contact, by a more rapid impetus being to the hinder more than the foremost has acquired, and thus roll over each to the danger of their lives. 3 boys, in New York, had their necks broken by that means in the winter of 1832.

During the Winter of last year, 1833, the frosts & thaws came in such rapid succession, that Sleighing was both dangerous & rare. *The Kingston Spectator*, American paper of January, 1834, records the following

> Extraordinary escape from drowning and deliverance from death, which occurred at the upper part of Lake Erie. "Mr. John Wigle, of Gosfield, set out with his wife and child in a sleigh, for Point Pele Island, eighteen miles from land. When he had got about 12 miles from the shore, his horse broke through the ice. The shock was so unexpected and so violent, that they were thrown into the water. Mr. Wigle fortunately was thrown on the breast, from which he sprung on the ice. Mrs. Wigle was so stunned from being thrown

against the fore part of the sleigh, that she was insensible of her danger until she was rescued by her husband, which he did by grasping her when in the act of sinking, with one hand, and the infant with the other; the mother having dropped it from her arms. He then succeeded in cutting his sleigh loose, but lost his horse and harness. They were then between six and seven miles of the nearest house, with a strong wind ahead, with squalls of snow, which hid the island from their sight. In this situation there was no time to be lost. Mr. Wigle put his wife and child in the sleigh and covered them with the wet blankets, which soon becoming frozen, protected them from the wind. He then drew the sleigh by the shafts towards the island, but was soon forced to pull off his boots, in consequence of their being so frozen that he could not stand on the ice. He got some irons off his sleigh, which he tied to his feet, without which he never would have reached the shore. This he succeeded in reaching after about five hours painful toil, his hands badly frozen, and his feet so worn with the irons, that they bled profusely. His wife and child were not materially injured, except being much chilled."

Stage-coaches & carts are commonly converted into Sleighs & so travel during winter, and it is no uncommon occurrence to see one lying, upset in the Snow, with all its wares helter-skelter.

Skaiting & sliding are also very popular amusements in America, far more so than in England, and have led to the most melancholy accidents, from the utter absence of regard for human life that prevails. Very little care is taken as to what state the ice may be in, and numbers lose their lives in consequence—indeed, such numbers perish by drowning, through the breaking up of the ice, that the papers scarcely deem them a novelty worthy of insertion in their columns.

Bathing is of course a common exercise in hot weather, as much so amongst the female as the male part of the American population. One young lady I knew, who had lately emigrated from England, desired me to tell her mother she had "become an expert Swimmer." Females bathe as publicly in the river as the men, only selecting different spots. There are no public Baths in America.

CHAPTER IX

MATRIMONY UPON MATRIMONY—YANKEY COURTSHIPS—FEW QUESTIONS ASKED AND LESS CEREMONY—DIVORCES EASILY PROCURED—NUMBER IN THE STATE OF OHIO IN ONE YEAR—CEREMONY OF KISSING THE BRIDE—GROUNDS FOR PRESUMING A PROMISE OF MARRIAGE

IT is with matrimony as with all other matters in America, there is no decent observance of ceremony, nor any importance attached to a Union, such as should lead the parties seriously to consider it as entering on a new and obligatory state of life, imposing duties upon the observance of which the well-being of a social & civilized community chiefly depends.

Any marriage contract is lawful in the United States, whether the parties go through a clerical ceremony, or a man simply says, on entering a room, in the presence of a 3rd person, who signs a paper as a witness, "I take this woman for my wife." Thousands, indeed the majority of marriages, are so made in America, and it is a very common thing for a girl to tell her husband, after they have lived together as man & wife for a few weeks, that she is "tired of matrimony," and forthwith She packs up her moveables, should she be so fortunate as to have any, and walks off to her friends. Her husband has no alternative but to live alone, unless he can obtain a divorce, which is not a very difficult thing to do in the United States, and thousands have not scrupled to make a fresh contract without troubling themselves with tedious appeals to a court of law.

In New York, the only question a girl of the lower & middling classes will trouble herself to put, on receiving an offer of marriage, is—"Have you a wife in New York?" It is no uncommon thing for the American to have one or two in another state. But each one being governed by its own laws & customs, in respect to marriage, no danger is apprehended on that head, and on the girl's being answered in the negative, a paper is signed by a witness, probably *instanter*, and the twain become one flesh: unless they should have the decency to prefer the assistance of a divine or magistrate, the expense of which is about a Dollar.

Sometimes the ladies are even less scrupulous than this. I

am acquainted with an English gentleman who emigrated to the United States about a year & a half since, who had previously married an English lady with a handsome property, but becoming politically prejudiced with his own country, he resolved to transfer his wealth to the United States & settle there. He, however, had the precaution to go alone to make the trial, taking with him a considerable sum with which he purchased a tract of land on arriving at New York & the necessary implements for clearing it, &c., and went up the country to his *location* without delay. He found it in the neighbourhood of a farm, the owner of which had a family of several daughters, and the new-comer being a man of wealth & education, our American soon sought & obtained his friendship. Every art was used to make him a constant visitor at his residence. The result was, that though he had in the outset told them he was a married man, & that his intention was to return to England & fetch his wife, if he liked his situation in the new world, they used every species of manoeuvre to influence him to remain & marry one of the daughters. But this only disgusted him the more with his lonely life & solitary & unprofitable situation—being obliged to do all the duties of husbandman, wood-cutter, dairy-maid, &c. though he had ample means to have paid for labour, but none was to be had. He no sooner declared his intention of leaving the country than his Yankee neighbours (which is generally the case) persecuted him with every annoyance, and the result was he sold his land for mere waste paper, though he had paid down his sterling gold for it, & it is doubtful whether he will ever realize a penny of the purchase money.

This is the fate of hundreds. And fortunate indeed is the emigrant who goes over without his family to make the trial, for hundreds are now living in America in a state of the greatest misery, who would not have remained, had it not been from a dread of again encountering a tedious voyage with a wife & children. I knew some disgraceful instances of fellows who had left a wife and family behind them in England, and made no scruple of taking a second wife in America. One man had a wife & family living with him in New York, whom he drove away to England by his brutality, and though this was known to hundreds, he found no difficulty in contracting a *left-handed* marriage with an American girl possessed of 1000 dollars, and his oldest child, a boy of 12 years old, was a witness to the whole transaction and continued to live in the same house with his father.—In fact, it is so common a thing for a man to have one wife in one state and a 2nd in another, that it is a proverbial saying, "An American has one wife in New York and another at Brooklyn."

Another man of 2 wives, who had married an American girl with a small fortune, was a Methodist preacher within a few miles of New York when I was there. When he left England he had never mounted a pulpit, and his wife expected to be sent for with her 6 children, as soon as circumstances permitted. Finding, however, that she recd no summons, and suspecting all was not right, she came over to New York, assisted in so doing by her parish, and inquired for her husband. She was told there was no person of the name in New York, but there was a Revd of the name at Newark. The poor woman posted off to that place, and there found that her husband had abandoned her & been married to an American girl who had borne him two children.

There is, however, a law by which persons may be punished for bigamy in America but it is so expensive a proceeding, from the difficulty of obtaining evidence, &c. that not one injured person out of 5000 could avail themselves of it. In fact the law is in such a state in North America, as regards marriage, and morality is so lax in consequence, that their own papers are continually complaining of it. One of the most ably conducted Journals, the *Sun*, a short time since took an occasion to observe, that such an enactment was much wanted in the United States such as had lately been passed by the South American states, which made it imperative upon all emigrants entering their country to produce a certificate whether they were married or not, and for the truth of which their resident Consul must vouch.

A short time before I left New York, a poor woman presented herself at the door of her runaway husband who had married an American girl on reaching the United States, and upon her knocking, he opened it himself. He asked her "what she wanted?" She told him *she was his wife*. Upon this he slapped the door in her face. The poor creature in vain tried to redress herself, and she must have perished in the streets of New York with her helpless children, but for the compassion of a few English Emigrants, who provided her with food & shelter, and she is now living decently, as a washerwoman, within sight of the dwelling of her recreant husband.

But this state of concubinage is universal in America. I lodged for a few days in one house where there were 14 couples living, as man & wife, and the person who kept it declared to me that she knew they were all living in a state of adultery. As for divorces, they are granted in all the States upon very trivial evidence. According to a late number of the Sun American Paper, in Ohio alone there were 5000 in less than two years. My readers may easily imagine what must be the state of morality where such things can be with impunity, and what are the prospects for a family of daughters, should any such contemplate emigrating to the United States.

The customs observed at such marriages as are celebrated with a kind of public recognition by their friends & relatives are anything but such as would be desirable in well-regulated societies. A houseful are invited, and of course there is a feast, which terminates with the ceremony of the bride being saluted by every *booby* of the party. I was present at one where the bridegroom by no means relished this part of the proceeding, and stood peeping from behind a corner of the room half blushing, half clenching his fist with rage, as the operation proceeded, & no sooner had it closed, than he seized his bride's hand, dragged her to a table where there stood a basin of water, and himself well-washed her face. And this precaution was the more necessary; as all the gentlemen present, with the exception of myself, had been chewing tobacco & spitting about the room the whole time they were present.

With marriage vows or contracts so loosely observed, an American Judge has lately decided, in New Hampshire, that if a gentleman for a considerable length of time pays particular attention to a lady of the same rank & standing in life with himself, such as to visit her (whether relation or not), or take her to visit at his father's, or friends, &c. from these facts the *jury have a right to presume a promise of marriage*.

CHAPTER X

All in America Gentlemen—Not True—A Cowhide Lashing Their Way of Paying off a Grudge—O'Connell & Spring-Rice—Gouging Eyes out Common in America—Duelling—Anecdote of a Barbarous One—Assassination Common at New Orleans—Savage Disregard for Human Life—Children Infected with It

EVERY rule has its exception, and so, it appears, has the proverb "two of a trade can never agree": for Mr. Stuart, in his *Three Years in America*, as cited by an American paper entitled *The Free Enquirer*, after declaring it as his opinion, that the United States contains "an infinitely greater number of gentlemen than any other country which exists, or ever has existed, on the face of the earth," adds, "I am glad to be supported in this opinion by at least one late British traveller in America, Mr. Ferrall, who says, that all in America are gentlemen." And this opinion adds Mr S. I put forth "*without fear of contradiction*, if the most generally accepted definition of the term (gentleman) be admitted, that it includes all persons of good education and good manners." Had Mr S. said *tact in turning the penny*, I should have fully agreed with him: but as it is, I deny his Statement *in toto*, and, like him, *without fear of contradiction*. I have never read either his or Mr Ferrall's work; but I must say I think that it is truly disgusting to find men of sense, and what pass for sensible men, and travellers too, whose every word should be a lesson to mankind, transmitting to the historian such *fulsome trash*—nay not fulsome trash alone, but absolute untruths—until even the Americans themselves, much as they love to be bespattered with compliment, must, when they read it, exclaim—

Undeserved praise is satire in disguise.

What extroadinary notions of *gentility*, "good manners," as Mr. S. expresses it, must that people have, with whom it is a habit, when secretly cherishing a grudge, to induce a *friend to* take a morning's walk with them, into the woods or forests, and coming to a convenient spot, tie their *dear friend* to a tree, &

Plate 6. A Member of Congress Receiving a Cowhide Lashing. By permission of the Syndics of Cambridge University Library.

with a thong from a cow's hide, to lash him till he is ready to expire with pain and loss of blood, and that, perhaps, merely to revenge themselves for some fancied injury—For instance: what would the British people say of Mr O'Connell, what would Messrs Stuart and Ferrall say, if, after the defeat his motion for a repeal of the Union received in the British House of Parliament, he, imagining that the Right Honourable Thomas Spring-Rice had been the cause of that defeat, had, with that honest effrontery which characterizes him, pretended to make matters up with his Right Honourable opponent, and induced him to take with him an early breakfast, but first, upon a pretence that it was healthy and good for the appetite, persuaded him also to accompany him in a ride as far as Epping Forest; and having reached its borders, in the *genteelest* way imaginable, said, "Now I should like to tie my horse to a tree & penetrate a little into this place. Suppose, my dear Sir," turning to Mr Spring-Rice, "we quit our horses for a brief space, and penetrate as far as Turpin's Cave?" "With all my heart," exclaims Mr R. and forthwith they grope their way till they come to a secluded spot, such as, in America, no cries of distress can issue from. "Now, Sir," says Mr O'Connell, who perchance is the stronger man of the two, "I intend to tie you to this tree and pay you, with a *cowhide lashing*, for spoiling my motion for a repeal of the Union." Mr Spring-Rice begs 10,000nd pardons, threatens & entreats—"No," says the hard-hearted repealer, "no whining—I'll have my revenge." And in the *genteelest manner imaginable*, he lays the back of Mr. Spring-Rice bare to the bone, and leaves him in a dying state, to take his chance of relief from some backwoodsman, and off rides Mr. O'Connell to his breakfast & his seat in the house, without fear of consequences for the *gentlemanly* assault he has committed?

I can assure my readers that this is no imagined picture. A similar thing was perpetrated in America, & by a Member of the American Congress upon another, too, the operator now representative of Tennessee. The fact is set forth in the autobiography of Colonel Crockett, the said American gentleman alluded to. But I can further assure Messrs Stuart and Ferrall, and they must have known the fact, that a cowhide licking, as the Americans would call it, is the ordinary way of paying off a grudge in many parts of the United States, and that the practice of soliciting the company of a friend in a pleasant ramble into the forest, the *Thurtell-like manner* of seducing the victim into the Snare, is a common occurrence in America. I have no doubt but many Americans will cry "shame," on perusing this chapter—but I answer, let them rather blush that there is cause for noticing such atrocities—or *gentlemanly* habits, if they please; and they will hear no more of them. Several cowhide lashings were administered during my stay in America, the last, to my knowledge, only a few days before I quitted New York for England.

Everybody acquainted with America must know & lament, that many other atrocious methods for revenging injuries are practiced by the Americans, even in their most civilized State, and in their great commercial depôt, New York, where their actions, manners, & habits are constantly under the eye of strangers; 3 cases of gouging eyes out occurred in that city but a very short time before I quitted it, which was in the latter part of May, 1834; and the following is the manner in which the disgusting & barbarous operation is performed. An American gentleman (of course, since Messrs Stuart & Ferrall agree that "all in America are gentlemen") watches his opportunity for springing upon his victim, and catching the long lock of hair, which is generally suffered to grow a little above each eye, between his two fingers nearest the thumb, he with a twist and dexterity that would throw our operating-surgeons far in the background, digs out the eye with his thumb, before you can say "Jack Robinson." And here I would recommend all persons emigrating, who may have any *contradictory* blood in their veins, if they have a wish to preserve their eyesight perfect, to *crop* their hair as close as possible.

Any person who is in the habit of reading American Police-Reports will see accounts of such attempts. The *Sun* American Paper, dated the 9th of April, 1834, one of their best for Police accounts, lies by my elbow whilst I am writing this chapter, and in it occur the words, John Rogers "attempted to gouge out one of the eyes of Israel Louis," for which John "ought to have been 'burnt at the Stake,' but he was only committed." Higher up the country the thing is a frequent occurrence. It is a common saying, if you go into a house of entertainment where Kentucky men abound, you will be sure to see some with but one eye—

having lost the other by being *gouged*, very genteely no doubt, and a practiced hand will recognize if such is the case, from the *drooping* of the eye-lid. Indeed the Kentuckians have the credit of being perfect masters of the art.

Duelling also is very common in America. But that, you will say, is a practice of revenging an insult common to the most civilized societies in all nations. True. But in no country is it accompanied with such barbarous characteristics as in America. For instance, duels are fought from the upper windows of two opposite houses. The parties take their loaded rifles, present them at each other, and fire from the opposite windows, at a concerted signal. An instance of this kind occurred between a Judge & a General, Americans, with which no doubt my readers are familiar.

Another instance of the Savage way in which duelling is conducted occurred not more than 3 months since, at New Orleans, in which a father, a husband, and a relative were shot. The old man's son-in-law had occasion to visit England, and during his absence his wife fell a sacrifice to the arts of a seducer. This the husband discovered on his return, and after upbraiding his wife with her criminality, she fell on her knees, acknowledged her guilt, and ultimately gave up the name of her paramour. The husband then communicated his disgrace to her father, a venerable old man, to whom he sent her. He was, it is said, one of the last of the republicans of the Washington School. The old man insisted upon taking the affair into his own hands. This was granted; and, his daughter having in the meantime been divorced from her husband, he at once waited upon the seducer and extorted from him a promise, that he would marry his daughter and wipe out the stain of disgrace, or meet him in 12 days to settle the affair in some other way. They met at the end of the 12 days, and a duel followed, though the old man's eyes were dull with age. The result was the old man was shot through the heart by his daughter's seducer, who was a practiced duellist, or what is called *a dead shot*, and knew, it is said, he had no danger of being hit. This disastrous result caused the injured husband to take up the affair, and he too was shot dead. The seducer was next called out by a relation of the old man—a 3rd victim fell. And such is the deadly spirit these circumstances have called forth in the breasts of the old man's relatives, said the New Orleans' Paper, a short time before I left, that God only knows where the matter will end.

But duelling and assassination are continually happening in that part of America. Persons are not infrequently shot with rifles, as they are mounting the sides of the Steamers, to take their departure from New Orleans, for no apparent cause but that of revenge, nor has there been a single instance, as yet, of one of these American *gentlemen* being brought to condign punishment for their murders. One assassination of this kind was perpetrated so publicly in the early part of the present year, 1834, that the Captain of the Steamer saw the fire by which his passenger fell, as he was mounting the side of the vessel, and rushed in the direction with a hope of securing the murderer, but it proved useless, as the villain had taken shelter in some one of the neighbouring houses or grog-shops. And I here state my conviction, from a careful observation of men & manners, in America, that there is such a savage disregard for human life abroad in that Country, that the very children are infected with it.

CHAPTER XI

MORAL STATE OF YOUTH IN AMERICA—STATE OF EDUCATION AT NEW YORK & ELSEWHERE—LANCASTRIAN OR NATIONAL SCHOOLS THE ONLY PLACES PROVIDED FOR THE CHILDREN OF THE BETTER CLASSES—PRIVATE SCHOOLS NOT PATRONISED—NUMBERS OF CHILDREN WITHOUT EDUCATION—NO PLACE OF EDUCATION PROVIDED FOR COLORED CHILDREN—HARVARD UNIVERSITY IN A STATE OF INSURRECTION

THERE is such a savage disregard for human life abroad in America, as I before observed, that the very children are infected with it. And this fact was acknowledged to me by an able physician in New York, to whom I mentioned it, with the observation, that they (the children) would "think no more of seizing hold of a cat or dog and strangling it, than they should of twisting a piece of rope." I was at another time in company with an American lady, & her little son of about 2 years old, when she remarked to me, what "a bright little rogue" he was. "He is so very mischievous," she added with a smile, "he will sometimes hold the cat by the tail over the fire and singe his whiskers off." It is a melancholy fact, that you may in America, daily hear mere infants swearing in the most frightful manner; and I have heard the Dutch women exclaim (of whom there are many resident in New York) as the oaths issued from their infantile lips, "Oh good English! Oh good English!"

As for the conduct of the American boys in the streets, I have been frequently obliged to run to avoid the stones & brick bats they are constantly in the habit of hurling from one side to the other, at the beastly pigs, boars & sows, with which the streets are beset, or at one another, without regard to age or sex passing by, and it is no uncommon sight to see a pig with its leg broken by them. I had named this more than once to Americans whom I was in the habit of meeting, by whom it was flatly denied; and by one gentleman in particular. But at the very instant he was one day contradicting me in the subject, I pointed out to him 4 parties of boys so employed, in the same street, and he acknowledged at once, that "seeing was believing." Boys, mere children, may be constantly seen to enter the grog–shops, throw down their 3 cents, drink of their glass of neat spirits (generally rum or brandy), light their cigar, & walk out with as much *sang froid* as their fathers. Indeed, there may be every day seen in New York, boys of 12 or 13 years of age, at the Hotels or grog-shops, *playing at Dominoes* for beer or spirits, with all the gambling ardor that marks their Seniors.

And I may here remark, that gambling is carried to a fearful height in America, and though there are laws for its prevention, there is abundance of houses open all night where these experienced are in waiting for their prey. More than once was I beset by born American gamblers—gamblers by profession, but I was not come-at-able. Suicides are very common, particularly at Boston, of young men so reduced to despair and beggary—so much so, that it has of late been a subject for comment amongst the American journalists. But gambling in America is not confined to houses in their towns & cities. It is carried to a shameful extent on board their steam-boats, wherein professed gamblers commonly take their passage for the sole purpose of fleecing the unwary.

In some states of America boys are regularly trained in the art of pistol & rifle shooting; not, be it observed, for any necessary purpose; but that they may become expert duellists. In an American paper of the other day is the Announcement of "a Seminary for teaching the art of *pistol firing*"; and the Kentuckians not only make it a chief part of the education of their youth, but they are constantly trained to hit their object *through a mist*, as it is called—the method being for the boys to kindle a fire, and place a rushlight so that its blazing wick can just be discerned through the rising smoke, at which they practice firing, and thus become expert duellists. No one is there esteemed a good shot, it is said, who cannot drive a nail into a board without turning it, for though he should "hit the nail on the head," were it bent in any way it would be sure to create a general laugh at his expense.

Under such circumstances, it is not surprising that there is a boy (named Elliot) 12 years of age now in Boston Gaol, awaiting his trial, for shooting another boy of his own age, whilst out practicing at a target, with a horseman's pistol. He returned home without his companion, and to several questions declared he did not know where he was. This was on a Saturday. The poor wounded boy had in vain entreated his murderer would assist him to his friends. The hardened reply was—"I intend to bury you"—and he actually went and returned with a spade to dig a grave for his victim, who had in the meantime crawled & hid himself under some projection—and lived to describe his murderer's chagrin at missing him. The poor wounded boy, whose name was Buckland (son of a person of that name at Springfield, Massachusetts) was not discovered till the next morning, and then in a dying state. All this time his murderer denied any knowledge of him, but the youth recovered sufficiently to communicate the whole of the diabolical transaction to his friends. The result was the apprehension of Elliot.

But what must we expect from a state of Society where parents (I have heard them as seated on their knees) are in the habit of *teaching their offspring infidelity*, and swearing grossly in their presence. I heard one *gentleman*, a distinction to which his property & rank in life entitled him, and in fact a Quaker of considerable influence in New York, address a child not 3 years old, that was annoying him, certainly, when writing, by climbing upon his knee, with "Get down you young ——!"

One would naturally suppose that the first care of a free and an enlightened government, such as America claims to be considered, would be the moral and religious education of the people. But this has certainly not been the case. "It is computed that in the states South and west of New York," says the intelligent editor of *The Man*, American Paper, dated 13th of May, 1834, "there are more than a *million* of children, between the ages of one & 15, who attend no Schools, and are growing up without the simplest rudiments of an English education. But of 400,000 children in Pennsylvania, only 150,000 were at School in 1830. In New Jersey, 11,700 children are destitute of the means of instruction, and 15,000 adults are unable to read. In Kentucky, out of 143,700 children between the age of 5 & 15 in 1833, only 103,300 attended School."

In New York itself there is but poor provision made for the education of the better classes. I could not learn that any encouragement was given in any part of that city or its neighbourhood to respectable private Schools. So that the children of the opulent as well as those of the poor must either attend the National Schools, or none. This has a most pernicious effect upon the upper classes, of which I witnessed some painful instances both of language & manners, and is a heavy drawback on the advancement of civilization. And here I must remark, I never could learn that any provision was made in America, either in the state of New York, or elsewhere, for the education of the children of the *free-blacks*. I have often watched at the doors of their National Schools but I never could discover a coloured child, either male or female, issuing from one, nor do I believe they would be permitted to attend them. Alas! for the poor blacks, education, like freedom, is not necessary for them, in the eye of an American—it is with him as Longinus has declared it is with some who ascribe the sublime to an effort of nature alone:

The only Art to attain it is to be born to it.

What is the state of their Universities may be imagined from the *Boston Transcript* of May, 1834, which says—"Some of the Sophomore Class of Harvard University having injured the furniture of one of the public halls, President Quincy threatened to send the whole class to *Concord*. The next morning they evinced their contempt of his authority by hissing & scraping at prayers. The consequence was public rebuke, and the dismissal of the class. On the order being announced, the other classes took against the Government, and the rebellion became general. At the last accounts, all studies were suspended."

CHAPTER XII

American Patriotism—Paltry Grant to The Poles—Narrative of a Pole—State of Swiss Emigrants in New York

IF an engrossing love of self, if a belief that they are the cleverest people in the Universe, if an utter contempt for everything not purely American, constitute patriotism, then are the People of the United States the most patriotic nation upon Earth; for in all those qualities do they excel in a superlative degree. What must the poor expatriate Poles, what must the poor Swiss Emigrants, think of Republican America, of that land and people to whose thresholds fame has drawn them, as a greatly favoured spot, where they were welcomed with cold looks & colder words (instead of being rec$^{\underline{d}}$ with outstretched arms & a brother's benison) and are suffered to starve in the midst of plenty? Several hundreds of the former (says the *New York* American *Advertiser*) who cannot speak our language, are actually starving in New York, nor has an effort been made by the Americans or the American Govt. to assist them.

I happened to be in New York when the 300 or 400 expatriated Poles arrived who sought the American shores, and sadly must the poor fellows hearts have ached at the utter indifference with which they were *welcomed* by the American part of the population. Indeed, but for the attention they excited from the English Emigrants, but for their congratulations, not the slightest countenance would they have received, & it was publicly remarked, that not a single American evinced a feeling of approbation at their landing. The English Emigrants, on the contrary, went amongst them and showed them every attention their humble means would afford. I took one of the Poles, a fine handsome man, into an Hotel, where about 20 persons, mostly Americans, were present, to endeavour to raise a subscription for them. Myself and another put several dollars into a hat and went round the room with him—Shall it be told, that the only half dollar added was by an Englishman, and that of all the Americans present, but one added a paltry shilling? Yet these men were *republicans* & mostly well off in the world.

The very editors of the newspapers blushed for their countrymen, and by spirited articles endeavoured to rouse the money-loving Americans to a sense of the disgrace their apathy would draw of them in the eyes of Europeans—it was, however, in vain. For a benefit it was proposed to give them at one of the Theatres was absolutely postponed for a time, from the small inclination evinced to support it, and when it did take place, scarcely a single American was present. Their audience were mostly English.

At last the Government felt themselves obliged to do something for the poor fellows, shamed into it by the outpourings of the papers, the murmurs of the Emigrants, and the effect, perhaps, of their being reminded by the Poles, that two of the distinguished men of their country had fought for them during their struggle for independence, one of whom had perished on the field of battle. Will it be credited by Englishmen, by *Aristocratic* England, that whilst her Parliament voted a Sum of £10,000 for the relief of the Polish Exiles in London, swelled by ample donations from various sources to a munificent sum, that America, the Republican Government of America, the land of Liberty & independence, as it is called, voted them the paltry Sum (I believe I am correct) of 500 dollars (£100 English) for the relief of nearly 400 Poles?!—I confess this Act appeared to me the very consummation of national degradation—who shall henceforward talk of America as the land where they boast all men are equal?!—Yet an American had the effrontery actually to name it to me with exultation. But when I told him that the poor town in England of which I was a native had subscribed the sum of £1500 (6,000 Dollars, American Money, for the Polish Patriots), I did for once silence an American, and a lady present exclaimed to him, with the pride of an English heart as yet unsullied with American selfishness, and long may it remain so, "God bless you, you don't know England."

But let my readers judge of American patriotism, from the following abstract of

A Narrative of a Pole,

which was translated from the original, published in an American paper entitled The *New-England Galaxy*, in April, 1834.

There was not a happier family in Warsaw than ours at the close of 1830. The wrongs of our oppressed country, it is true, would often dash with gloom our most joyful moments. But the savage & iniquitous Constantine had not yet broken in upon our little circle, by his tyrannical measures. None of our friends had been among the victims of his ferocity. And though the scenes which we daily witnessed were sufficient to rouse our indignation, yet my father's constitutional gaiety forbade him to look wholly on the dark side of things, and prevented us from falling into utter despondency and grief. He was one day accosted in the street by a friend, who, in cautious language, deplored the national degradation, and recounted some fresh act of cruelty and oppression. My father assented to his remarks, and, on parting, exclaimed, in a tone of voice, which was indiscreetly loud: "*Eh bien; vive la joie! Le bon temps reviendra!*" (Well, be of good heart—better times will return.) Just Heaven! those words were his doom! A Russian emissary of the tyrant had heard him utter them, and from that moment he was a marked man. The next day a commissary of police, with a number of Soldiers, entered the house. My father was forcibly torn from his family, and imprisoned in an unwholesome dungeon in the vicinity of a filthy drain. My mother strove to intercede with the grand Duke for his pardon, but was ignominiously repulsed. We soon afterwards heard of his death, and the wreck of our property ensued. My sister, who was transcendently beautiful, became the forced paramour of a Russian officer. My mother declined gradually in health; but lived to see the first dawnings of the revolution. The vision of regenerated Poland seemed to rouse all the energies of her soul, and fill her emaciated frame with new life. I was by her bedside. She spoke with animation which surprised me. A glow kindled in her cheeks. An angelic brightness burned in her eyes, as she prayed to the Most High in behalf of her son and of her country. It was her last effort. She sank back exhausted. A quivering motion of utterance flickered along her lips, and ended in a peaceful smile. Convulsively her attenuated hand clasped mine. Paleness, like a shadow, chased the hectic from her face. I listened in vain for the sound of her breath. I laid my hand upon her forehead. It was cold—and then did I know that she was dead!

Firmly and briefly did I give directions for her funeral,

and saw her remains consigned decently to the ground. I was now alone.

How did I hail the unfolding of that spirit, which the 3 days of Paris raised to its highest pitch! The 29th of November was the day fixed upon by the Patriots for a general rising. On the evening of that day I witnessed the concerted signal—the burning of a house near the Vistula. No sooner had the flames burst forth from the roof, than the cries of "To arms! Poland forever!" resounded from every quarter of the city. The cadets, headed by Schlegel & Wysocki, attacked the barracks of the Russian Guards, with a view of arresting the Grand Duke. The hireling soldiery were soon routed, but Constantine, as is well known, escaped. The cadets returned to the city without the loss of a man. In the Norvy-Swiat they were joined by two companies of infantry, while Potocki and Trembicki, who opposed the revolutionary movement, were almost torn in pieces by the people. In the course of the night we attacked the arsenal, and supplied ourselves liberally with arms. I was present early next morning in the Ulicka Dluga, where the assemblage of the patriots took place. You have already had descriptions of the singular & heart-stirring scene. A faint glow was just beginning to crimson the east, but it was still dark. Fires were kindled in different parts of the city, which threw a strange light along the streets. It was on this occasion that the assembled multitude knelt down and with electric devotion, returned thanks to God for the success which had thus far attended their armies, and prayed that he would ever bless their cause.

It is needless for me to go through the events of the revolution. Dwerkecki in the course of his manoeuvres in opposition to (the Russian General) Rudiger, unfortunately invaded the Austrian frontier. After a warm action, the Austrian cavalry appearing in sight obliged us to lay down our arms, while the Russians were permitted to retire to Volhynia. With a companion, I escaped the vigilance of these tools of tyranny, and after many imprisonments and releases, after continued hardships & vexations, I arrived in Paris in March 1833. The sympathies of the French had been with us during our struggle but not their assistance. I managed to subsist by various subordinate occupations for a considerable time, and finally passed over to England. Wherever I went, I found shoals of my countrymen, many

> of whom were in a condition of abject penury and humiliation. I reached Liverpool at the commencement of the present year, and immediately took passage in an American vessel for New York.
>
> As we approached the American shores, my emotions grew painfully acute. I pictured to my self a reception, which, contrasted with that which it was my fate to experience, would be painfully ridiculous. I fancied that I should find enthusiasts in the cause of liberty, who would welcome with open arms, the survivors of those martyrs in her defence, who had bled for subjugated Poland. I believed that the countrymen of Kosciusko and of Pulaski would be everywhere hailed with respect and with hospitality. I dreamed of plenty, of sympathy, of honourable employment, of good feeling, and of kindness.
>
> * * * * * * *
>
> After spending all my resources in New York, I went forth and made application to several persons of wealth & standing. The commercial interests of the country were, I was told, destroyed. Others asserted that their liberties were at stake, and that a monied aristocracy was making efforts to put down the free spirit of the people. *One man told me to go back & kiss the feet of the aristocrat of all Russias*, for that a baser despot ruled here. He added, "I am a ruined man. Don't apply to me."
>
> * * * * * * *
>
> I am weak, discouraged, and ill at ease. I feel like a weed flung on the vast ocean of events, and tossed from wave to wave without respite, without an abiding place. But there is a heaven, a shore of peace.—It is glorious to reflect that the hour may be near at hand when I shall join those friends & compatriots, who have gone before me to the world of spirits. The hope is my sole consolation now. I would not part with it for the treasures of the world.

Everybody knows with what horror an Englishman would listen to the bare idea of employing foreign troops. Your American is less careful to whom he entrusts the duty of fighting his battles or coercing the refractory. Several of their newspapers recommended the employment of the Poles as troops, observing they would make excellent horsemen and fight better than the Irish, of which country nearly all the dragoons of America are either natives or descendants—and many of their marines are English.

CHAPTER XIII

POLICY PURSUED BY AMERICA TOWARDS THE INDIANS—THE LATTER BETRAYED INTO MURDERS BY THE FORMER—DESPERATE CONFLICT—ANECDOTES OF THE INDIAN CHIEF BLACKHAWK—HE CAUSED THE REPEAL OF THE LAW OF IMPRISONMENT FOR DEBT—WHICH IT IS SINGULAR THEY ARE ENDEAVOURING TO RE-ENACT—THE AMERICAN GOVERNMENT REBUKED BY ANOTHER INDIAN CHIEF—ANECDOTE OF A 3RD INDIAN CHIEF—PRESIDENT OF AMERICA REBUKED BY AN INDIAN CHIEF IN THE COURSE OF A TREATY

THE selfish & barbarous policy which the Americans have pursued towards the Indian nations, of which but a remnant now exists in the United States, and which, there is reason to fear, the inhabitants are plotting to extirpate, is a stain on their character, as a civilized nation, of the blackest dye, Slavery excepted, especially when viewed in reference to their republicanism and *vapourings* about equality. No sooner do the Indians settle in any favourable district, than your American finds a pretext for despoiling them of the soil, either by intrigue or open aggression. The consequence is that the most bitter feuds are created and kept alive, and murders are daily perpetrated on the frontier of the most barbarous character, by the Indians, as many well-informed persons think, at the instigation of interested settlers, for the artful purpose of exciting public odium against them and rousing the country to such a pitch of excitement as to cause a kind of the general crusade for their extirpation, that the whites get possession of their lands & property.

The following is an account of a Desperate Conflict that occurred under these exciting circumstances, from the *New Orleans Bulletin*, American paper, in consequence of which the writer, a native of Middletown, New Jersey, and agent to a Colonel Austin, died at Bexar, the 23rd of March, of the wounds he recd in the affray:—

BEXAR, March 13, 1834.

DEAR SIR—The lamentable situation in which I find myself, causes my mind to revert to my friends in New Orleans. I have had one of the most dreadful adventures that man ever had and told of it afterwards. I left this place on the 15th of last month for the capital, Monclova, having business with the legislature. I was so imprudent as to start only with a youth, although it is customary to travel in large companies on the frontier. I had proceeded about forty miles by 9 o'clock at night, when something like 20 Tawakanies presented themselves in the road, stepping out of a thicket—firing 8 or 10 muskets at me in almost touching distance. One ball entered my side and lodged near the back bone. I fell to the ground with great violence, which caused my pistol to go off; the ball of which also entered my hip, but came out again. I had all my presence of mind; I returned the war whoop; I tried to throw myself in the midst of them, knowing that in desperation alone there was any thing to hope. I charged on them, and they retreated into the bushes. After several unsuccessful attempts to come in close quarters with them, and having a great many guns shot at me, I took a stand behind a bush, and they approached and commenced firing—I took deliberate aim at one of the most daring—put a ball and four buckshot through his body—he gave a slight scream and fell—it was enough—they were whipt. His companions dragged him off and all immediately disappeared.

By this time the pain occasioned by my fall overcame me. I flung myself on the ground and rolled in agony till morning; the Indians got our horses and saddles, we only saved the saddle bags. I was several miles from water and started to go back on the road. When I came up to it, I could not swallow, in consequence of an arrow I had received in my throat. Here I staid two days and nights, sitting against a tree, without a blanket or any thing to cover me with. The first night the young man was with me; the next day I dispatched him to Bexar, and remained alone till they came out to bring me in. When the company arrived, I went back to the battle ground, got our saddle bags, saw where they had dragged off the dead Indian, and picked up fifty arrows. My wounds were no part of my pain; my body appeared mashed, and it is that which has caused all my sufferings. On the road I met Dr. Beal, who cut the ball out of me and tendered every service that hospitality could suggest.

When I arrived here, there was neither physician or medicine to be had, not even the commonest articles of food. I desired greatly to get a dose of medicine to relieve me from choking, but it was not to be had. I have now lain twenty-one days on my back, not being able to bear any other position. I find myself no better; I thought for some time I should die, to which idea I was perfectly reconciled. I have a place selected for my grave, being excluded from the church yard as a brute or heretic.

This situation for a sick man in this place is indescribably unpleasant—he can get nothing that he wants to either drink or eat. People here have been so long tributary to the Indians that they bear every indignity as a matter of course; they have stolen all the horses from their neighboring ranches, yet no campaigns are started against them. There is nothing sinks a nation so much in my estimation as a fear of the Indians—yet so cowardly are the latter, that five and twenty Americans can whip two hundred of them. Two or three years ago, thirty Shawnese attacked and routed between two and three hundred Comanches within a few miles of this place. The Comanches applied to their friends, the Mexicans, for assistance, and obtained it, causing the Shawnese to lose a Comanche cavalcade which they were driving off.

I wish, if I ever get well, to return to civilized society. Whatever my circumstances may be, I never want to be a hundred yards West of the Mississippi again. Yours, very affectionately.

T.W. McQUEEN.

This is only one out of a number of Murders that had been perpetrated during the few months previous to my departure from the United States, which were looked upon but as the commencement of a series of reprisals begun by the oppressed Indians. *The New York Commercial Advertiser* of the 29th of May, 1834, says, it is apprehended, "that the Indians entertain the design of committing degradation, both upon the property & persons of the whites, secretly, if not publicly. Dr Burnes, a gentleman belonging to Etawah, Cherokee County, (Georgia), was shot on the 13Inst. about 2 miles from Cassville, by an Indian. He was riding along without the slightest apprehension of an attack when the shot struck him in the head & glanced off, wounding him severely but not mortally."

Much as some persons will attempt to depreciate the character of these Indians, they are by no means that unintellectual people the Americans would lead us to suppose. It is not long since the celebrated Indian Chief, Blackhawk, happened to be passing along the streets of New York, when he saw an officer conveying a man to prison. He inquired what for. The answer was, "drunkenness." "A pretty republic this," was the rebuke of the *savage*. "You first sell men poison to make them drunk, and then send them to prison for drinking it." It was the same Indian Chief that caused the Americans *to abolish arrest for debt*. During a visit he made to a New York Prison, observing some decently drest persons amongst the prisoners, he inquired "what brought them there?" "Debt," was the answer. "What!" exclaimed Blackhawk, "put men into prison for debt! How are they to get the means for paying their creditors in prison?" This was said in a similar spirit in which our own Dr Johnson wrote his celebrated paper in the *Idler*, some 50 years since, and this Indian Chief has the credit of thereby Shaming the American Government into the repeal of the law. But it is a little singular, that at this very period, whilst the English Government are considering the propriety of a measure for repealing the law of arrest for debt in Great Britain, the American Congress have been occupied with discussing a measure for the re-enactment of the law, which was only recently lost by 3 votes.

Another Indian chief was one day standing amidst the crowd at levees of the President of the United States, when he attracted the eyes of an American Senator, who went up to him and inquired if he had a petition to present? "What is the use of bringing a petition here," was the answer of the Savage, "when you white men never keep your word?" If this rebuke was not a stigma upon our national character, it was observed by the Editor of an American paper, at the time the incident occurred, he did not know what was.

But the truth is the Americans have no regard for national character, nor do they treat the poor Indians, chief or not, with more respect than they do the free-black population, and with much less regard for justice. A gentleman with whom I am acquainted was lately on his way from New York to Canada, on board a Steamer, when his attention was much taken with the fine figure of an Indian chief among the passengers, and he was no less struck with his intelligence, on conversing with him. He found he was one of those attached to the English cause during the recent war with the United States, and held a commission in the British-American war, the half pay of which he had just been to receive and he was on his way to join his Indian countrymen. The English Gentleman wished him to dine with him in the Cabin, but on requesting he might invite him to the meal, the Captain of the American Steamer reminded him of the prejudice that existed against people of colour, which made it impossible to grant his request, without the permission of the passengers generally. They did *stoop* so far as to concede the point to the Englishman, whose address & manner had made him a general favourite, but when the Indian Chief sat down, no one besides the Englishman paid him the slightest attention, or exchanged a word with him. He knew he was looked upon as an intruder, and he seized the first opportunity for escaping the humiliating situation in which he found himself, with half a meal.

The Indians are well aware that they have neither forbearance nor justice to hope for from the Americans. They who were the original possessors of the soil are treated as outcasts & intruders. Well was the American President rebuked by an Indian chief, when he proposed to treat with him for the cession of a part of his territory: "White man & Red man (said the Savage) sat on a chair together, & the White man keeps hitching, & hitching, till the Red man is pushed off. And thus, it is," he added, "that your White men despoil us of our Country. What use is there for a treaty?"

CHAPTER XIV

Americans' Ideas of Independence—Helps—Servants—And Boss—Dr Johnson, Mrs Macaulay, and American Equality—Masters, Helps, and Apprentices—American Society One Great Hodge-podge

"We Americans," is an expression constantly in the mouths of the people of the United States, and the Emigrant will scarcely have been a month fixed in the republic before it seasons everything he says. I was so provoked with this in one person I knew, that I could not help exclaiming—"D—n it, have you so soon forgotten the old country, friends, relatives, and English comfort!" But I suppose it is the effect of association and the loss, in a degree, of self-esteem: for it is impossible for any Englishman to pride himself honestly in the change he has made, when he finds himself surrounded by Americans, American habits & usages, & coolly compares them with what he has abandoned. He will tell you, "but I have acquired *independence*." Independence forsooth. What is the independence he has purchased by the change?

The only idea of independence an American has is that of treating his compatriots and customers with *vulgar* insolence and indifference. As if the practice of the amenities of polished and social life were inconsistent with that of independence, either civil, political, or religious. They will, for instance, sift their cinders, in their best rooms, under your nose, without any intimation of their intention so to do, and call it impertinence if you remonstrate. If you go into one of their Grog-shops and order a dish of stewed oysters, a greasy host, from a corner, smoking with his heels on the table, will tell you, in the most *independent* manner imaginable, he can't or won't rise to serve you. Or, if you have succeeded in getting a cup of coffee and eatables, should you ask for a 2nd cup, you will most likely be told, as I have often been, "you can't have it." If you order a glass of spirits of which you only take a *sip* at first, as a moderate Englishman is accustomed to do, you no sooner put it down than before you can take it up again to finish it, it is popped into the receptacle for waste. "Keeping moving" is their motto.

I one day desired the Servant might be sent to me. I was overheard, and in bounced my lady of the mop & pail with, "We have no servants in this country, I guess." "Pray what are you, then?" was my inquiry. "A help," was her answer. "Well," said I, "and a help means one who assists a person, and a Servant does no more." "But I tell you," said my lady, "We have neither masters nor servants here." "Pray what do you call your master?" I inquired. "Boss"—was the reply. "Well," said I, "and Boss is Dutch for master." This puzzled our free-born American, and out of the room she bounced, probably to make further inquiries as to the truth of the latter assertion.

At one lodging-house where I staid for a time, a gentleman gave some offence to a dirty wench, a help, save the mark, and into the breakfast-room she flung, mop in hand, and addressed her mistress with, "if you don't send Mr —— about his business, I shall leave your place." No reason was given, and mine hostess had the sense to resist. Upon which Dolly packed up her wardrobe and walked out of the house without so much as saying "by your leave."

Another help had been hired by an English Emigrant, who mistaking her for a person whom he had engaged to do certain offices as a remuneration for her food & the wages he was to pay her, gave her orders to do certain things, as he was wont to do to his well-ordered establishment in England. My lady, however, refused to do more than she thought meet, and flatly told him that she was "no Servant, but help, and that she should only perform what she thought *necessary*." This roused our Englishman's choler, and *radical* as he called himself, he turned Madam into the street, bags & baggage, where she had not been long before she would fain have returned & done her duty. Were this course pursued in more cases, your Americans would soon find it their interest to be good servants, instead of *dirty* helps, which they generally are; for, catching their habits from their betters, they will pass the whole winter without so much as once washing their hands & face, nor do I think they often indulge themselves with such a luxury in the Summer Season.

Before I visited America, I had often been told, that your American *helps* dined at the same table with their *Boss*: but this I found to be false, as I did many other tales. The custom is for the master & his family to dine first, and the white Servants then sit down & make a dinner off the remains, at the table where they have just been waiting. Servants in England beat them here. They have generally a comfortable table fresh set out for them. As for the black servants in America, they are never allowed to dine any where but in the cellar, where they mostly pass their time, their commons being composed of the *scrapings* left by the White Servants.

It is well known that the famous M[rs] Macaulay was a great advocate for the principles of equality, engendered by the French Revolutionists. D[r] Johnson was one day dining at her table, when she very dogmatically insisted that there ought to be no distinction between men, whatever their stations in life might be. The Doctor listened without saying any thing, and having swallowed his dinner with great haste, rose from his chair and desired the liveried servant, John, who had been waiting behind him to take his place between the two ladies, who had supported our English sage. "Bless me, D[r]," exclaimed M[rs] M. rising from her chair in great agitation, "what are you about?" "Only carrying into practice your doctrine of equality, Madam," was the reply, given in his characteristic manner. And I can assure my readers, that though America is, according to their Constitution, the land *where all men are equal*, were a help or servant to attempt to take a seat at the same table with an American Boss & his lady, they would both rise with as much agitation as did M[rs] Macaulay—nay, I would not answer for the Boss in a fit of Yankey choler, kicking the free-born American, otherwise help, out of the room, probably into the street.

I was one day passing through a thoroughfare in New York, and saw a help kicked out of a house, for what offence I cannot say, but it was an evidence of the fact, that American servants are no better treated than English ones: I even doubt if they are either so independent or so well off. In England, if a servant is sent away, without sufficient warning, or cause, upon appealing to a magistrate they will have their complaints listened to & redressed—I inquired if such was the case in America, but the persons I appealed to stared at me with a credulous expression, as if they doubted my Sanity. It is, however, no uncommon thing for a help or an apprentice to take themselves off into the country, for a week or 10 days, without asking leave of their Boss, & at the end return to their employ & places without taking the slightest notice of the delinquency, and their Boss commonly satisfies his anger with 10 minutes *swearing* at them, in no very gentle terms, well aware, that if he turned he or she off, he should not better himself.

The truth is, no American has an exact idea of the relation he bears, in Society, to another. To be vulgar & insolent is esteemed the height of independence. No one seems to know his position or duty. Master & help, Statesman & Citizen, Host and Sojourner, Dealer & Customer, high & low, rich & poor, seem one eternal hodge-podge—now insolent, now obsequious, ever talking of independence, but never really practicing it—this is literally the case from the President to the Sweep—by the by, the latter class are all *blacks*.

Plate 7. All Men Are Born Equal. Vide American Constitution.
By permission of the Syndics of Cambridge University Library.

CHAPTER XV

SLAVERY—TREATMENT OF RUNAWAY SLAVES AT NEW YORK—INIQUITY OF SUCH PRACTICES UNDER A REPUBLICAN GOVERNMENT—MURDERS PERPETRATED IN CONSEQUENCE—RIGHTS OF THE BLACK POPULATION TO THE SOIL

THE American Constitution says—All men are born equal:—so said Thomas Jefferson, late President of the United States, author of the *Declaration of Independence*, wherein the above is especially set forth. Yet this same Thomas Jefferson was the father of a *race of Coloured Slaves, that worked as such upon his own estate*, & even the present Head of the United States, Andrew Jackson, is said to be one of the *largest slave-owners, in America*. Is it then to be wondered at, that in those states where slavery still prevails, most extraordinary scenes are exhibited, & that it is shewn up with all the obscenities and savageness which characterized it in its worst periods?

An American gentleman, a Quaker, told me, that not long since, visiting some of his Quaker friends in Virginia, he was one day invited to dine with a slave-owner, and took his Children, grown-up sons & daughters, with him, as requested. But what was his horror to see the feelings of his children shocked, by their being waited upon at table, by female Slaves, in a State of perfect nudity; and upon his remonstrating with his host, he actually expressed himself insulted. He assured me that the condition of Society there was such, it was quite impossible for any one to hope to save their children from the taint of the immoralities they must witness, and that many whites were emigrating in consequence. In Richmond the negroes are kept in such a state of subjection, by the republicans of the United States, on the appearance of a white man in the streets they are obliged to stand in rows till he is past. Any white seen speaking familiarly to a Slave, in more than one state, probably in all, would be *cut* and looked upon with horror for so far practicing their declaration of equality, and it is a capital offence, in some parts of America, *for any one to teach a Slave to write*.

What a contrast does *Republican* American bear to other parts of the world, in this respect. England has emancipated her

Slaves at a sacrifice of £20,000,000: and, says the American Quarterly, as cited by the Sun American Paper, April the 9th, 1834, "On the declaration of independence by the Mexican provinces, a law immediately followed for the entire abolition of slavery." What a reproof for an older country, boasting free institutions. We find America still barbarously encouraging & protecting this infamous traffic, even to death. "A German sailor," says the paper quoted, "was shot at Baltimore in attempting to get on board the brig *Hope*, lying in the bay (of New York), bound to New Orleans, in which were confined 200 Slaves destined for that place, and for their security a guard was placed over them": a guard composed, be it observed, of *republicans*, or, as they are called, of the free-born sons of America. If a slave escaped from any slave-owner & could reach a place subject to Great Britain, he no sooner got his foot on the soil, than he became a freeman: as Cowper so beautifully expresses it—

> If once a Slave
> Breathes but our air, that moment he is free.
> They touch our country and their fetters fall.

But in America, republican America, forsooth, the case is quite altered. For even in the State & city of New York, where slavery has been abolished (into which act, it is notorious the American Government was harried by the English Emigrants), no protection is afforded to a negro who may escape from the lash of a Yankey Slave-driver. "Nine negroes (meaning free-blacks) were committed on a charge of assembling at a Coffee-House Slip," says a New York paper of April, 1834, "armed with clubs for the purpose of rescuing a runaway slave which the Recorder had ordered back to prison."

And "a black man & woman," says a New York Standard, of the 29th of June, 1833 (citing the *Detroit Free Press*), "who had formerly been slaves in Kentucky, were arrested in this city a few days since, in accordance with an act of congress, and after examination were committed to prison, to await the pleasure of the owner. On Monday last, they were taken down to the lake. *Two gentlemen*, agents of the owner, had come to Detroit for the purpose of arresting them. On Sunday evening a successful attempt was made by the colored people of the city, to rescue the woman; and their movements then indicated a spirited desperation and audacity quite incompatible with the due enforcement of the law with the ordinary means. On Monday afternoon, about 3 o'clock, when it was expected the prisoner would be taken from the jail to the steamboat, a large number of black people assembled on the commons. When the carriage drove up, they drew nearer to the prison. One lusty fellow planted himself on the steps, armed with a tremendous club, and swore that the man should not be taken away. As soon as the door was open, Sheriff Wilson received a blow on his head which brought him to the ground; when a party of negroes rushed up, caught the manacled slave in their arms, and carried him to a cart which was waiting for him. He took the reins & drove towards the woods on the Gratiot road, accompanied by the ringleaders of the mob. We have heard that Sheriff Wilson was dangerously wounded, & two negroes were shot, but neither of them have yet died."

This scene was enacted, be it noted, in republican America. But a worse still remains to be told—A runaway Slave was lying in the prison of New York, committed a few days before I took my departure for England, who had escaped from Richmond, and solemnly declared he would suffer any death rather than be sent back to his merciless owner. And so determined was he, that he stabbed the Sheriff in the act of arresting him, whose life was only saved by the knife being turned from the direction of his heart, by one of his ribs. Several constables were next wounded in attempting to take him, and he was only secured & taken to prison, at last, by a party of butchers sallying from their slaughter-houses upon him. For which service, observed the Editor of the New York *Sun* paper, in recording the fact, we heartily wish them in the poor fellow's situation.

But still more harrowing to the friends of humanity must be the fact, that a number of slaves from different states who had escaped to, & settled in New York, during the last 20 years, & had in the meantime married and become fathers of numerous families, were recently betrayed by a mercenary wretch, who possessed himself of their secret & gave information against them: In consequence, when I left New York, the authorities were occupied with the *humane* task of arresting the poor fellows & tearing them from the bosom of their fond families, as fast as they could find them out, most if not all being married &

settled.

In this same America, where their *infamous* Constitution declares *all men are born equal* (I call it infamous, because everything is infamous that bears a lie upon the face of it—) there was lately another scene enacted, at Maryland, where a slave having escaped, was arrested by two *gentlemen*, who placed him in a room for the night, and themselves slept in the apartment, with a rifle by their sides, for the better security, or, as they would say, **protection** of their prisoner. It was natural that he should project his escape, and to lull their suspicion, he pretended illness. Both his gaolers fell asleep; upon which he seized the gun, killed his keepers, and escaped into the woods.

Are these the scenes upon which the Americans would found their claims to be considered a liberal & civilized nation? Rather are they becoming the creatures of a Caligula or a Nero. When they (the Americans) rebelled against the mother country, did they hesitate to liberate themselves? Did they hesitate to slay thousands to that end? I tell them in their teeth that every American who upholds Slavery, and the barbarous policy they now pursue towards the poor negroes in the United States ought to have "Traitor" branded on his forehead.

But the *humane* Americans have made provision for the free-blacks, they will tell you, in their new Colony of *Liberia*, in Africa, to which they annually transport as many as their funds will allow them to liberate who chose to go there. But how will they reply to the fact, that for every score they liberate, or transfer to this African pest-house, they import into the United States 100 fresh slaves, dragged from the bosoms of their friends, in the most ferocious manner, and conveyed in American ships to the ports of the United States, *where free-men are shot* upon a suspicion of any attempt to communicate with them—Shot by the very Soldiers of republican America, that America where all men are born equal? By what right, I would ask, do the Americans pilot the transporting of the free-blacks to this new State of *Liberia*: "Have not I become climatized," said an old free-black to me, one day. "Have not I, who was born in America, as great a right to the soil as they have? Nay more, for my fathers were brought here by force? Besides," he added, "are they not intruders as well as we?" I say again, that every American who upholds slavery and the barbarous policy they now pursue towards the poor negroes, in the United States, ought to have "***Traitor***" branded on his forehead.

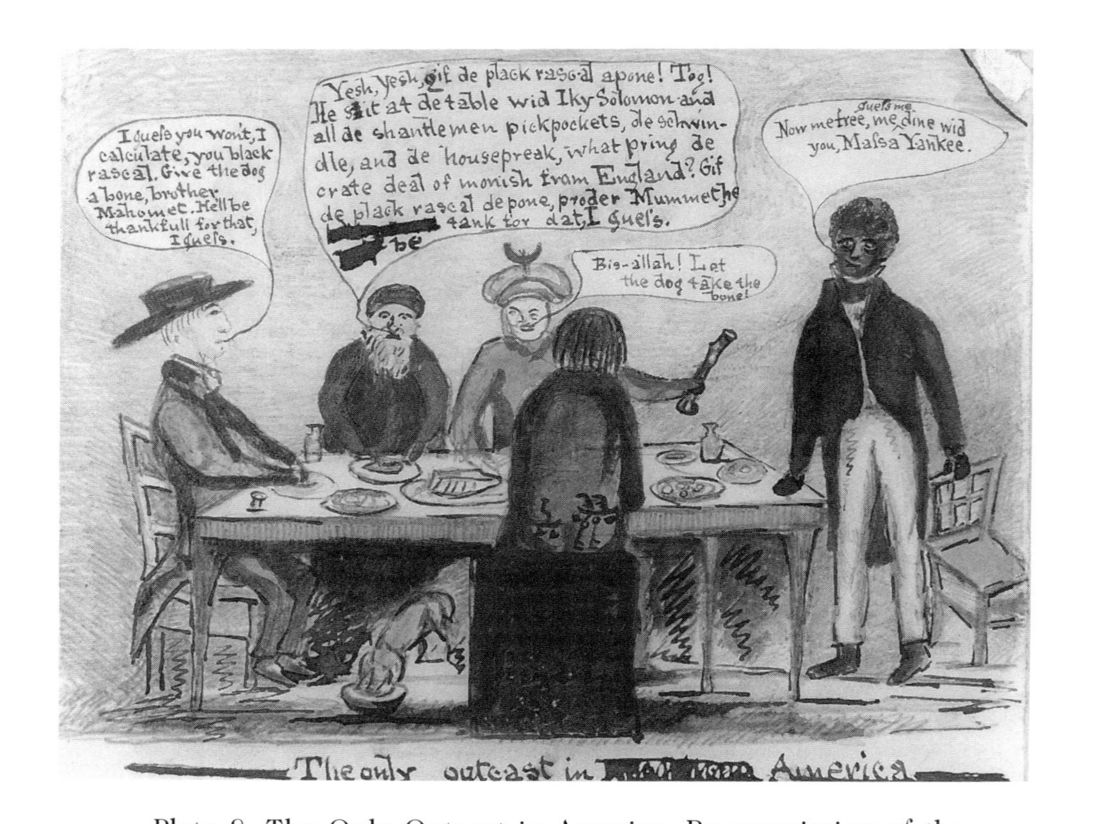

Plate 8. The Only Outcast in America. By permission of the Syndics of Cambridge University Library.

CHAPTER XVI

Free-Blacks the More Moral & Intelligent Class in New York—Crime for a White to Marry a Black—Free-Blacks Tenderly Devoted to Their Families—Yet Universally Despised by Americans—Permitted to Serve God but Not Man—First-rate Mechanics—Anecdote of a Slave who Purchased His Freedom—Washington Died a Slave-Owner

IT is painful when writing of a people who occupy so much of the attention of Europe, as do the Americans at this time, to have so little to say of them by way of commendation. But severe as I may appear to write of the Americans as abject slave-owners, they deserve scarcely less censure & contempt for the course they pursue towards the free-black population of New York—whom I here pronounce, fearless of disproof, as Mr Stuart would say, to be by far the more moral and intelligent portion of the inhabitants of that city. Nor are they one step behind the Americans in civilization: Nay, I say to the American portion, they may learn much that would improve them both as social characters & citizens of a rising Empire, from this poor despised race.

Though it is a fact that ought to fix eternal disgrace upon the Americans, that these same blacks are the *only outcasts* in their misnamed republic. For whilst they gladly receive amongst them the *monied swindlers* (Several were pointed out to me in New York, moving in what is called good society), the free-black finds neither mercy nor Sympathy, save amongst the English Emigrants.

One American had the effrontery to tell me, that it ought to be made a *crime* for a white man to marry a black woman. Let the American *gentleman* go study the character of the free-black, and he will behold a fond husband and father and a man social, sober, & industrious in his habits. Their affection for their offspring not only far surpasses that of the American, but they are tenderly, nay devotedly attached to their wives, and far, very far exceed the Americans in their gallantry and estimation of the weaker sex. It is truly delightful to see the free-blacks walk forth, well-dressed & well-behaved, on the Sunday, with their wives & children. Their contented, happy, cheerful faces are by far the most attractive feature that characterizes a New-York Sabbath. As for gallantry & attention to their females, an American is not to be named with a free-black. Yet these same Americans affect universally to despise them, and many have often expressed their astonishment at seeing me converse with them. But I confess their intelligence, their wit and general information, their natural acuteness of intellect, was a source of far greater attraction to me, than any the society of whites, born Americans, afforded.

They are, too, more moral than the Americans, though, as one old black told me, from the universal contempt in which they were held, "They had no motive for being so. Do what we will," said he, "we never can gain the respect due to man. They will tell us that we should render ourselves more worthy of respect. But," said the poor old man, "are not the doors to distinction shut against our race?" In New York, where freedom has been conferred upon them, they are not allowed to be *Cartmen* (in England a *menial* employment) though they may possess considerable property, the fruits of honest & the most patient industry. They are not allowed the privilege of voting unless possessed of 400 dollars. They can neither hold state or corporate offices. They may, however, be *preachers*—that is, they are esteemed worthy to serve God, but not man—and this in what is called a free country, a country, forsooth, where all men are born equal!

And here let me observe, that the ridiculous anecdotes told of the Sermons of black preachers, which are handed about in print, are libels upon them. I have heard far better language and far better notions of futurity and moral obligation from the mouth of a black preacher, in America, than you will hear 9 times out of ten from the mouth of the raving fanatical declaimer who holds forth from the pulpits of many American churches or conventicles; and what is of greater importance than either their pronunciation or language, they have the recommendation of sincerity. I was one day pointing out to an American my conviction that the blacks possessed every mental quality necessary to make them good and useful members of society. Upon his questioning it, I pointed out one as an example. "Ah," was the exclamation, "but he is an *educated* black!"

"Well," said I, "and so are many others and so might they all be. But let me ask you if the Americans are *all* educated?" To this question Jonathan had nothing to reply.

The truth is the free-blacks in New York and elsewhere have a natural Suavity of manners, fluency of speech, and what is termed *quickness of parts*, to which the Americans have no pretension, though neither so money loving, nor so eternally talking of dollars. Your Americans are notoriously deficient in a taste for the fine arts, and in singing, either naturally or in a cultivated style, they are on a par with the fettered tribes that inhabit the wilds & forests. The Blacks, on the contrary, have great taste for pictorial beauty; I have visited many & have generally found the walls of their dwellings covered with such prints as they could procure; & I have often been charmed with the sweet tones & dulcet melodies that issued from their humble dwellings. And several English artisans assured me that where they had had the advantages of experience, they were inferior to no mechanics in the world.

And here I am reminded of an anecdote of a handsome young black whom I have often seen & conversed with, that by his industry, good conduct, and ability, as a Cabinet-maker, saved sufficient to purchase his freedom, in some distant state. He came & settled in New York, with an excellent recommendation from his master, as a first-rate hand, and soon got employment as such, in a large establishment. But notwithstanding his ability & intelligence, his American fellow-workmen were so besotted with their illiberal dislike of the black population, that they were continually taunting him on the subject of his colour, and reminding him of the approach of the festival held in New York in commemoration of the freedom of the slaves being granted in that State, asking him, if "he did not mean to join in the rejoicings of the 2nd of July?" His manly reply was, that he "thought it beneath him to do it, as every man, white or black, had a right to his freedom; besides," he added, "I am not indebted to the government, I purchased my freedom." This want of gratitude to republican America, however, was not to pass with impunity. A spirit of persecution was raised against him, and they refused to work until he was dismissed. And not only was the poor fellow cast forth without employment, but a combination was formed, denouncing such masters as should take black mechanics into their service.

Indeed, many well-educated & intelligent blacks have in consequence been driven to take upon them the most degrading employments, and have thereby been reduced to despair and crime. Under these circumstances an American will point them out and say, “There, are they a people fit for freedom?” And if any crime should be committed by a black man, it is a notorious fact, that the magistrates and even some of the newspapers are sure to seize upon the occasion to heap odium upon the race generally. But what is to be expected from a people the *father* of whom, even

Washington
Died a Slave-Owner!

And it is scarcely credible, but it is nevertheless true, that notwithstanding this treatment of the Free-Blacks in the State of New York, notwithstanding the people of every other state in America are Slave-owners, the following passage occurs in *The Crisis*, American paper of the 2nd of March, 1834, as the words of a resolution at a public-meeting of Citizens of these same United States, held 3 days previously—“That in Kingly Governments, there are different classes, but that in Republics all men are ***free*** & ***equal***, and therefore when the road to comfort & wealth is open to all *as it is in the United States*, we know no such distinction of classes of the poor & the rich.”

VOLUME II

Plate 9. New Year's Day in America. By permission of the Syndics of Cambridge University Library.

CHAPTER I

Peculiar Custom of Drinking Healths of American Girls on New Year's Day—Drunkenness in Consequence—Reflections thereon of an Old Republican—The Whole Scene a Perfect Saturnalia

MOST nations have their peculiar customs and America is behind none that I am acquainted with for the number & peculiarity of hers. One of them is celebrated on the 1st of January, or New-Year's Day, when all the youth of New York & other towns are early on the move, trimmed out in the most approved fashions of the day, & adorned with all the trinkets & ribbands they can muster. Each one has previously made out a list of the names of those ladies whom he intends to honour with a call 2 or 3 weeks beforehand. One young American exhibited to me a catalogue of 50. Thus prepared, they sally forth, and "rat, tat, tat," is the universal din. At every house they enter, "Is Miss —— at home?" is the inquiry. Miss is all the while simpering in the corner of the room, and upon receiving an affirmative answer, the next observation is, "I am come to drink her health & wish her a happy New Year." This is accordingly done, and where they are acquaintances, a salute is thrown into the bargain. It is, however, no matter whether the parties are strangers to each other or not, every house is "liberty hall" on this day, and the Cogniac and kisses are all given gratis.

One may very well imagine, that by the time young Corydon has got through his list of 50, he is pretty well 3 sheets in the wind, or "rather hazy" as the sailors say. But very many of the more respectable classes seem to forget themselves on New Year's Day, and to reel from house to house, in no very tempting condition to make love in. I saw numbers led home on New Year's Day, 1834, in New York, who, by the force of gravity, ever & anon came to the ground. You might here & there see men, more sheepish than others, stand peeping round a door, half hesitating whether they should knock or not, whilst Miss might be discovered through the window, every moment expecting the "rat, tat, tat." In some Streets you would see one peeping, whilst a bolder youth demanded admittance, and all New York seemed to have poured forth her male population to do the *gallant* on this day. "They call it *social*," said an old half-bred testy republican to me. "Pretty sociality it is for mothers to have their daughters placed in a chair, *like a stuck pig*, for every fool to run his grizzly beard against." "I guess," added the old man, with a laugh, "there's many a match concocted in New York on New Year's Day, if nothing worse happens."

I was told, that I should be fully expected to pay the *honours* & take my dose of Cogniac Schnapps with all the pretty American girls I had been introduced to. I was, however, too much amused with what I saw to make a single effort on my own account. Myself & a friend took the round of several streets, to "spy out the nakedness of the land," towards afternoon. We saw old maids & Bachelors, or what ought to have been such, "frosty with age," trudging about in all directions. One youth had made his entrance & exit so often, that after mounting the steps & knocking with great difficulty, he fell upon them *oblivious*. How he was received by his fair one, I did not wait to learn. The whole scene, in fact was a perfect *Saturnalia* throughout the city. No wonder there are so many divorces annually in the State of Ohio.

CHAPTER II

Serenading in America—Cracked Voices & Cracked Instruments—Gainsborough & the Fiddler—Anecdote of the English Divines, Drs Clarke & Sykes—American Gents' Custom of Expressing Their Regard—Rothschild upon Change Hugging Jew & Gentile—No Taste for Such Habits or Customs—Dr. Hague's Ballad on Shaking Hands

IN lands where minstrelsy and melody are the order of the day; and in countries where tournays, chivalry, and beauty and bright eyes were the burthen of the harper's songs; when ladies' favours were the rewards of valor & victory; & where lovers wooed to the light guitar amidst bowers of thyme & myrtle, beneath Italian skies; one might still dream of midnight-songs and serenades. But will it be allowed that your money-loving American, whose hands are eternally in his breeches' pockets, fumbling his dollars, who has less voice & fewer notes than a cuckoo, is to be seen in the streets of republican America at one, two, or 3, in the morning, serenading his mistress, with "Hard is my fate,"—"My Lodging is on the cold ground," & various other pathetic melodies, to the annoyance of more peaceable citizens? Yet such is the fact. One unhappy swain, to whom his mistress had, I suppose, "given the bag," as they say in England, woke me out of a comfortable sleep every night for a fortnight. And he had no sooner made his exit, than another love-sick swain took up the like trash a few doors further from my lodging, with something very like the tones of a cracked clarinet—probably Apollo had not blessed him even with an *American* voice. I might very well liken the tones of his instrument to the cracking of a whip in the hands of a lusty English waggoner.

This "Yankee-doodle" reminded me of an anecdote told of our divine Gainsborough, who had a taste for the fiddle and went with a friend to hear the most eminent violinist of the day. The piece was one of those brilliant concertos for the execution of which modern instrumental performers have of late years been so celebrated. Everybody was delighted, and the friend of Gainsborough amongst the rest. But Gainsborough loved the simple melody, and the fine rich tone & expression of our older schools, and did not express himself much pleased with the music. "You know, my dear Gainsborough," said his friend, "the

Plate 10. A Yankee Serenading His Miss, after a Quarrel, at New York. By permission of the Syndics of Cambridge University Library.

piece is very difficult to perform." "I wish it had been *impossible*—" said Gainsborough. Just such a wish did I express when my American musician struck up "Lost is my quiet," with his *own* variations: or that the gods had given him an ear and taste for the divine art: for no knife-grinder's machine could be half so inharmonious, as was his performance of the above melody, and I don't know what besides. I wished him & his pipe at the d——l—and from the length of time he kept it up, I concluded his mistress did the same. I rose on one occasion to survey the evening, and could almost have found it in my heart to have pitied the poor moon-struck wretch, as he ever & anon made a pause & cast his rueful look at the closed casement, where not even the *ghost* of a pocket-handkerchief could be seen, much less a lily hand or a pair of bright eyes. I only wonder he was not either carried to the watchhouse, or belaboured by the sturdy hand of some old money-loving republican papa, for presuming to disturb him and his family. This is one of the few customs Jonathan will do well to *whip* out of the rising generation, for they will find the necessary accomplishments of no use upon "*change*," either at New York or elsewhere.

Whilst I am upon the subject of "*Change*," I am reminded of another American custom, which reminds me of a story of the celebrated English controversial Divines, Doctors Samuel Clarke & Arthur Ashley Sykes—extant in Nichols's *Literary Anecdotes*. The former would often visit the latter, when "his usual way was to sit with him upon a couch, and, *reclining upon his bosom*, to discourse upon subjects agreeable to the taste & judgment of both." In the same manner will your American Gents come & seat themselves upon a couch by those to whom they proffer their friendship, *passing their arm round your neck or waist* and recline upon the bosom of their *male* acquaintances. Sometimes they will go as far as kissing & *slobbering* like great babies. God forbid that I should quarrel with the customs of any people, but I at once confess that I never see men salute each other, but it gives me a *chill*. Sometimes they will salute one another in the open street, perhaps on their way to "*Change.*" When I saw them hugging each other, I used to fancy what a figure our great monied Colossus, *Rothschild*, with the destinies of half the world upon his shoulders, would cut upon *Cornhill*, hugging & *slobbering* some 50 of his monied compatriots, Jews & Gentiles, before proceeding to business, on a *settling day*. One young American, who was anxious to *court my acquaintance*, commenced operations with an embrace. I declined a salute & frankly told him I preferred the English fashion of a hearty shake of the hand, and recommended him to an excellent ballad on the true spirit with which it should be performed, the composition of Dr. Charles Hague, late Professor of Music at our English University of Cambridge, the words, I believe, by the late Theo^{n} James Plumptre, B.D., Fellow of Clare-Hall in the same University.

CHAPTER III

UNHEALTHINESS OF THE CLIMATE OF AMERICA—FEVERS—AGUES—RUPTURES AND CONSUMPTION VERY COMMON—DANGER FROM DAMP SUMMER NIGHTS—FREQUENCY & DANGEROUS CHARACTER OF TORNADOS AND FRESHETS

THE city of New York is commonly supposed to contain more widows and widowers, in proportion to its amount of population, than any other city in the known world. This is to be attributed to more causes than one. The most prominent reasons are the unhealthiness of the climate, and the excessive indulgence in *dram-drinking*, by all classes. I once heard it quaintly observed that at least half the population of New York went to bed drunk every night—and from my own observations I am inclined to believe it. These habits no doubt are one great source of the shortness of the term of human life in every part of America, and are powerful incentives to the cases of consumption and ruptures with which the population of New York in particular are afflicted. Great numbers are carried off by the former. But one great check upon the increase of population in America, notwithstanding the shoals of emigrants that annually set foot on her shores, is the variableness of the climate. A burning hot day in New York, during which you will see persons quarrelling for the shady side of the street, is frequently followed by the most searching cold night air, loaded with agues and fevers and death to as many as rashly expose themselves to its baneful influence. Numbers fall down dead after drinking a glass of cold water during the hot season. An article extracted from the *New York Gazette*, in the *Times* of the 16th Augt 1834, states, "The heat for the last 3 days has been excessive. Each day the mercury has been up to 92, and as high as 93, in the shade. All Animal strength has been nearly prostrated. Several men & horses have dropped down in our streets & expired, some from drinking cold water, & others from exposure to the heat. Nearly all the carpenters, masons, & labourers employed out of doors have suspended their work. Such was the general prostration of working men the other day, that not half the usual number performed their daily work. 3 labouring men died of the heat in Hudson Street in one afternoon." Indeed.

Funerals are so frequent that coffin-making is a trade of consideration in New York, where stores with "Ready made coffins" over the door are common. I know a case of an old farmer "well to do," but bitten with the emigration-mania, who sold his little property and departed from England for the purpose of settling in the land of *Liberty*, as he called America. He reached New York where he landed with some £2000 of Sterling English gold, but had scarcely set his foot in the city, shouldering the most valuable part of his luggage, when his eyes were attracted by a showy store headed "Ready Made Coffins." "What," exclaimed the old man, "do people die so fast as that in America?" He was told such establishments were common and a great source of profit. The old man had only to turn round to catch a sight of the Bay, where he had just landed, & seeing a packet about to clear out for England, he ran to the wharf, hailed it, and having secured his passage, was on his way back to England without so much as eating a meal in republican America.

One person with a large family, whom I know intimately, a hale temperate man, had stood the change of climate well, but his wife & children had not been many months in New York before they were so constantly afflicted with agues & fevers, the common pests of the place, that no alternative was left him but either to return with them to their native air in England, or make up his mind to see them drop off like half ripe fruit under the influence of a noxious blight. Thousands of adults so perish annually, who have not the means of flying from the death they are conscious daily threatens them, and they fall before their despairing family-groups, who have only to sigh & wait their turns. The number of funerals that are daily passing in New York, at the most healthy times, are sickening to an English heart—I have watched them from the windows of my lodging till I have been ready to die of *ennui*. What a scene must New York have been during the rage of the cholera, when people died at the average of 300 a day; in some other American towns it was still worse.

And here I cannot forbear making a few remarks on the indecent haste with which the corpse is committed to the Earth, and the mob-like character of an American funeral. It is a custom always to bury persons on the same day their decease takes place, whether from any malignant cause or not, and I have known great numbers who have expired at noon to be interred the same evening, and no doubt many have been buried alive. But this is not the only indecency for which American funerals are remarkable. They are a perfect mob. 300 or 400 persons may be seen constantly following, *en train*, many with cigars in their mouths, in all sorts of colours & fashions, some with their garments torn, without regard to decency. The custom is for a public notice to be given, stating the hour of interment, when all friends, relations, & acquaintances of the family are invited to join the procession to the grave—and I can assure my readers, that an Irish funeral is a farce to what I have witnessed in America on such occasions. The corpse is not infrequently committed to its resting place without any sort of religious ceremony: for though there is no church establishment in republican America, their pastors' creed is—*no pay no work*—and if the friends are too poor to raise the *necessary dollar*, the burial must proceed *without a prayer*. I pointed out all these things to my American friends, who unhesitatingly declared that there was less decorum amongst the English residents in New York, but at the moment I was one day so rebuked, a corpse passed the house covered with a decent pall and followed by a few sorrowing friends in sable, in the same silent unobtrusive manner that characterizes funerals in England, and my American friends had the candour, for once to acknowledge it was more decent.

I found the winter of 1833 very mild in comparison with what I had been led to expect, but the Spring of the present year, 1834, proved as severe—indeed it was so inclement, that the general opinion was the cotton crops as well as others would be destroyed, and I was told, as Jonathan has always a ready excuse for every American failing, that the severity of the season was uncommon. But on referring to an American paper, *The New York Standard* of 1833, I find it stated "There was a slight fall of snow in the North part of Montgomery county" in *June*. At the same time "more or less frost occurred also in different parts of the State, to the injury of corn & garden vegetables in many places. And it is thought the crop of corn will be a very short one."

The truth is the climate of America is so uncertain, so constantly varying, like the natives, between the two extremes of hot & cold, that it is utterly unsuited to English constitutions, and the consequence is that those whom necessity keeps much abroad, seldom live long after their arrival. The longer livers, amongst the emigrants, who do not yield themselves victims to the beastly habit of dram-drinking, are those employed indoors. The only period when I found the climate any thing like steady, was in the latter part of Summer, when there is such a continued oppressive heat, and such a glaring Sun, as to be overpowering to the strongest sight, and the consequence is ophthalmic diseases are very prevalent.

The Thunder, lightning, and rain, in America, surpasses any I ever beheld elsewhere. Four children were struck dead by the $2^{\underline{nd}}$ one day in New York, as they were sitting in a school-room, and I do not exaggerate when I say, that after a week's rain in New York, it is a perfect race with the doctors' cabs, driving to the homes of the multitudes of patients caused by the change of the weather, so prevalent is sickness after heavy showers.

Another fearful visitant in America is the Tornado. Three occurred but a short time before I quitted New York, by one of which, besides the awful destruction of property & the tearing up whole forests of trees, 20 persons were killed, and 16 by another. *The Petersburg Intelligencer*, a Virginia paper, of the $8^{\underline{th}}$ of May, 1834, says, "The most terrific Tornado ever witnessed in this part of Virginia, occurred on Monday last," May the $5^{\underline{th}}$. "The destruction of human life and of property of every kind is truly appalling. It would be impossible to give more than a faint outline of its desolating fury. The scene is represented by those who had an opportunity of witnessing it as one of surpassing and inexpressible grandeur and sublimity. Every thing within its range was laid prostrate, the largest trees were torn up by the roots, & carried a considerable distance; dwelling & outhouses were levelled with the earth, and their fragments scattered in every direction. The day had been cloudy with occasional showers. About 3 the clouds assumed a black & lowering aspect. In a few minutes, after the whirlwind commenced its ravages. It took the form of 'an inverted cone,' says an eye-witness, 'and every cloud near seemed to rush into the vortex. As it approached, you might see the limbs of the forests careering through the darkened air.' Its general course was from West to East: its width varied from two hundred yards to half a mile: its duration at any point was not more than two minutes: and its extent could not have been less than 70 miles. Besides various other details of the loss of life & the destruction of property, a gentleman writes, that 'it appears to have commenced in the county of Lunenburg, near Hungry Town, where almost all the heavy timber was torn up by the roots, and where it proved very fatal. Near this place, it seems that the poor (who lived in log houses) were the principal sufferers, several negroes & children were killed. Hence it passed to Notaway Courthouse, where the storm increased—the public road being rendered impassable. From Notaway Courthouse, or near that place, the wind passing in a Northeast direction, reached the plantation of Mr. R.

Fitzgerald, where great injury was done, but no lives lost. Near his residence was that of Mr. John Fitz who suffered immensely, having one negro killed, another's arm broken, and various others injured. Hence it pursued its course to the house of Mr. Justice, where a great injury was likewise sustained, several persons severely injured, and the life of one despaired of. The next death was that of Mr. Joshua Hawks, an honest, upright citizen, literally crushed—his wife at the same time receiving injury so severe as to leave but little hope of her recovery.'"

Scarcely a week passes during the Summer season without a recurrence of *Tornados & Freshets* that devastate & destroy life & property to a ruinous extent. *The New York Advertiser* of the 2nd of June, 1834, says that a severe Tornado lately passed in the neighbourhood of Florence, Alabama, which destroyed the lives of many persons; the hail that fell during the time, is said to have been as large as a man's fist; and the storm was accompanied by an incessant blaze of lightning. In Pulaski, Tennessee, it raged with great violence, carrying away fences & houses. In fact it is no uncommon thing for a man to be entirely ruined, up the country, by the terrible effects of these fearful Tornados, and the overpowering sweep of the *Freshets*, as they call their floods. The same paper of the previous 29th of May mentions a hail storm of such violence between Spartanburgh & Greenville, S.C. which raged for near 20 minutes, during which the hail storms that fell measured 7 & 8 inches in circumference.

Plate 11. A Night Scene in New York. By permission of the Syndics of Cambridge University Library.

CHAPTER IV

Doctors and Their Patients—Castor Oil—Calomel, & Drugging Generally—Extensive Quacking—Exorbitant Fees—Refuse to Attend Free-Black Patients

NEXT to grog–shops, the most numerous class of establishments in New York are those of the Apothecaries and Doctors of all sorts—from the shirtless vagabond to the thriving quack, Monsieur Chabert inclusive, who is now an Apothecary in Broadway, New York, and, if we may believe his announcements, gives *instantaneous* relief to all kinds of diseases. But he is "beaten into fits," as I heard a man say, by a lady physician in Delancy Street, New York, over whose door may be read—"*Mrs Bird, Doctoress*," of what faculty is not said, but she no doubt deals both in & with *simples*. All professors of the healing art, Quacks, Chemists, Druggists, Apothecaries &c. are dubbed *Doctors*. In fact there never was a country where *empiricism* reigned more widely than it does in America. Persons are employed to vend drugs totally ignorant of their qualities, and it is not, therefore, surprising, that people are frequently poisoned by them. I personally knew of 3 cases of death by such means, in one street in New York. Blue-pill is given in such doses as would stagger the most daring English practitioner. I was told by some respectable persons, that 200 grains of calomel was commonly given, and in almost every case your Americans resort to bleeding their patients.

I was one day in an Apothecary's shop when a fellow came in & asked for 2 ounces of castor oil. The apothecary asked him for his vial. He was not provided with one, but said he could take it in his pocket—When told it was a liquid, he added he would take it at once, coolly swallowed it in my presence, and walked out as if he had simply taken a dram of spirits. It is no uncommon thing to see *Doctor* conspicuously written in front of what in England would be mistaken for a cow-shed. There is no particular regulation of fees, physicians, apothecaries, & quacks—all charge *ad libitum*. A gold beater told me he sent for a kind of Chemist & Apothecary, a *Doctor* nevertheless, to see his sick wife. The poor fellow had no money, but the doctor condescended to pocket some gold leaf, value 2 dollars. In agreeing that the charge for merely calling would not exceed a dollar, he visited the doctor a few days after, as he agreed, to receive the difference, but learnt there was no balance, or rather there was an exact balance, the *Doctor*'s charge being 2 dollars.

If Doctors or Apothecaries in England conducted their business in the same manner as do those of America, it would be necessary for them to be furnished with a pawn-broker's licence. It is a usual thing for them to take goods in lieu of money. I was one day in an apothecary's shop, or store, when a fellow entered & demanded his watch, which it appeared he had left in the *Doctor*'s keeping till he could pay his 2 dollars due for medicine, & the *Doctor* declining to give it up without payment of the debt, he came the next day with 6 stout assistants and threatened "to knock the Doctor's head off." And the Doctor was finally obliged to have them ejected by the police. But this practice of taking articles in pledge I found was very prevalent amongst the medical *gentlemen* in America.

The most respectable of the profession have a sorry habit of driving about in dirty vehicles, themselves unshaven and otherwise wanting in that decent appearance which is a marked characteristic with respectable apothecaries & the physicians in England. Another discreditable habit is that of lounging about & gossiping at shops or stores. But all this is in character with the habits of the people, who are nearly all tinctured with a plague of gossiping, and what is worse, they are *listeners*. Even the boys will walk behind you in the street and catch up your words as you pass along conversing with a friend. And on several occasions my words were exported to me through this disgusting eaves-dropping habit. It is held not to be respectable, however, for a physician to keep an apothecary's shop: but in this, as in all other cases, your American makes lightly of a difficulty where dollars are in question, and gets some ignorant fellow to have his name placed over a medical store, in which he is employed to preside at the rate of 2 or 3 dollars a week & his board, the physician taking care every night to balance accounts & pocket the profits. But all this is transacted under the rose. There are a few exceptions, no doubt, but I am speaking of them as a body.

One thing I believe them to be all scandalously remiss and unfeeling in, which is their neglect of their poor colored, or free-black patients, and to my knowledge it more than once occurred that physicians in New York refused to rise to attend a patient in a dangerous state, when called upon at night, on discovering that it was a poor black man or woman that required their assistance. I ought to add, that Morison's pills are esteemed infallible across the Atlantic, and that all Doctors are inveterate chewers of tobacco in America.

The following admirable specimen of quack-puffing, printed in the *Sun* American paper of April, 1834, is equal to any thing I ever met with of The Hygeist School, or any other in England:–

COMMUNICATION.

> For more than a year I was prey to the following sufferings; violent headache, dimness of sight, weakness of stomach, attended with whites; night and morning a raking cough, with yellow and fetid risings, during the night, renting pains in the arms and legs, attended with awful dreams. Such were the torments under which I had labored for a long time, without receiving any help whatever, from the many Doctors I had applied to at various times, when at last it was my good fortune to be directed to Doctor X. Chabert, No. 322 Broadway opposite the Hospital, who in the course of one month has totally relieved me from all my sufferings, and enabled me to resume my daily avocations, which I had been obliged to abandon: considering my recovery as mysterious, I think it my duty to publish it for the benefit of the public, and also to pay a just tribute to Dr. Chabert, to whom I vow an eternal gratitude, for the great good he has done me in renovating my health, and thus prolonging my existence. MRS. ANN NEESON, 204 East Broadway.

CHAPTER V

American Peaches—Bread—Butter—Fruits—Water—Meats—Fish—A Harmless Joke—More Yankee Smartness—Coals & Wood Dear

A stranger would suppose, after being but a few days in New York, did not his stomach teach him the contrary, that *peaches* were the staple article of food in the United States. So proud are they of their peaches, that however foreign may be the subject matter of any conversation, American peaches are almost sure to be *lugged* in. They are eternally talking of their peaches. I confess I was not so marvellously struck with their superiority, though I was told that up the country they grew in their hedge-rows. Nor are their fruits cheap, as might be imagined. *The New York Advertiser* of the 3rd. of June, 1834, observes, "Strawberries are becoming tolerably plenty in our markets. The little baskets were this morning selling for 9d. each—or about 2/6 per qt." A New York Gardener assured me (who had emigrated from England, from one of the Royal Horticultural establishments, in the neighbourhood of London) that the English fruits generally were far superior to those of America, especially in Harrow—and I may here add, that he was so far from being gratified with his change of situation, that he would gladly have returned to his own country. It appeared to me that there was a heated dryness in the air, which prevented their fruits ripening as deliciously as do those of England. It is for some such reason as this that their apples possess a quality, on account of which their cider is given as a warm drink for the stomach.

But whatever their peaches or apples may be, their bread is very far inferior to that of England, and is of so spongy a nature, that you might take in your hands a sixpenny loaf, American money, and without much effort squeeze it into a substance not thicker than a common Captain's biscuit. This you will say is light enough—truly so—and I was told it was a common thing for the bakers to ruin the most delicious matter with it. No yeast or balm was to be had in New York, the consequence is that all home made bread is as heavy as the baker's bread is light. Nearly all American butter has the taste and appearance of the common Irish salt butter in London, and even in the depth of winter it is difficult to procure it sweet, or fresh. All vegetables in America, especially potatoes & turnips in New York and its neighbourhood, are poor and dear, and for a moderate sized cabbage you must pay sixpence.

Their spirits are universally inferior, rum and brandy, which are usually drunk, are very bad, and their wines are *thin*. The only tolerable beverage to be had in America is their cider, and strangely enough it is scarcely ever drunk. Their coffee is trash, tea tolerable, and beer very poor. Their water is generally brackish, and the *saline* taste is at first very disagreeable to Emigrants. I speak of New York. Up the country it is better. Spring water may be procured a short distance from this city, but it is so expensive as to be out of the reach of the poorer classes, and will not keep sweet long in hot weather.

There is a toughness in all their meats, flesh & fowl, which render them inferior to those of England. Mutton is always lean and the carcass runs small; beef, which is by far their best meat, is the same, and fetches a shilling per pound, American money; their veal is very moderate in quality, indeed it is accounted by far their worst meat, and the calf's head is so small, that when I first saw one on the table I took it for a sheep's head. Their turkeys, about the size of which I had heard so much, are scarcely so large as those of England, and are unquestionably inferior in the quality of their flesh—as are likewise their ducks, fowls, & geese. The price of a turkey is about 4 shillings & sixpence, English money, or 9 shillings American. And here I am reminded that should you chance, at a boarding-house to begin the week with dining off a tough old American settler, in the shape of a goose, it is 10 to one but a portion of the same will, in some shape or other, be served up for Saturday night's supper. For your Americans are very clever at re-dishing up all sorts of things, much longer than they are *sweet*, and a peep into their kitchens, where there is a want of order and economy, and a continual messing, hissing, frying, phizzing, stewing, and chopping, would, I fancy, satisfy any fastidious stomach for a week.

I recollect one day sitting down to a gander of the first water, on the first day of the week, felicitating myself on the treat which awaited me, mistaking it for an American roast goose. But upon trying my masticating powers, I gave up eating in despair, it was so tough. Of course I concluded I should see it no more. Supper came and there again was the gander. Gander again for the next day, dinner & supper. Well, I thought, there must be an end of it now. Alas! how deceitful are our anticipations. Our gander was the 3rd day served up for dinner in a pie, the remains of which graced the supper table. I was resolved to see no more of it, and to that end contrived to pocket a leg. But who shall say what to-morrow may bring forth—I had scarcely sat down to breakfast the following morning, when forth came the giblets of our gander, cooked I know not how, and they kept possession of the table for another day. I resolved there should, however, be an end of my tormentor, and between tearing & gulping, I spoiled the dish—nor did warrior ever triumph with greater glee over a fallen enemy, than I did in the final destruction of our American gander.

Here I may add, that American Venison, of which I had heard much, is so much inferior to that same delicious dish in England, as I have eaten it in our good city of London, at Oxford & Cambridge, that it is absolutely like carving a mahogany board—and as for fat, you might as well expect to discover the philoso, her's stone, as find any attached to an American haunch. All fish is of inferior quality in America. I heard a shilling per lb, sixpence English, asked for Eels.

Adulteration is carried to a great extent in every species of article that will admit of it in America, and not satisfied with that, it is a notorious fact that they carve nutmegs and hams out of wood and manufacture cigars of oak-leaves. When I mentioned this to an American gentleman, he called it "a harmless joke." It is no uncommon thing, upon going into a shop & offering a dollar in payment of any purchase, to be told it does not weigh its proper weight, but they will accommodate you by making a correspondent deduction. This is a species of fraud, for such it really is, very widely practiced upon strangers in New York—& I have been more than once shocked to see all this kind of *Yankee Smartness*, as they call it, put in practice by respectable persons. Another piece of *smartness* is their taking advantage of the ignorance of strangers & paying their tenpenny pieces for shillings. I found the Yankee *too smart* for me a great many times in this respect. It was no use complaining.

And here it would be unjust to suppress an instance of *Smartness* in a New York *translator*, which I was a witness to. A fellow called one day upon a friend of mine, to inquire if he had any boots or shoes to mend. My friend replied he had a pair of the former & asked his charge. "A dollar," was the reply. "Very good," said my friend, and handed him the old boots. He had not departed an hour, when back he came with them. My friend stared at the man & exclaimed, "Very quick, I guess,"—and after telling an impudent falsehood or two, by way of giving a polish to his *Smartness*, I suppose, he acknowledged that he had brought him another pair which stood ready at hand, that he might not keep his employer waiting, for he "guessed it was no matter provided he had a pair, which they were."

Fuel in America, both coal & Wood, is very dear. During one violent Winter the latter sold for 7 dollars a load. The consequence was the poorer people were scarcely able to save themselves from falling victims to the severe frosts with which America is visited. They are, indeed, so piercing, that no European can encounter them without suffering greatly. Their coals are of such a quality, that to light a fire is considered an absolute undertaking. As soon as lighted, they give forth a hissing & cracking noise not unlike that of eels frying, and the room is continually filled with a most disagreeable sulphureous stench. It is difficult to keep in a coal fire even with a blower, upon removing which it is sure to drop out, and it never emits that comfortable heat & lively blaze that English coals do. Wood is their best fuel and now sells, on the average, for a dollar & a half a load.

Plate 12. Congress versus the President. A Scene Lately Enacted in America. By permission of the Syndics of Cambridge University Library.

CHAPTER VI

Americans No Finer Principles—Bad Politicians—Black Population under No Obligation to Those Who Established Their Rights by Rebellion—No Republicans Just or Liberal—Except the Mexicans—President of America's Nose Pulled Publicly by a Member of Congress—Received Threatening Letters—Would Run Their Heads against a Stone Wall Were *Liberty* Written thereon—Banking System of America Licensing Swindlers—Jewing—Mordecai Noah—City of Ararat—Monied Aristocracy—No Concentration of Her Resources—Wealth Chiefly Swallowed up in Building Speculations to the Neglect of Manufactures—A Sordid Love of Pelf Common to Americans—Sketch of a Disappointed English Democrat—Love of Titles by Americans—Saying of Andrew Jackson—Americans Long Bankrupt as Republicans

THE minds of the Americans as well political as social, in whatever way considered, are made up of a chaos of selfish prejudices and animal passions. I have often endeavoured to elicit from them the shadow of one finer principle by which they thought and acted, but in vain. And such a paltry feeling is there abroad at the present time, that several respectable Americans told me "it was now no honour to hold a State office, so many '*snobs*' had got in." But I was scarcely surprised at this from people who had hinted to me, on my arrival, that I must *not* speak against my own country, but invariably abused me if I attempted *to speak in favour of it*.

As politicians they are perfect babies, short-sighted and prejudiced on every subject. Well might the editor of the *Cosmopolite*, American paper, scoff at them by saying, that Englishmen were republicans by principle, Americans only by birth. I have asked many of the more sensible of them "why they rebelled against the King of England?" "Because he wanted to enslave us," was the general answer. "But have you not held the blacks in Slavery?" was my query. To this they had nothing to reply. And well might they be silent. For the King of England, had it been true that his desire was to enslave them, had right on his side. But the black population of America were under no obligation to a people who established their rights upon rebellion; they had not the plea even of conquerors upon which to found a pretext for holding them in slavery, setting aside the infamy and wickedness of their policy.

But when, where, in what age or country, ancient or modern, did *republicans* ever shew themselves just or liberal, save only in their clamour (*vox et praeterea nihil*) towards the weaker part of the people they governed? I know of but one instance, and that a recent one, the Mexicans. Yet a member of the American Congress had the effrontery to declare, at the time Mr. Canning entered into his commercial Treaty with the States of South America, that they were not sufficiently advanced in civilization to justify the United States' government in taking a like step.

But what must we expect of America, where every institution is of mob-origin, where power can only be maintained by mob-popularity, and the President of which people had but the other day his nose publicly pulled by a member of Congress on the deck of a Steam-boat; to whom *threatening* letters were also lately sent, stating that his life would be taken, unless he restored the Deposits to the United States Bank—in other words, be governed instead of governing. Well might we say to such a people, as the *Montreal Herald* did lately to the French Canadians—"If your man Papineau should write 'Liberty' on a stone wall, your people would all dash their brains out against it." There never was a country, on the face of the earth, where there were so many separate, selfish, and incongruous interests to satisfy, nor a people so totally unacquainted with the true principles of government, especially with its conservative duties, as the people of America are. And in such a state of confused incertitude are they at this time, that were a Buonaparte or a Washington to arise amongst them, and only to hold up a shadow, or a semblance of some Utopian object of desire—some state of political beatitude which exists only in theory—away would go the whole bevy, as observes the writer last quoted, "as madly as a dog with a kettle at his heels, and as heedlessly as a flock of sheep intent on nothing but following their leader." Everything in America is in a state of rottenness, and it is more than probable, whether the President gives way or not on the Deposit question, that the Union will be shortly broken up.

As for their banking system, it is little better than licensing swindlers. A man has only to prove himself worth a hundred dollars, in old tables & chairs, any kind of property, in fact, & he may commence Banker—that is, issue *his paper*, which he quickly gets into circulation by some specious trick or other.

Many have set up the business of Banker without *a cent*, and having got a certain quantity of notes into circulation, they break. The next step is to employ a broker to buy up their notes, which, the law permitting, they shortly issue again. And thus they proceed, from time to time, till they realize a fortune, to the ruin of thousands.

This is one species of *Jewing* under which America has suffered largely: but it is not the only one. "It is not generally known," says the Editor of the *Sun* American paper of April, 1834, "that the Chatham Street Jews in New York cause nearly the whole of the silver coin which passes through their hands to undergo the process of '*Jewing*.' Yet such is the fact." They place whatever piece of money it may be "on an instrument similar to that used by type founders for cutting leads & rules. A knife then passes the edge of the silver in such a manner as to cut off a very thin shaving, which is carefully preserved in a buckskin pouch. The piece of coin is then fastened to another machine, and a punch resembling that used by a cobbler, is made to cut out a circular piece of the metal but little larger than the head of a pin, which is also preserved. The money is then put back into the money drawer to be dealt out to customers by way of change." But even this is not the last system of "Jewing" going on in America. It is pretty well understood, that the State Bank of America is principally under the control of the monied Jews of London, and that it is chiefly with their influence & funds that the present quarrel between the American President and the United States Bank is kept up. Pretty picking have your wealthy London Jews been making out of republican America for the last quarter of a century, and pretty picking they will continue to make, whether Andrew Jackson gives way or not. It is as natural for a multitude of Jews to be found where there is room for plunder, as it is for a multitude of birds of prey to scent carrion. This accounts for their being so numerous in the United States. The paper last quoted computes them at 50,000—"no wonder the times are hard," says the editor. The truth is, the wealth, power, and government of America has and still is chiefly in the hands of Jews and Dutchmen, and even Andrew Jackson, with all his acuteness and common sense, has been more than once gulled by the former.

The whole civilized world has heard of Mordecai Noah, the "Grace of God man," as he has been & is still called, whose fame principally rests on his notorious project for building a city on *Mud Island*, to be called the city of *Ararat*, to which all the Jews

Plate 13. Mordecai Noah Inviting the Jews to Settle in Mud Island in His City of Ararat. By permission of the Syndics of Cambridge University Library.

were to be invited from every quarter of the World. What Mordecai Noah's ulterior views were have not transpired, but one thing is certain, that the sprinkling of Jews already possessed by America is found to be no blessing, what the Yankees would have done with the 12 tribes, Heaven only knows. "When Greek meets Greek, then comes the tug of war," and no less might be said of Mordecai & his adherents, for he no sooner wanted to levy a contribution of a dollar each on his Israelitish Brethren, than, having touched them in a tender part, they turned their backs upon Mordecai. Mordecai, however, though obliged thereby to abandon his projected city, had wit enough to make the friendship of the President of the United States, was elected High Sheriff of New York, and actually succeeded in so completely gulling him, that he nominated Mordecai to a Government office, in opposition to the will of the Senate, and consequently upon his own responsibility. Mordecai, however, no sooner began to *Jew* Andrew Jackson under his own eyes, than Andrew Jackson seized an opportunity for dispensing with his further services, and Mordecai has now taken upon him the office of Editor of the most violent paper in America, *The Evening Star*, opposed him to the measures of Andrew Jackson, his original benefactor—report says the Bank has furnished him with ample reasons for the propriety of the part he is now playing. But "The President," says *The Man*, American paper, of the 13th of May, 1834, "is not a man to be Wheedled from his resolution by a set of soft-tongued vagabonds with pens stuck behind their ears. If my readers were acquainted with the history of the life of this famous man; nay, with only a fiftieth part of the wonderful acts of that life, they would laugh to scorn the idea of his being diverted from any settled resolution of his mind. ***Washington*** was a mere baby, compared with ***Jackson***: his deeds shrink into nothing, when placed before those of his present successor."—"Every thing necessary for America to know," adds this writer, "is kept from it by that base hireling press, which has been its curse for so many years. And, at this very moment, the important intelligence from the United States, is either smothered or totally disfigured by that press; and the people of England are actually believing, that the President is a sort of harum scarum fellow, under the guidance of mere passion, and that he will be obliged either to give up his measures, or give up his office. To make head against the delusion of so infernal a political machine is next to impossible."

There is no doubt but President Jackson, upon whom that

part of the American press opposed to him, which includes nearly all its leading journals, has heaped as much obloquy as one man could be well expected to bear, has a game to play, in opposition to the Aristocracy of America, that will require all the nerve he may be supposed to possess. *The Sun* American paper of the 9th of April, 1834, one of the most ably & independently conducted that the United States can boast, I speak from my own feelings, says, "The two political parties into which the country is at present divided, charge home upon each other with the design of subverting our Republican institutions. These parties, amongst various names they bear, are denominated Jackson & Anti-Jackson. On the one hand, the Jackson party accuse their opponents of a design to rule the country by a monied Aristocracy, through the instrumentality of the United States Bank. On the other hand, the Anti-Jackson party charge the other side with usurpation, and a design to establish a despotism on the ruins of the Republic. It must be admitted," says this writer, "that these are serious & high charges on both sides; and it behooves every citizen to inquire into the merits of the case in a cool, dispassionate manner. To do this, it is necessary to divest himself, as much as possible, of party prejudice, and instead of listening to the inflammatory harangues of pothouse politicians, to examine official documents. Let him peruse the constitution of his country, and learn, if he knows not already, the duties of the respective branches of the General government, and the limits to them prescribed. Let him compare the course pursued by the Executive with the provisions of that instrument. Let him read the United States Bank Charter, and compare it with the course pursued by the Executive in relation to that. Let him learn the number of dollars & cents discounted by the Bank since the removal of the Deposits, and compare the Amount with the prior discounts, to see whether or not the Bank is the cause of the present pecuniary pressure. Let him, in one word, inform himself on the various political topics, which at present agitate the community, and he will then be prepared to vote understandingly."

This was said prior to the Elections of May, 1834, and was good advice no doubt, but it was not such as the *republicans* of America could comprehend. Your American is capable of nothing so rational, & the consequence is, that which ought to have been made a question of *principle*, has become the touch stone of discord, hatred, and all the worst feelings to which political prejudices can give rise. Jackson is undoubtedly the most consistent man in the United States: He openly declared, when he last offered himself, or rather was pressed to become a candidate for the office of President a second time, that those who supported him must take for their motto "*Andrew Jackson & no United States' Bank!*" He was elected on those grounds & with that understanding, and he has hitherto *kept his word*. Should he succeed in crushing the *Hydra-head* of monopoly in his distracted country, without endangering her Commerce, he will undoubtedly be the greatest benefactor America has yet been blessed with, notwithstanding the pains *Major Jack Downing* has taken, in his *Letters*, which are a master-production of their kind, to prove him the contrary. Some have endeavoured to raise a prejudice against him by saying that his wish is to drive the emigrants *up the country*. Whatever foundation there may be for this, one thing is certain, that America has never yet shewn a disposition to concentrate her resources sufficiently to make the industry of her people available. It is pitiable to think of the wilderness over which you must traverse to discover the few spots of her vast territory as yet under the plough—added to which, her manufactures are contemptible, and instead of the wealth of the country being employed in extending them, and opening fresh fields for the industry & enterprize of the thousands of able artisans that flock to her shores, mostly to perish for want of employment, it is chiefly swallowed up in building Speculation, the source of *exactions* that are a disgrace to a *free* people. If the object of the President of the United States of America is to correct these evils, he will live to observe, and I make no doubt will have, the praises of the people who are now taught to heap odium upon his head from that basest of all human feelings, a *sordid love of Pelf*.

"Before I conclude," says a correspondent of the paper last quoted, of May, 1834, "let me relate what I have recently heard. A man who left England for America, some 16 or 17 years ago, and who was so determined a democrat, that the very sound of nobility, bishop, or King, almost threw him into hysterics, has, I am told, written to a friend in England, expressing his determination to return to his beloved native land, to his allegiance, to his natural sovereign; though he citizenized himself 17 years ago; and, as I have heard, really quarrelled with some Englishman (I forget whom) because he would not do the same: *this very man intends to return to England with all convenient speed*; saying, that his own dear native country *is advancing in civilization*, and that the United States *are retrograding*; and that d——d scoundrel, ***Jackson***, had *destroyed the constitution*, and broken up the credit of the country, and has severed, with his Goth-like sword, all the ligaments of civil society, of social order, and of regular government." "In justice to the much-censured President," adds this writer, "I think myself bound to observe, that I believe, that the man, from whom this censure has proceeded, has, for many years, been zealously engaged in upholding the '*Social system*,' by discounting bills at 2 1/2 per cent. per month; the bills being guaranteed, not by acceptances or indorsements, but by *deposits of goods* or pawns, more than sufficient to cover the amount advanced."

Whilst I am upon the subject of English Democrats, I may observe, that when I took my departure for the United States, I was charged with a letter from a staunch *English Radical*, to a radical citizen of America, who had emigrated from England some 8 or 10 years before, to inquire, whether, if the writer came to the United States, he had a chance of success in life? I was asked, "If he were the same democrat he had known?" My answer was—"I had never known him to change." "Then," replied the Americanized-Englishman, "tell him he will never do for America." The truth is, the Americans never were republicans at heart, in the true meaning of the word—and though they are continually affecting to laugh at English titles, have they not their *Honourables*, their *Bishops*, *Doctors* of all sorts, *Generals*, *Colonels*, *Reverends*, *Captains*, and *Squires*?—Aye—& are as fond of them as children are of toys—they only wait for the additions of King, Prince, and Lord—but who shall be the *first* to "bell the cat" is the startling question. Not a notice appears in any of their papers announcing meetings to be held by *Republican Societies*, but half their names have ***Esq***. affixed to them. In the *Crisis* American paper, of March 22nd, 1834, is the following—

> ***Republican Young Men***
>
> There was an overflowing meeting, at Masonic Hall, of the young men of the city of New-York opposed to the arbitrary & heinous measures of the national Executive, &c. The call of the meeting having been read a series of spirited resolutions were successively proposed by David Graham, Jr., ***Esq***., Mr. Gould, Jonathan Nathan, ***Esq***., Joseph H. Patten, ***Esq***., William Hall, ***Esq***., and Mr. Morse, &c.

The same paper attributes to President Jackson the saying—"that all who trade on borrowed capital ***ought to break***"—Americans, as *republicans*, never traded with any other but *borrowed* capital, and have long been thoroughly bankrupt as such.—

CHAPTER VII

THE GOVERNMENT OF AMERICA NOT A CHEAP GOVERNMENT—LIST OF SALARIES PAID THE PRESIDENT & OTHER OFFICERS OF STATE—DO PAID TO CUSTOM-HOUSE OFFICERS IN NEW YORK—NEW YORK CORPORATION PATRONAGE—AMERICAN TAXATION

IT is a common practice with the advocates of cheap Government, in England, to hold up that of America as an example for England to follow. But these same declaimers lose sight of the fact, that besides the expence of the chief Executive Government of the United States, each state has its own executive to pay—and when persons speak of the Salary of the President of America and compare it with that received by the Heads of English & other European Governments, they should be reminded that each State in America has its Governor & other officers, all of whose Salaries are extra, and as well as that of the President of America, &c. are drawn from the pockets of the people, by direct & indirect taxes. And when the American Government is so considered, & its resources are compared with those of this & other countries, it will be found that the Government of the United States is by no means that cheap & desirable system which its admirers are accustomed to paint it. Another source of expenses to which the people of America are subjected, is that of paying large salaries to their chief magistrates of their Corporations, Aldermen, &c. whilst those of England, receive no compensation but the honour the dignity of the office itself confers. Another thing to be noted, as part of the Government Expense to which America is subject, is the large Salaries paid to Members of Congress, whilst the Members of the British Houses of Parliament do not receive a penny.

The following is a List of the Salaries paid the American Executive, and the Custom-House & Corporation Officers of New York, as given in *The Crisis*, American paper, of the 22d of March, 1834:

> ANDREW JACKSON, President of the United States, is paid $25,000 a year of the people's money, or nearly *five hundred dollars a week*.
>
> MARTIN VAN BUREN, Vice-President, gets $5,000 a year of the people's money—almost one hundred dollars a week.
>
> Louis McLane, Secretary of State.

Roger B. Taney, Acting Secretary of the Treasury.
Levi Woodbury, Secretary of the Navy.
Lewis Cass, Secretary of War.
William T. Barry, Post-Master General,
all these are paid $6,000 a year, or more than one hundred and fifteen dollars a week.

Amos Kendall, Fourth Auditor, and author of General Jackson's Manifesto against the United States Bank, is paid $3,000 a year of the people's money, or more than fifty dollars a week; saying nothing of extra pay for his deposit Bank agency.

Messrs. Cambreleng, White, Lawrence, and others, attached to the interests of Messrs. Van Buren and Kendall, are paid already more than fifty dollars a week, apiece.

LIST OF OFFICERS OF THE CUSTOM HOUSE IN N. YORK,

With the Amount of their Compensation.

S. Swartwout, collector,	4400
David S. Lyon, dep. do.	1500
M.S. Swartwout, do. do.	1500
Daniel Strobel, do. do.	1500
Henry Ogden, cashier,	2300
Nath'l Shultz, auditor,	1700
Joshua Philips, Ast. cash.	1450
And'w Martine, ast. aud.	1250
C. Duryee, liquidat'g cl'k.	950
Eben. Platt, export clerk,	do

[The list continues for many pages, deleted here—Ed.]

Aggregate Amount of Salaries, $340,000

CORPORATION PATRONAGE

Salary per annum.

Gideon Lee, Mayor	$3000
Jacob Morton, Clerk of the Board of Aldermen and of Common Council	2000
Do. preparing minutes for publication	150
John Ahern, Assistant Clerk in Mayor's Office and of Board of Aldermen	1000
Dow D. Williamson, Messenger Common Council	700
Jacob Hays, as Sergeant at Arms, Board Aldermen	250
Do. as High Constable	500
John Sidell, First Marshal	900
John W. Richardson, Clerk of Boardof Assistant Ald	1000
Do. preparing minutes for publication	150

George B. Butler, Assistant do	200
David T. Valentine, Sergt. at Arms, do	500
Do. as Marshal attending Marine Court, 12s. per day, (except Sundays)	469.50
John Flemming, Treasurer	500
Talma J. Waters, Comptroller	2500
Wm. Thompson, Deputy Comptroller	1200
Wm. B. Smith, Collector of City Revenue	1200
Geo. B. Smith, Street Commissioner	3000
Edward Doughty, Asst. Street Commissioner	2000
Jacob Lozier, Clerk in Street Com's Office	750
____ _ ____, do do	500
Lewis Jamison, Porter attending the Record Office, 8s. per day, (except Sundays)	313

[Again, the list goes on at length.
A few highlights are included here.—Ed.]

Ogden Hoffman, District Attorney	3000
Henry Meigs, Clerk of Oyer and Terminer and Sessions Courts	2000
John P. Roome, Crier of Courts	300
Samuel Jones, Chief Justice Superior Court	2500
Josiah Ogden Hoffman, Associate Justice do	2500
Thomas J. Oakley do do	2500
Isaac Asten, Sweeper of Fulton Market, $2 per day	730
George Duryea, Deputy Clerk of do	500
Leonard Baum, do. Washington Market, 500 and Sweeping, 469 50	969 50
Sum annually expended under the control of the Commissioners	$124,852 92

548 Watchmen, at 8s. per night, Marshals, who receive fees, and Sunday Officers, &c. &c. are appointed by the Mayor—Amount of salaries annually 124,484 11

Many English no doubt imagine, that the people of America pay no taxes. But I can assure them they are grossly deceived; added to which, the Corporation exactions in many cases exceed anything of the kind in England. An American cannot keep or drive a common cart, as a Cartman, whose business is to convey luggage from place to place, without paying a heavy licence-duty; and it is a fact, that the Americans feel their taxes so heavily, that at the time I left they were crying out for a property-tax in lieu of such exactions.

Plate 14. Our Quiet Ballot Box. By permission of the Syndics of Cambridge University Library.

CHAPTER VIII

Vote by Ballot a Failure in America—No Protection against Bribery & Coercion—Drunkenness, Rioting, & Fighting Common at Their Elections—The Better Classes Arming & Heading the Mob—Near a 100 Killed & Wounded—One Irishman Put to Flight 6000 Americans—Ballot-Box Fixed at Grog-Shops—Beastly Scenes at Nearly All—Drunken Voters Brought to Ballot by Cart Loads—Masters Bribed to Coerce Their Men & Spoil Their Tickets—Manner of Forging & Marking Tickets—The President's Rejection of Petitions—Standing out for Judges—Our Quiet Ballot-Box—Mordecai Noah's Advice to Disfranchise the Irish—Jackson's Notion of a Slanderer

WHATEVER clamour may be roused by political theorists in England in favour of *vote by Ballot*, one thing is certain, that it has proved a complete failure in *Republican America*. Nor could any honest man entertain the idea for a moment, who had seen half as much of its operation as I did in April, 1834, during the late New York Election and that only for a Mayor, aldermen, &c. *They must at once acknowledge, that it is no protection against bribery, or coercion, nor that republican America was on that account one step in advance of the other nations of the Earth, in either political honesty or independence*. Several days before that on which the election commenced, I witnessed such scenes of drunkenness, rioting, and fighting, in the streets of New York, as I never beheld in *aristocratic* England, in the most exciting times, at the hottest contested election. Persons were continually carried to the hospitals wounded, and so great was the animosity of parties during the election itself, that little less than an hundred persons were near being victims to popular fury, and several died of their wounds on reaching the hospitals. Military, both horse & foot, were called forth to quell *the riots*, and this, be it observed, in a country where neither the Ballot or Republicanism can be said to be in its infancy; but where men are accustomed to boast of their honesty & political independence, and to hold themselves up as an example to the rest of the world.

I pointed this out to several American gentlemen, at the time, as an absolute stain upon the country. "Ah," was the reply, "but this is a period of unusual excitement," referring to the animosities that have been engendered by the Bank question. "Never before," says the *Sun* American paper, "have we witnessed such excitement at any election in our city, as exists on the present occasion. The whole community seems in commotion. Hardly a neutral is to be found. The two great political parties are straining every nerve to its utmost tension in their efforts for victory. We do not exaggerate when we say, that it will tell on the destinies of the Nation."

But from what I saw going on, I was doubtful whether this excitement, though partly springing out of the Bank question, was not more deeply rooted, and referred to the files of American papers to satisfy myself. I there found, that the Elections of 1833 were accompanied by similar exhibitions. Nor are these scenes of riot, drunkenness, and every vice that the most corrupt constituency could practice, confined to New York; they are common all over America, and are participated in by the high as well as by the low. "It is worthy of remark as a Sign of the times," says an eye-witness, in a letter published in the *Sun* American paper, dated Albany, the 7th of March, 1834, speaking of the Ward Elections, "that some citizens occupying elevated Stations in Society, were led by their intemperate excitement, to join in the mob before the Governor's door (which they designed to fire) and to direct and sanction its proceedings. And one man, characterized by his unusual courtesy as a gentleman, was guilty of the contemptible meanness of giving a dollar '*to buy a barrel of tar to burn Governor Marcy's door.*'"

But worse than this was perpetrated by influential men in New York, several of which class broke into the arsenal & stole fire arms, and afterwards handed them from their windows to the mob, loaded and with fixed bayonets. This I saw. And one American whom I could name and with whose person I am well-acquainted, actually gave the word, "fall in," and headed a party so armed. The commander of the military disarmed several whose pieces were loaded with ball. And in such a state was the city of New York kept, that had it not been for the prompt conduct of the old Mayor & the soldiers, the most bloody scenes would have followed. I saw old men, & others, trembling with fears of some dreadful explosion during the night before the election closed, and I question if the people in all New York slept that night in their beds, dreading a revolution, or a bloody conflict. "Last night," adds the writer above quoted, "the city (of Albany) was filled with riot, roar, and drunken carousal; all the

Plate 15. Jackson Dismissing the New York Delegates and Petition. By permission of the Syndics of Cambridge University Library.

main streets were illuminated with tar barrels, and the little boys screamed, the big wigs swore, and the bullies fought the Irish, wherever they could find a *single one* going peaceably about his business *without* company or cudgel to protect him."

The Irish, it appears, are generally the supporters of President Jackson's measures against the United States Bank, and it seems they are everywhere in America marked men in consequence: for the same persecution of them as above described was followed up during the progress of the election I witnessed at New York, where several were most severely beaten as were many English whom the *free-born* republicans of *enlightened* America mistook for Irish. One resolute Hibernian I saw attacked by a crowd of several thousands, the paper said 6, who gallantly faced his enemies, & actually made them fly—upon which incident the *Sun* American paper had the next day an exclamation inserted in its leader to this effect, "O! Shades of Washington, &c. would you not blush for your countrymen, had ye beheld 6000 Americans put to flight by one Irishman!" One American paper, the *Evening Star*, cried *Shame* upon the proceedings of his countrymen, adding that they would render republican America "the laughing-stock of all Europe!"

I had been told, before I crossed the Atlantic, that their *Ballot-Boxes* were placed at the Church-porch, and that everything passed in the most orderly manner. But I found the whole either a fiction or a deliberate falsehood. They were, on the contrary, placed at *Grog-shops*, or *Hotels*, and during the time the votes were taken, I saw & heard drunkenness and rioting proceeding both within and without them. In fact, the most beastly scenes were exhibited at nearly all of them. One fellow, we did not inquire to which party he belonged, said the *Sun* American paper, at the time, who "was lying in the gutter near the polls of the Fourth Ward yesterday," April the 8th, —"the rain pouring upon him—and one of his legs forming a complete dam by which the course of the little stream was turned from its 'natural channel'—was asked why he did not go home. He replied, 'cause I'm waiting the *result*.'" I saw hundreds of *independent voters* brought up to *ballot* in vehicles after the fashion of London Omnibuses, many of whom were so drunk they were obliged to be lifted out, & nearly all were in a state but little removed from drunkenness.

Many of these men have been no doubt artfully made drunk by some of the opposite party, for the purpose of *spoiling* their tickets, as it is called—which is thus effected—Each man has what is denominated a "charter ticket," and another marked "Mayor." Upon the first is printed the names of the candidates for the office of *Alderman*, &c; upon the other the *name* of the candidate for the office of *Mayor*, all *correctly* spelt. The opposite party having procured false tickets, with a letter left out of a name, get the correct tickets from the drunken voter and give him a forged one instead, or, I was told, another practice was to ask the intoxicated man to let them look at his ticket, and after having *scraped out* a letter, or altered or blotted out one in the name, return it to the owner, who unconsciously puts it thus altered into the *Ballot-Box*, by which as well as in the case of a forged ticket, his vote is rendered a *nullity*. By these tricks, ***5000*** *bad votes* were given during the late election for Mayor in New York, and it was publicly asserted that the Bank Candidate, Verplanck, thereby lost his election, he having, it was said, a majority of the *good votes*.

And that this is possible my readers may believe, from the manner in which the *ballot* proceeds. Persons are appointed to each *Ballot-box* whose duty it is to watch & mark down each vote as given. But there is no means given used for preventing persons putting in *more than one* Ticket, which it is said is frequently done, and the injury it may cause to the opposite party (and it is precisely the same as regards *forged* or *spoiled* Tickets) will be understood from their plan being, at the close of the Ballot, to cast aside whatever the excess of tickets (forged, spoiled, or extra) may be over the number of checks, suppose 100; fifty would then be placed to the account of each candidate, or should there be more than two candidates, they are deducted from all in equal proportions: no matter on whose side the evil originates. There is no doubt but both parties were guilty of all the above species of fraud, to a great extent.

One system of coercing voters, very prevalent in America, is for the masters to ascertain which of their men intend to vote opposite to their *interest*, as it is called, then dismiss them from their employ some time previously to the election, in order to reduce them to such a *necessitous state*, by the time the election comes round, as to force them to vote for their favourite candidate. I was personally acquainted with one instance of 50 men being so treated by one Master, resident in Broadway, New York, previously to the late election for Mayor, in the interest of the Bank; and it was openly asserted in New York, at the time, that the Bank had distributed no less a Sum than 65,000 dollars to indemnify such masters for losses they might sustain by a temporary suspension of their business, from thus coercing & dismissing their men. By this means, not only were hundreds of men sufferers by being reduced to penury, but they were at last forced into a compliance with their masters' demands, and to vote for men whose political principles they detested. Yet this is the system your English Radical is anxious to tag to our Constitution, in place of that open honest-hearted system of polling, which has preserved to England all that security both of persons & property, for which she stands pre-eminently before all countries in the world.

One system for coercing voters in America is the following—Each master takes care to supply his *coerced men with tickets*, that have some ***secret*** *notch*, *dot*, or *mark* upon them, and knowing well who of his party will have the *overlooking*, or *scrutinizing*, the tickets after the Ballot-Box has closed, they communicate their secret marks to their friend, the Scrutinizer, who takes care to ascertain if such as held these *marked* tickets have voted, and such as have failed to comply are instantly turned off from their work, to seek new masters, in some cases to starve. I am personally acquainted with a great many instances of men being so dismissed, after the close of the New York election of last April. One American to whom I named these instances of tyranny in a country professing republicanism, flatly replied, that "persons ought to vote in their employers' interest—" and I fearlessly assert the truth, that, free-born as they call themselves, the great majority of Americans are imbued with the same principles, if principles they can be called. In fact the whole system of what is called Freedom, Liberty, and republicanism, in the United States, is a farce.

Nor are the enfranchised in America one jot better informed on the subject of politics than are the same class in England—nay I confidently believe that the same class in England are less liable to be imposed upon. A short time before the Election came on, the Bank party got up a petition, which was called The New York petition, to be presented to President Jackson, praying him *to restore the Deposits*. A committee was formed to push this petition and it was circulated in all directions for signatures. Thousands of mechanics signed it without inquiring or in any way understanding what were its merits or purport—and when I remonstrated with some on thus blindly committing themselves, they would exclaim, "Well, I know nothing of politicks. I never trouble myself about them." Here again the masters were induced & even bribed to coerce their men to swell the number of signatures, & I knew a great many instances of men being turned off for refusing to give their names to countenance the New York, or rather the Bank petition. This petition was got up for more reasons than one. But the most fortunate circumstance connected with it, for the Bank party, was the manner in which it was received by Jackson. He was not to be frightened from his purpose by such a bugbear, and is said to have dismissed the Deputation of New Yorkers, who presented it in a manner and with emphatic words of a class it is not desirable should be here repeated. This circumstance was seized upon at the election, and there is no doubt but many opposed the candidate devoted to his interest in consequence, and that some were incited to acts of violence, spurred on by a recollection of what the mob were told was an *indignity*, not to the Bank Party, but to the citizens of New York. *The Crisis*, American paper, of March the 22nd, 1834, says that "*King Andrew*," meaning the President, "has usurped the powers of both Houses of Congress," and now, it is added, "insults the people themselves!" "The committee from Wilmington, Delaware, who presumed to ask the President to mitigate the public distress, were told to '*Go home, and go to work, and leave the government to him*.' Had Washington or Jefferson dared thus to insult freemen, the blood of '76 would have been aroused throughout the Union. But now we calmly & tamely submit to be trampled down & spit upon!"

The following instance of the sagacity of enfranchised Americans is recorded in *The Man* American paper, in a letter dated Philadelphia, 11th of May, 1834. "*Crockery* at the Southwark election, sent his hands down to stand out for judges. One of them came back before the rest. 'Well,' said his employer, 'how did you make out?' 'Oh,' says the fellow, 'we beat them, huzza! huzza!' and about the store he went huzzaing, scarcely able to contain himself, or repress his extacies enough to give his employer the desired information. 'How much did you beat them?' he asked. 'Oh, about 900! huzza! huzza!' 'Ah, so much as that; well, that is more than I expected, but,' said the employer, a shade of doubt crossing his mind, 'which side of the street did you stand on?' 'Oh, on the right, to be sure, on the West side, huzza!' 'You d——d fool,' exclaimed the employer in the bitterness of his disappointment, 'you were on the wrong side of the way'; and, sure enough, and his recruits had fallen into the ranks of the enemy."

It was a few days previously to the New York election, that the two Austrian frigates arrived in the Bay of New York with the expatriated Poles. I saw these officers walking the streets of the city, closely watching all that was passing, and a pretty specimen they had of *republican* Institutions. One of the American papers observed, whether *ironically* or not I leave my readers to guess, that "they were no doubt observing '***our quiet Ballot-box***.'"

Another Anecdote connected with this Election is the fact, that the editor of the *Evening Star*, the notorious Mordecai Noah, whose virulent abuse of Jackson & his friends is such that even his supporters cry "Shame" & blush, had a short time previously to the election coming on, descanted upon the brutalized state of the citizenized Irish Emigrants in New York, and attributed it to the "600 years of misrule of England," as he termed it. But a day or two after, when the election closed in favour of the *Jackson* candidate, for whom it is known the Irish voted almost to a man, the same editor called upon the American legislature to pass some act for *disfranchising* those same Irish!—It might be recommended to this gentleman to bear in mind the words attributed to Andrew Jackson, as set forth in the pages of a contemporary paper, *The Crisis*, like him a supporter of the Bank party, "that the *Slanderer* was worse than the *murderer*—the worse because *disgrace* was worse than *death*—and so much the worse, as death was no cure for calumny—that an honourable man would rather die than submit to have his character destroyed!"—

CHAPTER IX

Church & State in America—The People Divided into Two Great Classes of Atheists and Fanatics—New Persecutions—The Mormons—Methodists—Parsons Frey—Avery—and others

I certainly did not expect to hear any mention made of *Church & State* in republican America, save in the way of reproach. But I had not been long in New York before a book appeared, by a Methodist Preacher, entitled *Church & State*, in which it was attempted to be proved, that the Church of America had diffused the Spirit of Christian Faith more widely & with a more beneficial result than almost any other Christian Church upon earth, and also to shew its *connexion* with the State. But this I do most unhesitatingly affirm, that the only class of religionists that observe anything like a decent spirit of decorum in their forms of worship, are the Roman Catholics and the few English who retain the religious tenets & customs of the English Established Church. The people of America are literally divided into two great classes—*Fanatics* and *Atheists*—the few that do not come under these two heads, are scarcely worth notice, from the paucity of their numbers.

It would be a hopeless task to attempt to enumerate the tenets of the 365 sects of Fanatics that abound in America, and useless would it be to refer the reader to Girard's *Sketch of All Religions*, for that does not contain a tithe of them. "The number of sects in Philadelphia is such," says a recent authority, quoted by the *Times* of the 28th of July, 1834, "that Girard's College would barely have contained a representative from each denomination. There are no fewer than 9 Protestant Episcopal churches, 4 Roman Catholic, 19 Presbyterian, 10 Methodist, 3 Reformed Dutch, 6 Baptists, 5 German Lutheran, 6 Quaker, one Free Quakers, one Covenanters, 2 German Reformed, two Universalists, two Synagogues, one Bible Christian, one Mariners' Church, one Swedenborgian, 10 Unitarians, 1 Moravian, one Menonist or Dunkers, one Swedish Lutheran, one Mount Zion. In addition to these, the Evangelical Society have erected 4 in the Suburbs. None of them are remarkable for exterior beauty, but are generally so plain as scarcely to be distinguished from private houses." This description is applicable to all the large towns in America. In the city of Boston & its neighbourhood, where the fanatics are omnipotent, they are so numerous & so powerful, that a person who does not join some one of them and attend one of their Churches as they call their conventicles, would not only subject himself to general persecution, but be literally *hunted down* between the fanatical preachers & their half-mad followers. Indeed, Englishmen who have never witnessed it, cannot have the most distant idea of the extent to which the persecution of what they term *irreligious* persons, that is, non-attendants at their conventicles, is carried. But in this as in all other things, there is generally more selfishness than piety: for the erection & proprietorship of Chapels, as is the case with everything else in America, has been made the source of wealth to many a sordid disciple of Mammon.

And let it not be imagined by your irreligious democrats of England, that there is any thing like a tolerant spirit otherwise abroad in America, or that a *Taylor* or a *Carlile*, could publish and preach their impiety in Republican America with impunity, any more than they are permitted to do in England. Whilst I was in America, towards the conclusion of 1833, Alexander Keilden, I believe I am correct in the name, was prosecuted for animadverting too freely on religion & the Scriptures, at Boston. He was convicted and sentenced to a fine of 500 dollars and Six months imprisonment, and was still incarcerated in consequence, but had removed the case into a higher court, wherein the matter was pending at the time I left the United States. I happened to be one day in a Court of Law, in New York, when a man presented himself as a witness, who refused to be sworn upon the Gospels, as he declared he did not believe in them. Upon which the Judge bawled out, "Get down, Sir: you ought to be ashamed of yourself." On a similar case, occurring in another New York Court of Law, "Get out, Sir," exclaimed the person in authority, "none of your blasphemy in the court." Had these cases occurred in England, what would not the enemies of religion have said? But I can assure them, intolerant as they may imagine the English Legislature to be, there is still less tolerance in America, and that such cases as the above are not only frequent, but accompanied with a grossness of language & expression of which Englishmen are incapable.

One of the present Sects of Religionists in America, if they can be said to deserve the distinction, are a kind of wandering class called *Mormons*, who pretend to have intercourse with Heaven, and to be endowed with the power of working miracles. One of their pastors, for they have Bishops, &c. undertook some short time since to arouse his followers & convert unbelievers, by walking on the water, as Christ had done. A pond in the neighbourhood was selected for the exhibition. Some persons suspecting a trick, seized an opportunity for examining the pond and found a plank fixed across, about 3 inches below the surface. This they sawed nearly through in the middle. At the time appointed the Mormon preacher approached throwing & waving about his arms, exclaiming to the gazing multitude, as he approached the side of the pond—"Repent, repent, repent: the end of the world is at hand!" and other incoherent expressions. No sooner had he commenced crossing the plank, than it began to give way, but he, not suspecting treachery for treachery, continued crying out as before, as he ever & anon turned to the multitude. But as he advanced, he began to stagger in earnest & gradually to sink—the people shrieked, and the picture is described as most awful, as in a moment after he disappeared altogether, to the consternation of all present, as well as of those who had had a hand in thwarting the impostor, who had no idea of causing so tragical a denouement. It was a long time before his body could be drawn out, and then not till life was extinct. The result was, that the Mormons lost all credit in that part of the country.

One of the most singular persecutions that have occurred in modern times, was lately enacted in Jackson County, against this same sect, of which the full particulars are given in an American paper, of Dcr. 1833, extracted from the *St Louis Republican,* headed *Persecution.*

> A meeting of the citizens of Jackson county, to the number of four or five hundred, was held at Independence on the 20th of July. Their avowed object was to take measures to rid themselves of the Mormonites. Col. Richard Simpson was called to the chair, and Jones H. Flournoy and Samuel D. Lucas appointed Secretaries. A committee was then appointed to report an address to the public, in relation to the object of the meeting. After having retired for some time, they submitted an address, which was unanimously adopted; and in which the conduct and views of the obnoxious sect are exposed. They represent that the Mormonites number some 1200 souls in that county, and that each successive spring and autumn pours forth its swarms among them, until they have now nearly reached the low condition of the black population. That the citizens have been daily told, that they are to be cut off, and their lands appropriated to the Mormons for inheritances; but they are not fully agreed among themselves as to the man-

ner in which this shall be accomplished, whether by the destroying angel, the judgment of God, or the arm of power. The committee express their fears that, should this population continue to increase, they will soon have all the officers of the county in their hands; and that the lives and property of other citizens would be insecure, under the administration of men who are so ignorant and superstitious as to believe that they have been the subjects of miraculous and supernatural cures; hold converse with God and his angels, and possess and exercise the gift of divination, and of unknown tongues; and are, withal, so poor as to be unable to procure bread and meat. The committee say, that "one of the means resorted to by them, in order to drive us to emigrate, is an indirect invitation to the free brethren of colour in Illinois, to come like the rest to the land of Zion. True, the Mormons say this was not intended to invite, but to prevent emigration; but this weak attempt to quiet our apprehension is but a poor compliment to our understandings." The invitation alluded to, contained all the necessary directions and cautions, to enable the free blacks, on their arrival here, to claim and exercise the right of citizenship. Finally, the committee say—"Of their pretended revelations from heaven—their personal intercourse with God and his angels—the maladies they pretend to heal by the laying on of hands—and the contemptible gibberish with which they habitually profane the Sabbath, and which they dignify with the appellation of the unknown tongues, we have nothing to say. Vengeance belongs to God alone. But as to the other matters set forth in this paper, we feel called on by every consideration of self preservation, good society, public morals, and the fair prospects that if not blasted in the germ, await this young and beautiful county, at once to declare, and we do hereby most solemnly declare,

1. That no Mormon shall in future move and settle in this county.

2. That those now there, who shall give a definite pledge of their intention within a reasonable time to remove out of the county, shall be allowed to remain unmolested until they have sufficient time to sell their property and close their business without any material sacrifice.

3. That the editor of the *Star* be required forthwith to close his office, and discontinue the business of printing in this county; and as to all other stores and shops belonging to the sect, their owners must in every case strictly comply with the terms of the second article of this declaration, and upon failure, prompt and efficient measures will be taken to

close the same.

4. That the Mormon leaders are required to use their influence in preventing any further emigration of their distant brethren to this county, and to counsel and advise their brethren here to comply with the above requisitions.

5. That those who fail to comply with these requisitions, be referred to those of their brethren who have the gifts of divination, and of unknown tongues, to inform them of the lot that awaits them."

Which address being read and considered, was unanimously adopted. And thereupon it was resolved, that a committee of twelve be appointed forthwith to wait on the Mormon leaders, and see that the foregoing requisitions are strictly complied with by them; and upon their refusal, the said committee do, as the organ of this county, inform them that it is our unwavering purpose and fixed determination, after the fullest consideration of all the consequences and responsibilities under which we act, to use such means as shall insure their full and complete adoption, and that said committee, so far as may be within their power, report to this present meeting.

After an adjournment of two hours, the meeting again convened, and the committee of twelve reported that they had called on Mr. Phelps, the editor of the *Star*, Edward Partridge, the bishop of the sect, and Mr. Gilbert, the keeper of the Lord's store house, and some others, and that they declined giving any direct answer to the requisitions made of them, and wished an unreasonable time for consultation, not only with their brethren, here, but in Ohio.

Whereupon, it was unanimously resolved by the meeting, that the *Star* printing office should be razed to the ground, and the type and press secured. Which resolution was, with the utmost order, and the least noise or disturbance possible, forthwith carried into execution, as also some other steps of a similar tendency; but no blood was spilled nor any blows inflicted. The meeting then adjourned till the 23d inst. to meet again to know further concerning the determination of the Mormons.

The citizens again convened on the 23d day of July, 1833 which was composed of gentlemen from all parts of the county, and much more unanimously attended than the meeting of the 20th instant.

A committee was appointed to wait upon the Mormon leaders, who had intimated a wish to have a conference. After an adjournment of two hours, the meeting again convened, when the committee reported to the meeting that they had waited on most of the Mormon leaders, consisting of the bishop, Mr. Partridge, Mr. Phelps, editor of the *Star*, Mr. Gilbert, the keeper of the Lord's store house, and Messrs. Carrol, Whitmer, and Moseley, elders of the church, and that the said committee had entered into an amicable agreement with them, which they had reduced to writing, which they submitted; and that the committee have assured Mr. Phelps that whenever he was ready to move, the amount of all his losses should be paid to him by the citizens. The written agreement is as follows:

"Memorandum of agreement between the undersigned of the Mormon society, in Jackson county, Missouri, and a committee appointed by a public meeting of the citizens of said county, made the 23d day of July, 1833.

It is understood that the undersigned, members of the society, do give their solemn pledges, each for himself, as follows, to wit:

That Oliver Cowdry, W.W. Phelps, Wm. McClealand, Edward Partridge, Lyman Wight, Simeon Carter, Peter and John Whitner, and Harvey Whitlock, shall remove with their families out of this county, on or before the first day of January next, and they, as well as the two hereinafter named, use all their influence to induce all the brethren now here to remove as soon as possible—one half, say, by the first of January next, and all by the first day of April next. To advise and try all means in their power, to stop any more of their sect from moving to this county; and as to those now on the road, they will use their influence to prevent their settling permanently in the county, but that they shall only make arrangements for temporary shelter, till a new location is agreed on for the society. John Carrol and Algernon Gilbert are allowed to remain as general agents to wind up the business of the society, so long as necessity shall require; and said Gilbert may sell out his merchandise now on hand, but is to make no new importation.

The *Star* is not again to be published, nor a press set up by any of the society in this county.

If the said Edward Partridge and W.W. Phelps move their families by the first day of January, as aforesaid, that they themselves will be allowed to go and come in order to transact and wind up their business.

The committee pledge themselves to use all their influence to prevent any violence being used so long as a compliance with the foregoing terms is observed by the parties concerned, to which agreement is subscribed the names of the above named committee, as also those of the Mormon brethren named in the report as having been present.

The report of the committee was unanimously adopted

> by the meeting, and it was then adjourned.
>
> These proceedings (says the editor) may find some justification in the necessity of the case, but they are wholly at war with the genius of our institutions, and as subversive of good order as the conduct of the fanatics themselves. Perhaps, however, it was the only method which could have been effectually put in practice to get this odious description of population out of the way. Banished as they are from that frontier, it may well be asked to what place will they now remove; and will they enjoy any better security in the new abode which they may select?

This apparent acquiescence in the dictatorial proceedings of their opponents has not, it seems, been persevered in, and, according to the American Papers of a late date, parties of the Mormonites residing in other parts of America were arming themselves for the purpose of assisting their brethren, in Jackson County, in their subsequent determination to resist their forced emigration.

This is a case probably without a parallel in the religious history of the world. But all religious matters in America, like everything else, are conducted upon a System without a parallel in the history of any well-regulated community, as the foregoing facts and the following *truths* will shew. *The Sun* American paper of May, 1834, observes, "This is the season of the anniversaries of religious & charitable institutions. They are numerously attended, and their reports speak favorably of their increasing strength and usefulness. Having for the most part, the welfare and happiness of man as their grand object and aim, we wish them all success in their efforts. There are, however, one or two associations among them, which, whatever may be the purity or zeal of their supporters, are calculated to produce the most serious evils. Among them, is the Society for the *promotion of the Seventh Commandment*—or in other words, *the Society to prevent lewdness*. There are certain subjects which the common consent of all civilized societies has marked as too indelicate, gross, and disgusting in their character, ever to be brought—except in extraordinary cases, and where the moral sense of the community has been severely shocked—before the public eye. Of such a character must of necessity be all details connected with the proceedings of this Society. Its supporters defy all common sense of propriety, all received notions of decency, and do not hesitate in public assemblages, where ladies form a great part of the audience, to give the most disgusting accounts of low debauchery and sensual indulgence, such as can hardly be communicated to the delicate mind of a woman without polluting it. This society probably owes its existence to that record of the stews, *McDowall's Journal*, which has already been presented by the grand jury as a dangerous and immoral publication. In all charity, and without seeking to inquire into the motives of men to profess to be guided by a desire to promote public purity, and public morals, we must say that this association, unless opposed by the same general spirit which demanded that a public example should be made of *McDowall's Journal*, will exert a most pernicious influence upon the morals of this community. Every friend of decency & morality should frown upon and discountenance it."

The same authority stated in the previous month of April, that "a religious sect had sprung up in the county of Surry, one of whose tenets is to salute each other at a holy meeting with a holy kiss. One of the female devotees, a young lady of a thousand charms, happened to encounter a young gentleman, of whom she was enamoured, and gave him a more cordial & loving salute than was quite becoming. The next day she received a message from the high priest of the sect, saying she had been excommunicated for 'kissing with an appetite.'" I could relate anecdotes of their camp-meetings would make the ears of decency tingle and the cheek of modesty burn with shame, enacted, not only under the eye of their spiritual teachers, as they call their *vagabond* pastors, but in which these same pastors were principal actors. I shall not, however, dwell upon them. Those who would be better versed in the history of an American camp-meeting, I must refer to the writings of Mrs Trollope, and to the more recent publication of Mr Ferrall. I have never read the latter, but I am told he has fully entered into the subject. It is a fact that the females of all classes of fanatics in America are under a complete state of subjection to their *spiritual* pastors, and that they alone ought to be looked upon as their hearers & their supporters. One would suppose from appearances that the American women were all *fanatics*, & the men all *atheists*—Indeed, I believe it to be near the truth. I have been in many of their most crowded congregations, and amongst several thousands never saw above a hundred men present at the same time; in fact the disproportion of the sexes never fails to create surprise in strangers. It is to the women all their appeals are addressed, it is upon them all the baser purposes of fanatical preachers are made to operate.

Let us then inquire who this great class of preachers are, and we may thus draw some conclusion as to the value of their influence upon female society in America. I have elsewhere recorded the fact, that several abandoned characters who emigrated from England leaving wives & families destitute, became *popular* preachers after reaching America, settled as such & married American women with property, and on their wives & families arriving in the United States & claiming their protection, these same *pious preachers of the word of God* declared their wives & families to be impostors, in which they have in most instances, nay in all that I am acquainted with, been countenanced & supported by their American congregations. One man, now a popular preacher no great distance from New York, emigrated from a city in Norfolk, where he was a dyer & scourer, by trade, and little better than a confirmed sot—now he is the Rev[d] Mr —, in America. I know a lady who lately emigrated from England, that went with some American acquaintances to hear a popular preacher at Brooklyn, near New York, which has been recently made a city. The party were persons of influence, and after the service concluded, the new settler was taken to be introduced to the Rev[d] favourite. His name was no sooner uttered, than she recollected that such a person had fled from England with a large sum of money belonging to a society for the *Conversion of the Jews*. She no sooner looked him in the face than she recognized the renegade Jew, and she confessed to me that the blush of shame mantled in her face as she put out her hand to shake that of *a known thief*. After she retired with her American friends, she named the fact to them. But they did not profess to be at all surprised or ignorant of the matter, and exclaimed—"Ah! but he is a *fine* preacher!"

This is only one out of many I could relate. But there is a more recent case before the American public, the remarkable one of a preacher being retained in his office of pastor, an *acknowledged Seducer & adulterer, a convicted liar, and a darkly acquitted murderer*! This man is the *Rev*[d] E.K. Avery, the father of a family, who was & is still a Methodist preacher of note in the vicinity of Boston. He had for one of his congregation a poor factory girl of the name of Sarah Maria Cornell, represented as interesting & intelligent. For some indiscretion, it is said, she had come under the bann of this fanatical *Moloch*—designedly, there is too much reason to fear, to make her a sacrifice to his baser passions, & this he accomplished during one of their *infamous* Camp-meetings, about the middle of 1832. She became *enceinte*, in consequence. Her health obliging her to seek advice, she first learnt her situation from Doctor Wilbur, a member of the Society of Friends, in the month of October, of the above year, and to whom, after a promise of secrecy, she declared the father of her offspring to be the ***Rev***^d E.K. Avery. It was with great astonishment the Doctor heard her, as he supposed the Rev^d delinquent a man of character, and after several interviews with this physician, at every one of which, it is affirmed "she appeared to be deeply affected, with a sense of her conduct, and always shed tears," she persisted "in naming Avery as the author of her difficulty."

Upon the Doctor's expressing his incredulity, his surprise and horror, at the bare imputation of such an offence on a minister of the gospel, his penetrating eye, and searching inquiries, it is said, lest he should be imposed upon, seemed to produce no other emotion in her than those of heartfelt anguish, and the additional information that Avery had advised her to make use of the oil of Tansy, in doses of 30 drops, with a view to destroy her offspring, or rather to kill the poor girl herself, and remove as he thought all the living evidence of his guilt, as 10 drops, the doctor informed her, were sufficient to lay her dead at his feet. She further confirmed the truth of what she had stated of Avery by shewing the Doctor a letter she had rec^d from him. Upon this Doctor Wilbur insisted she should demand an interview with Avery and negotiate with him for a sum sufficient to enable her to retire from the labour of the factory, & support her comfortably till she should be again able to support herself—proposing a sum larger than she thought her seducer could afford, upon which she generously refused to demand it, alledging that she knew Avery was poor, and that she would do nothing to distress him & his family. She finally consented to ask for a smaller sum and to request an interview.

She shortly afterwards called on Dr Wilbur & shewed him a letter she had received from her seducer, appointing to see her in a secluded & very solitary spot, at night, near the Fall River, in which neighbourhood the Doctor lived. This struck the Doctor as remarkable, & he begged of her not to go alone. This advice was not attended to. The scene of the meeting was so near the Doctor's residence, that when he arose in the morning, he was surprised at seeing people hurrying by in evident anxiety and on inquiry was told that a young woman had hung herself. He put on his hat & hastened to the spot to which the people were crowding, when the 1st object that met his view was the poor girl in whose welfare he had taken so much interest, suspended from a tree quite dead. There was no evidence how she came there, but Avery had been seen in the neighbourhood the night of the proposed interview, which had proved so tempestuous, that Avery, as it afterwards came out had in vain endeavoured to bribe a boatman to take him across the river to the opposite side, the direction in which his dwelling laid.

Upon taking down the poor girl's body, it was found that the rope by which she was hanging was tied with a double knot, and that it had been drawn so tight on the first being tied, that it must, as the medical men stated, have caused instant death—so that it was impossible the poor girl could have been her own executioner. All the medical men, from the distorted angry look of her features in death, testified that she had died by the hands of a murderer; and it further appeared, that she had on her hands a pair of clean white gloves, which must have been soiled had she hung herself, as the rope was in a dirty state. And it was found, on examination, that the flesh was violently pressed in on both her sides, with finger marks, below the stays, as if by the grasp of a powerful man, which Avery is. In short there were so many circumstances that shewed her death to have been the work of a murderer.

But all these facts did not all come to light at the time her body was first discovered, and much pains were taken by the Methodist preachers and their friends, in the neighbourhood, to defame the poor girl's character, after death. They actually refused to bury her in consecrated ground, & an honest old farmer, of the name of Duffee, who lived near the scene of death, was so moved with the barbarous persecution that was going on, that he declared she should have a decent funeral, in a spot he had appropriated to be the resting place of his own family.

At length public rumour bruited so many suspicious circumstances against Avery, that he was apprehended on a suspicion of being her murderer, & her remains were exhumed for further examination, but the evidence not being deemed sufficient to commit him upon, he was suffered to go at large. Other evidence, however, was procured sufficient to make a different impression upon the minds of a coroner & jury, and a warrant was granted for his apprehension. Upon this he fled and was traced by the officer to the cottage of an old woman, who to the officer's inquiry denied that he was there. At the instant, however, the constable thought he perceived something to flit behind the door, and darting forward, he found it was Avery, who faint-ed on being seized.

He was soon after brought to trial for the murder, during the progress of which many singular circumstances occurred. Amongst others was that of a woman coming into court & stating to the Judge, that she had dreamed for 3 successive nights, that the man who had murdered Maria Cornell had a wound on one of his hands. It was then recollected that Avery had, from the commencement of the trial, kept one of his hands *gloved*, and upon his removing the glove by the Judge's order, it was found that there was the remains of a wound, as if caused by a *bite*.

What makes this trial one of the most singular that ever, perhaps, took place in the known world, is the shameful conduct pursued by the Methodist preachers of the district, the friends of the accused, who are said not to have spent a less sum than 5000 dollars in their endeavours to establish Avery's innocence. Every means was resorted to by them, with a barbarous ferocity, to blacken the poor girl's character with lewd practices; females were intimidated by them from coming forward to give evidence who had been eye-witnesses of familiar scenes between the poor girl & her seducer.

Amongst other instances, says a writer in the *Free Enquirer*, American paper, "of the shameful manner in which witnesses were tampered with and their testimony kept back," is that "of a person who was heard to say, previous to the trial of Avery, that he saw him & Miss Cornell walking together during the camp meeting at Thompson, and that he knew them both. This information was communicated to the gentlemen who conducted the prosecution, and one of them went to Connecticut to procure the witness. *But he was one day too late*. On his arrival at the residence of the man, it was found that no less than 3 Methodist Clergymen had stolen the march upon him. The result was, that the witness refused to answer any questions put to him, and as no compulsory process could be had, nothing could be elicited from him. If any person shall think proper to question the facts relative to the 3 clergymen," adds this writer, "their Names, and that of my informant, shall be promptly given to end all doubt."

It was sworn by a respectable witness, that he saw Avery & his victim "walking arm in arm" on the evening of the 20th of October, in the neighbourhood of the Fall River, and "Mrs Bidwell also, wife of the Revd Ira M. Bidwell, testified that, on that night, Avery, who was expected to lodge at her house, was out so much later than usual for a minister, that she went to the house of a neighbour to inquire for him. And Mr. Bidwell himself stated that on the previous evening he saw Avery & Miss Cornell within '3 feet' of each other, & left them together, because he supposed Miss Cornell wished to have some conversation with him. All this does not look like a desire on the part of Miss Cornell, to avoid an interview with Avery as was pretended by him, and also by M[rs] Mayo, at the Thompson Camp meeting."

Evidence the most conclusive was produced on the trial shewing the intimacy that had subsisted between Avery & his victim, more than one witness swore to his being seen in the neighbourhood where the poor girl was murdered, yet Avery was acquitted, but acquitted only upon the Judge suggesting to the jury that any doubt in their minds ought to be given in favour of the accused.

One American paper observed upon this termination of one of the most interesting & exciting trials that modern times have produced, *that they were glad he was not to be hanged, as he was a descendant of one of the old Republicans who had fought for their independence*: so much for American love of justice. The report of the trials is before the American people, and but few who are not living under the despotic influence of the Methodist preachers have the smallest doubt in their minds but that he ought to have suffered an ignominious death instead of being now at large and actually forced upon a congregation by the influence of the *Bishop* of the district (Methodists have their Bishops in America), and the party of Methodist preachers, upon whose shoulders he may be said to have been triumphantly borne from the tribunal of murder, to defile God's temple with his unholy breath.

Some of the more moral part of society have attempted to resist this man's being continued in his office of a teacher of the Gospel, and they have, in consequence, been dignified with the soubriquet of "*The Avery Knobs*!" and there is every reason to believe the fanatical part, preachers & followers, will succeed in retaining him. Had he been tried in New York there is no doubt he would have been hanged. His own child, being called upon to give evidence during the trial, stated that his father's horse having kicked him, he drove a stake into the ground, tied the horse's leg to it, and kept it in that position till it was nearly starved. Another characteristic of the man was that of his having defamed the character of a brother preacher, for which he was tried & convicted. Those who would know more of the foregoing melancholy tale, or read the exposure that took place on the trial, relative to their Camp-Meetings & the vicious state of what are called the religious in America, may be satisfied, as the whole account forming a large volume, has been published & circulated in America.

I notice it that the true state of things may be understood in England, that the veil may be partially torn from the faces of that vile hypocritical set who denounce the Church of England for intolerance, whilst they preach, teach, & practice persecution of a more bitter & blacker spirit than ever disgraced any established church upon earth. In Aristocratic England, in those places of public worship under the control of the Established Church, if a *black man* were to enter either a cathedral or a parish Church he would find himself seated in the midst of his white fellow creatures, the poorer class, probably, but no such respect would be paid him in ***Republican*** America. In the places of worship in this land where they tell you *all men are born equal*, no man of color, *free-man* though he be, is permitted to seat himself in any church, of whatever denomination, on the same side with the *Whites*—they have a portion of the church set apart for their use, and your free-born American would hold himself utterly disgraced to sit on the same form or in the same part of a church where a *man of color* was seen. It is a well known fact, that in this same aristocratic England an educated man of color finds no difficulty in getting into the better sort of society, and several, to my knowledge, have been bred at & have graduated at our English Universities. But in America, the boasted land of Liberty, if a man of color had the wealth of the Indies, the learning & sagacity of a Newton, the wisdom of a Bacon, or the piety and knowledge of a Jeremy Taylor, he would still find himself despised & an outcast.

Good God! English Exchange their habits & institutions for those of America! Uproot the venerable Church Establishment upon which all their moral dignity is founded, to substitute a vile system of mob-fanaticism of the offensive & persecuting character such as now overwhelm society in America!—I call upon the English nation to pause before they consent to such a sacrifice, at the call of the ignorant self-deluded demagogues she numbers amongst her Representatives; to ask these same demagogues, if they are acting upon the test which ought to govern the minds of all good men—Experience?—Who shall upon this subject expect the truth from a Hume, a Cobbett, and others, their compeers, the professed enemies of the Established Church, in answer to such a question? I, like many others of my countrymen, had been accustomed to listen to & read the declamation of these men, till I believed them honest and took their words upon trust. But a dear bought experience proved to me, and I will prove to all who make trial of the truth of their declarations, both in & out of Parliament, that they are moved to make the Avowals they frequently do, for party purposes alone. They live upon the delusion of the people, and they therefore practice, nay, they not only find it in their interest to practice it, but I verily believe they go on from time to time echoing the same false doctrines & theories, till they not only "lie like truth," but at length persuade themselves that their impostures are truth itself.

That there are some *reforms (renovations)* required in the Established Church of England, cannot be doubted. Her overpaid dignitaries ought & must resign a portion of their princely incomes for the benefit of their poorer brethren—it is in their interest to do it. But let not the unhallowed hands of political brawlers be laid upon the venerable establishment rather to uproot than repair it—the Protestant Church of England in its doctrines, forms, and institutions is so far removed from bigotry & fanaticism and approaches so nearly the spirit of the Gospels themselves, that it ought to be looked up to as the very ***Sun*** of the Christian World—the centre round which all the minor religious societies revolve with security—but for them to assume its functions were not less hazardous, less fatal to the well-being of the Christian community of these realms, than it would be for the great centre of the Universe to give place to those minor orbs who not only reflect the light of his countenance to the advantage of humanity, but upon whom their very existence depends. No Church has shewn itself so tolerant as the Church of England, no Church has abused its power less—and whilst we look round upon the broad plains of civilization, it stands no less conspicuous in its constitution as admirably adapted to the wants of a highly advanced, greatly distinguished nation, than do the British Constitution & government surpass all others in its adaptation to the wants of the greatest, most civilized, and most thinking people of the earth.

CHAPTER X

Sunday in New York—Horse Jockeys & Horses—Drunkenness—Boars Fighting—Salesmen in Church Porticos—Boys—Brickbats—English Emigrants—Was Told I Should Be Asked to Ride

IT is too bad for the Americans to have lately taken it upon them to *school* the English in their newspapers, for rejecting Sir Andrew Agnew's Sabbath Observance Bill, though a story is told of one of their *Saints*, a Bostonian (worthy of Drunken Barnaby's Puritan, who hung his cat on a Monday for killing a mouse on the Sunday). He is said to have stopped the entrance to a Beehive, that the "vermin" might not work on the Lord's Day. Notwithstanding, the observance of the Sabbath in America, as far as decency, sobriety, and respectful demeanour goes, will not bear the least comparison with the observance of the Sunday, in any part of Protestant England.

But to speak of New York particularly—I have seen in the vicinity of a church, whilst service was proceeding, Horse-Jockey looking fellows letting the horses for hire, around whom were crowds of boys and low fellows, many in a disgusting state of intoxication. Here and there, to complete the picture, you might see a brace of boars fighting for mastery, with hundreds of boys shouting and laughing at *the fun*, or flinging brickbats at each other to the danger of themselves & the passers by, consisting of numerous persons—crowding for Long Island, or other places of public Sunday-amusements. In the meantime I have observed persons selling nuts, oranges, & oysters, in the very porticos of their churches, where might be heard the crowds of Fanatics absolutely roaring, howling, groaning, and scraping their feet in one overwhelming chaos of discord. Some singing "Hallelujah!" incessantly; others crying "Lord Help me!" a dozen times without intermission; and a 3rd party screaming & playing such frantic pranks, as one would only expect to hear or see from madmen. This is applicable to the appearance of the entire city of New York on a Sunday, with the exception of the English portion at their Church in Broom Street, near the Bowery, where everything passes off with the same decent order & demeanour that characterize an English congregation in the Mother country.

Nor is the general appearance of the Americans more attractive on a Sunday. You will see crowds of children in the Streets, with dirty clothes & no shoes; the streets are in the same filthy state as they are seen on every other day of the week, and the eternal nuisance of the firemen & their Engines, bells ringing alarm, & the noisy multitude preceded by the horn-bellowers, and all the *etcetera* before described, are as prevalent on a Sunday as any other day, without the slightest abatement of cursing & swearing, which we might expect them to observe in a degree. Their dirty carts are everywhere left exposed and the lumber belonging to their stores remains abroad as on other days.

I was told that the Americans carried their holiness & attention so far, that I should be sure to be asked to ride, if I were seen walking on a Sunday. I took an early opportunity of putting this to the test of experience, by taking a walk, one Sunday afternoon, to that part of the outside of the city of New York, which answers to our Hyde Park drive—but no sooner had I set my foot on the public way, than your Yankee horsemen, who by the by would cut a sorry figure at the back of a pack of English harriers or fox-hounds, rode by me with so little ceremony & regard for my safety, that I was obliged to mount a bank to avoid the risk of their breaking my neck: nor did their drivers shew a spirit of greater regard for my safety. In fact they ride & drive in such a helter-skelter manner, that they cannot be supposed to have much regard for their own necks, much less have they for the necks of others. Such is a Sabbath in New York—I might add a great deal more, but enough has been said to shew that America is not the country should presume to "cast the first stone" at England.

CHAPTER XI

Courts of Law—Judges—Counsel—and Jurors—Magistrates—Police-offices, Officers and Reports—Road-side Law—All Crimes Attributed to the Black Population and the English Emigrants—Blackhawk's Reflections upon Seeing a Man Conveyed to Prison for Being Drunk

"Shew me your companions and I will tell you what you are":—was the answer of the wiseman to one seeking to know himself. In the same manner we might say to a People praying the like, "Shew me your institutions and I will tell you what you are; what progress you have made in the scale of civilization; and where you ought to take your stand amongst the more advanced nations of the Earth." But this is a scale by which the *touchy* American will not be tried. He has no idea of being or that he can be taught; but with a Spirit only becoming a spoiled child, he fancies he is already the most knowing and the most polished gentleman in Europe.

All classes in America are addicted to the filthy practice of chewing tobacco; my readers will, therefore, not be surprised to learn that in their Courts of Justice Judges, Jurors, counsel, &c. are continually supplying themselves with *pigtail* during the progress of the most serious trials, and spitting about in the most indecent manner. The same characters may be frequently seen in an unshaven condition—Judges drest in the most slovenly manner, counsel with beards of 3 days old, and jurors with little short of a week's growth upon their chins. I was one day in a New York Court during the progress of a trial, at the end of which the Recorder descended from his judgment seat and mixed with the barristers & others, laughing with a most obstreperous "Haw, haw, haw!" whilst the jury were at his elbow considering their verdict; and on their intimation that they had come to an understanding he coolly mounted his seat & received it with less decency than would have been observed at Bow Street, at the settling of a drunken brawl. A similar scene was shortly after repeated in a case of life & death. Up the country, scenes much more extraordinary than these are perpetrated.

One case I heard was that of an *American Colonel* being apprehended for horse-stealing by a constable who held the rank of Major. When brought before the Magistrate, the Colonel coolly threatened to thrash both him & the Major, if they attempted to prosecute him. Upon that the Magistrate turned up his sleeves and challenged him to follow him into the yard to fight it out, at once, when the constable offered to stand proxy, and settle the affair to the *satisfaction* of the Colonel, without the Magistrate's interference. The magistrate told the Major to mind his own business, and insisted on taking the matter entirely into his own hands. But to return to the Recorder of New York—I happened to be present when the notorious Sheriff Perkins was recently tried for assaulting an American with a *tailor's goose*. It appeared that many people aware of his eccentricities, were in the habit of annoying him in various ways and this the prosecutor had done, till flesh & blood could bear it no longer, & the Sheriff retaliated,—not he declared, with the instrument described, but with his *fist*. "I strike a man with a tailor's goose!" exclaimed the Sheriff in disgust, "We Englishmen resort to the manly art of self-defence, and strike our opponents with our fists so (throwing himself into a boxing attitude) right & left—we never resort to the mean revenge your Americans do"—here he was interrupted by the Recorder's rising & declaring he would not "sit & hear America insulted"—upon which the Sheriff made a most admirable defence. Notwithstanding, after the Recorder had gone through his accustomed ramble & gossip with the barristers & others in various parts of the Court, he mounted his judgment seat and a verdict of *guilty* was returned, much to the disgrace of both Judge & jury, from the nature of the evidence adduced.

Indeed, from what I saw, it is clear an Englishman has but little chance of justice being done him by an American jury. One case happened during 1833, of a man named Wilson, an English Emigrant, who was accused, in conjunction with two others, of robbing a packet. He was tried, convicted, & sentenced to 5 *years imprisonment*, with hard labour at their prison of Sing-Sing. The recorder was not satisfied with delivering so severe a *punishment* sentence, but he seized the opportunity for making the *atrocious* declaration from the bench, that almost all crimes, *especially those of a heavy nature, that came before him, were perpetrated by Englishmen*—a declaration that was not only false, but created a distrust towards all English Emigrants both in the minds of the natives & amongst the Emigrants themselves, and moreover greatly injured the business of the person with whom Wilson was a partner, in a large Cabinet-making business, who generously came forward to attempt to establish Wilson's innocence, on the ground, that, had Wilson been of a dishonest habit, he might have robbed him of 1000^{ds} of dollars: but he found on examining his books that every thing was perfectly correct. And the general feeling was, that Wilson was the victim of some enemy. This scandalous attack by the Recorder was severely animadverted upon in an able pamphlet published by some of the emigrants at the time.

It is notorious that both Judges & Magistrates, in America, never fail to attribute every crime to either the English or the poor free-blacks, and it was a general complaint in New York, when I was there, that from false-swearing of witnesses, and the prejudice of both Judges & Jurors, it was next to hopeless for an Englishman to expect justice when opposed to an American.

I had heard it boasted in England, by those who were accustomed to hold America up as a model for us to imitate, that its laws were of a humane character, and that in consequence crimes were less frequent & executions uncommon. I can only observe upon this, that England never exhibited heavier calendars, both as to number & the nature of the crimes, than did those of the United States whilst I was there. There were 7 executions in less than half a year, & two I saw in New York were for murder. And the *New York Advertiser* of the 31st of May, 1834, citing the *Brooklyn Star*, observes, the approaching Sessions "will probably be a long one, as there is a great amount of civil & criminal business on the Calendar—" & the same paper records the recent perpetration of several murders.

Indeed their papers abound with accounts of murders, Suicides & robberies. The way in which the police-magistrates of New York treat the unfortunate persons that are brought before them is either tinctured with disgusting levity, or unfeeling brutality. I was witness to a case of the latter kind towards a colored girl, a native of Hayti; in fact, it appeared she was the daughter of the chief minister of that Republic. She had, it was said, been seduced from her country by an English Captain of the name of Wright, whether of the King's or the merchant service did not appear. Her seducer landed the poor creature on Staten Island, in the Bay of New York, and abandoned her. From there she found her way to the city, and was picked up by the watchman for wandering in the streets late at night. An American paper stated, & truly, that when she was brought into the magistrate's office, in the morning, she looked more like a Princess than anything else—10though black, her person was beautiful & dignified in the highest degree. She was literally covered with jewels & precious stones, and her whole appearance excited universal admiration amongst the Spectators. After she had told her tale of misfortune, she burst into a fit of frantic grief, tore off her jewels & threw them about the court, and there was every appearance that the poor creature's reason was touched by her misfortunes—but never shall I forget the savage-like expression with which the American Magistrate, like herself a Republican, be it remembered, ordered the "Wench," as he called her, to be locked up till she came to herself. Had such a case occurred in Aristocratic England, it would have excited the compassion of thousands—your genuine Americans, however, high & low, rich & poor, are ignorant of the meaning of the word *compassion* in any respect, and—more especially (as in this case) where the object of it was *black*.

Another instance of the way in which police-magistrates dispense justice in America, is that of a poor fellow, an English agricultural labourer, who had been for some time working for a Yankee master, from whom he could get no money. At last he desired to remove to another part of the country & requested a Settlement. Being able to get none, he applied, as he was advised, to a magistrate. The master was summoned accordingly, & flatly told the magistrate that his reason for not paying was, he had no money. "Well," said the poor rustic, "What am I to do?" All the redress he could get from your American magistrate was, "Don't work for him any more," and with that he was obliged to depart satisfied. In fact your American masters are *smart* enough to know, that a poor fellow has little or no chance of *getting the law* of them, as it is called. I heard a workman tell one of whom he could not get his wages, that he should *sue him*. "Sue & be d——d," was the reply. I was present on another occasion when a person came into a man's counting-house to say Mr. wanted his wages. "Let him go to h-ll for his money," was the answer.

The following is a Specimen of what passed during one morning, in a New York Police-office according to the *Sun* American paper, of the 16th of May, 1834.

> POLICE OFFICE—(Yesterday Morning.)
>
> Mary Dehilton was charged with stealing a frock from Mrs. Van Venton, her landlady. Mary said she came from Plymouth, where our forefathers landed. Committed.
>
> Robert Kidd, of Charleton, near Varrick street, was charged with whipping his wife. The prisoner said he was a descendant of the famous Captain Kidd. He came home last night a little drunk, of course—for no sober man would

assault his wife—and commenced breaking the furniture. His wife begged of him to desist, whereupon he beat her most cruelly. He was committed.

Henry Jackson, corner of Delancy and Sheriff streets, was also charged with beating his wife. The prisoner made an apology to his rib, and was discharged with a reprimand.

Dennis McCarthy was charged with intoxication. Dennis said it was a terrible shame that he must be compelled to sleep in the watch house, merely because he got a little *in for it*.

Mag.—What do you mean by being a *little in for it*—were you not grossly intoxicated?

Prisoner.—Devil a bit was I intoxicated—only a little *boosy*, your honor.

Mag.—Only a little boosy, eh! What do you mean by that?

Pris.—Why, I was a little *shot in the neck*, ye see.

Mag.—A little shot in the neck, eh. Then you were not drunk?

Pris.—Drunk! I guess I wasn't drunk—only a little *swizzled!*

Mag.—Well, how came you a little *swizzled?*

Pris.—Why, ye see, I take a *swifter* of a little of the good old gin.

Mag.—Very good, sir—I'll not trouble you with any more questions. I shall fine you one dollar, and unless you pay it, I shall be under the necessity of giving you a little of the "good old Bridewell."

Pris.—Can't help it, sir—no money—d——d a cent—spent it all last night. He was committed.

Elizabeth Warren, was brought up for fighting with Charlotte Griffin. Elizabeth had the appearance of a "black and secret midnight hag." The complainant, who was quite a modest looking little woman, said that the prisoner was in the habit of flogging her, and she was determined not to stand it any longer. Committed.

William Johnstein, went into a house of ill fame in Church street, and kicked up a row. The prisoner was a well dressed young man—lived in Pearl street, and said he wouldn't have his name published for a thousand dollars. The complainant, Amelia Smith, said she had no disposition to proceed with the complaint.—as Mr. J. was a respectable young man, [!] and his being brought before the court, might have a tendency to injure his reputation. The Magistrate told the prisoner he should have thought of that before now—as, in all probability his name would receive the "Sun"-shine of notoriety for what he had already done. He was discharged.

CHAPTER XII

Labour Scarce and Ill Paid—Average of Wages Paid in New York—A Day's Labour from Sunrise to Sunset—No Leisure Time Allowed—Low State of Female Labour—Is the Cause of Much Vice—Masters & Workmen Paid with Goods—Money Scarce—An Author Paid with Pine-boards—What Trades Thrive Best—Some out of Employ for 5 Months together—Out-door Labourers the Greatest Sufferers from Climate

LABOUR in America is neither plentiful nor well paid. The account of wages is conflicting. The best hands get about 6 dollars a week, that is £1..4. English. Some masters will profess to give 7 and 1/4 dollars, 30/– English: but these are generally speculators, and the truth is, the men do not, in the end, get much above half that sum, as the masters will put them off by owing them 3 or 4 dollars a week, and either break in the end without paying them the balance, or defy them should they talk of redressing themselves by law. The average wages paid to Tailors is about 5 dollars a week, £1. English. One tailor told me he got but a shilling for making a pair of trousers. Carpenters, if tolerable hands, average about 6 dollars a week, £1..4 English. This is considered great wages for them, and for it they are obliged to work from Sunrise to Sunset, as are all other mechanics & labourers in America. There is no privilege allowed them of working *over time*, and thereby increasing their wages, as there are in England; nor have they leisure allowed them to do small jobs on their own account, as the English labourer has. I was assured by several apprentices, that they too were obliged to labour from Sunrise to Sunset, during which scarcely an interval of 10 minutes was allowed them for each meal. As for their having play-time, as is mostly the case in England, it is unknown.

A short time before I left New York, several thousand females struck for an advance of wages, and the *Sun* American paper of March, 1834, observes, "The low rate of female labour (in America) is a grievance of the very first magnitude, and pregnant with the most mighty ills to society. It demands the most serious consideration of those whose situations in life give them influence upon manners & customs. This unjust arrangement of remuneration for services performed diminishes the importance of women in society—renders them more helpless &

dependent—destroys in the lower walks of life much of the inducements to marriage—& of course in the same degree increases the temptations to licentiousness. It is difficult to conceive why, even in those branches, wherein both sexes are engaged, there should be such an extreme degree of disparity in the recompense of labor as every person acquainted with the subject knows to exist." I was told by several tailors that the reason why their labor was paid so badly was, a great many women were employed in the trade, who worked for next to nothing. None but the very best hands amongst the men could get what was called *good wages*.

The practice of remunerating labour with goods instead of money (the worst species of the English *truck-system*) is very prevalent all over America. I was told by a respectable Plumber & Glazier, in New York, that if he painted a Grocer's shop, or store, he should never get employed again if he did not take out the amount in goods, which of course he was under the necessity of retailing to his workmen. I knew another instance of a Bricklayer in New York, whose house was hung from top to bottom with hams, cheese, &c. and on a Saturday night he had the greatest difficulty to muster any money to give his men a trifle each of their wages in cash. It was a general saying that 3 fourths of the business of New York was carried on with the wages of the poor workmen, rather than with real Capital.

It is no uncommon practice for authors to subscribe their books & take out the value in goods. I was told an anecdote of one who called, in his rounds in search of subscribers, upon an old farmer up the country, who readily agreed to take a copy. Upon the author's asking him whether he would have it bound, or *in boards*, he replied the latter. The copy was sent to the farmer after publication, and at the usual time the author made his call for payment. "There they are," said the old farmer, pointing to 9 pine *boards*, carefully tied together and standing up clean & compact in a corner of his yard. The author stared at the sight, observing, that he did not know what to do with *pine boards*. "Oh," said the old man, "I told you I would have it *in boards*, & these they are. I can't spare any sheep just now," added the old man, in which article he was accustomed to pay. "But I want money," exclaimed the poor author. "Money!" said the old farmer. "Lord bless you, I never see any money in this part of the country. We scarcely know what money is." Our author was obliged to take the pine-boards or nothing.

One thing I would point out to English labourers & workers,

who have a notion of emigrating, that I made considerable inquiries amongst the Mechanics to ascertain what trades thrived best in America, & for what causes. I was told that Bricklayers & Carpenters not only suffered greatly during the Summer from their exposure to the dreadful heats, but that frequently, during a severe winter, they were out of work for 5 months together, the hard frosts making it impossible for them to proceed with their work either abroad or at home, and they were great sufferers from agues & fevers. Plasterers suffer in a like degree. One came back with his family in the ship I returned in, the poorer by £20 after a 4 months' stay, whom I saw the day after I landed at work in the British Museum. The *painters' cholic* is much more common than it is in England, and much more severe. In-door labourers stand the climate best.

CHAPTER XIII

Thousands of White Men Yoked in America like Hogs in England—Many Emigrants Would Be Fortunate Could They Procure One—The Employment Esteemed So Degrading Free-Blacks Will Not Engage in It—Good English Mechanics Can Frequently Get No Other Employment—Pay Not Exceeding a Parish-Allowance in England—Even This Is Fast Diminishing—Anecdote of an English Cabinet-Maker

I have often seen hogs in English villages yoked to prevent their invading gardens, orchards, &c.: but never till I arrived in New York did I see men so yoked, and white men too. It is a common practice for your *free-born* Americans to clamour in the ears of English Emigrants about their countrymen submitting to be *drest in livery*, as if there were nothing as servile, if servility it be, in the United States. But the truth is, they are sensible that, after all, they fall short of the meed of independence enjoyed in England, and find it necessary to search for something as a set off against the *abject* condition in which thousands are seen by English Emigrants, on their reaching America. That land to which they are, Alas! looking in vain for that milk & honey, which with ordinary industry they might obtain in England, Sweetened too with comforts they can never hope either to see or enjoy in America, not to name the experiences & dangers of a voyage across the Atlantic, and the horrors of disappointment & despair to which it is more than probable they will fall sacrifices.

"Sawdy Wood" is a term must be familiar to every man who has been in America and made any use of his senses. Thousands of persons, white men, in the most ragged condition, may be seen in the Streets of New York, daily, with their heads through a Yoke, *sub juge*, like a refractory English hog, & ever & anon will the hand be raised up to the tattered hat, with "any Wood to be sawed to-day, Sir?" And so difficult do Emigrants often find it to procure work on their arrival, that those who are not furnished with extra funds are frequently obliged to become, *Sawdy Woods*. Many are not so fortunate as to be able to raise a sufficient sum to purchase a *Yoke & saw*, with which to traverse the streets as I have frequently seen both Americans & English do, with scarcely sufficient rags on their backs to make it decent for them to be seen. And it is considered such toilsome & degrading work, that the free-blacks will never engage in it, if they can get anything else to do.

I have known many excellent English mechanics who were obliged to resort to it, to save themselves from absolute starvation, notwithstanding the fine stories that are told in England, of the plenteousness of both food & employment in America. Breaking stones on the roads in England is absolute amusement compared to this employment, nor do the Americans reward their labour with a payment that in many degrees exceeds an English parish-allowance. One shilling & sixpence, American money (nine pence English), sometimes two shillings American, or a shilling English, is paid for sawing a load of wood—that is, as much as a good-sized English cart would carry. This, be it observed, is a labour of the most exhausting kind and is all performed in the street, either under a burning Sun, or in the midst of rain, or during an inclement winter.

Yet no kind of refreshment is allowed by the American house-keeper employing them, either in the shape of a draft of poor beer or a mouthful of broken victuals. I have often asked myself, as I saw the poor fellows sweating over their task, can the people of America have any *bowels of compassion*? But even this hard resource for starving Emigrants is fast diminishing—coals now getting into general use, and no doubt they will become the universal fuel in cities and large towns, as wood becomes scarcer & coals more plentiful. I was told by one thriving English labourer, thriving by absolute toil, that though he had laboured like a horse for 6 months, as a Cabinet-maker, in different American houses, he never was offered the slightest refreshment. This man assured me, that he had just earned his master 20 dollars during the past week, by performing work in different houses, out of which he paid him 6 dollars, £1..4. English money. Not a moment, however, was he allowed to do the smallest job for himself. Had he laboured the same number of hours in England, his pay would have been not less than £2.10. More than twice the wages paid him in America. In short, if a man is so fortunate as to get work, he is consigned to slavery of the worst description. The wife of this poor man told me, with tears in her eyes, that she felt grateful to her husband for the manner in which he toiled to keep her from want, but she had a constant dread upon her mind, that he would shorten his days thereby, and that during the period of 4 years he had been in America, he was looking 20 years older than when he left England. I can assure my readers, that this is a true picture and applies to all English Emigrants, who labour for their bread.

CHAPTER XIV

AMERICAN POVERTY—PAWNBROKERS—BEGGARS PLENTIFUL IN NEW YORK—GREAT LOVERS OF LITTER—KNOW NOTHING OF ENGLISH CHARACTER—LABOURERS COERCED WITH ARTILLERY

IT has been said by one patriotic member of the British House of Commons, that *rags & penury* were unknown in America. It is, however, a common saying in New York, that "An American carries his whole wardrobe on his back," and in no place did I ever see more evidence of poverty, if dress is to be taken as a criterion to judge by. Hundreds may be met in the streets daily with their old tattered clothes patched, piece upon piece, till they are almost an inch thick, and not only do Pawnbrokers abound in New York, but the people may be seen, daily, in *files*, waiting their turns of entrance.

The Americans, too, will tell you they have no beggars in their country, that they think it a disgrace to beg. They have, notwithstanding, a custom amongst them extremely like begging. I was present on more than one occasion, when a young American entered the sitting-room, with a very confident air, truly, and said, "Mother's compliments, and will you please to give her a cent?" "Your mother has not got a cent, I guess," said the lady of the house. "No," was the answer, and off he walked, furnished with the sum in question, without so much as saying "thank you." At another time an Urchin came in with, "Have you got any cold victuals?" "Yes," was the reply. "Will you give it to me?" "Yes," and off he set with it. This they do not call begging. But I deny the non-begging assertion most confidently. I have seen thousands begging in the streets of America, and in those of New York especially, with their hands up to their hats in the most supplicating & humiliating posture imaginable—and born-Americans too. Though it is true they are liable to be sent to break stones in Blackwell's Island, for 6 months, for so doing: nor have the destitute any Mendicity Society to afford them temporary relief, as in London.

There is plenty of food to be had, such as it is, no doubt; but the means of procuring it is wanting. In fact, America is after all a *poor* country, and the majority of the people are scarcely a *grade* removed from beggary. An American bride with a fortune of 500 dollars (£100 English) is looked upon as a matrimonial prize; and a fortune of 1000 dollars (£200 English) is a thing to be widely talked of. But if any there be who doubt my statement, let them make the trial of Emigration as I have done, and they will confess, that in no city in Europe, of the same extent as New York, did they ever see more beggars, or beggars more wretchedly clad, both old & young, male & female, than New York contains. Never did I see in London, or any other town in England, so wretched a body of paupers as are those the corporation of New York occasionally send forth to cleanse the streets.

But the fact is "with poverty there is always pride," and the Americans are in possession of their share of both these characteristics. It is a common thing for them to denounce the English as a servile race, subject to the nobility of the land. But it is strange that they should have demeaned themselves so servilely towards an English nobleman who recently visited America, that their conduct became almost a proverb amongst the English Emigrants. The truth is, the very best classes in America are so ignorant of the relation that subsists between the nobleman & the poorer classes in England, that a young American who recently visited London, wrote in the greatest astonishment to his friends, in Philadelphia, on finding, as he expressed it, that in the British Metropolis a *Lord* was passed with as little respect as a *Sweep*. The truth is, the Americans are totally ignorant of the constitution, habits, & manners, both of England & English Society, with the exception of the few who come over for commercial purposes, and it is laughable to hear the *thorough* born Yankey, who was scarcely ever half an hour out of the back-settlements in his life, speak of England & the English with the confidence of a person who had been bred amongst them. Their blunders are truly ridiculous: but notwithstanding, they are recd as truth, and thus it is that false ideas of this country are, in a great measure, so widely spread in America.

I have been repeatedly laughed at, by Americans, for saying New York was *inferior* to London; nor would they admit that *St Paul's* was to be named in the same day with their *city*-Hall.— As far as the city goes, it is somewhat on a parallel with our Birmingham, cleanliness excepted—as for the city-Hall, it is pretty & stands in a commanding Situation, but is not to be named at the same time with the venerable buildings that adorn many English corporate towns, setting aside the British metropolis. It is not unlike the London University.

"England would be a fine country," I have heard them say, "if it were a *republic*," as if the bare name was sufficient to confer all that man requires, as they think & believe. "An

Englishman," they would add, "never speaks to a gentleman, but his hand is up to his hat, and he stands before him with fear & trembling." I never saw this spirit of servility exhibited any where to the same degree as it is in America. I have seen men in New York, *republicans* forsooth, stand quaking at the door of an American tradesman, not only with their hand up to their hats, but with a trembling expression in their countenances that in England a man would have been *kicked* for expressing. I have seen them start as if electrified, at the "*come in*!" of an American *gentleman*, save the mark, and if told to "*take a seat*," on entering the presence of the *august* personage, which thousands of the born-Americans are in their own conceit at heart, I have seen them *drop* themselves unto the *corner* of a chair, for they would not dare to be so familiar as to sit *plump down*, not only with a *servile* expression, but seen absolutely *frightened* at the condescension of the *great man*.

The truth is, though the Americans would fain disguise the fact from themselves, for they already begin to quake under it, the monied classes in America are already an *Aristocracy* of a far more dangerous, domineering, and oppressive character, than England ever knew; and there never was a country where the love of distinctive rank was so much cherished. Every fellow is an *Esquire*. An omission of *Colonel*, *Major*, or *Captain* would lose you the respect, probably, of your Yankey Grocer, Tailor, or Shoemaker. They have their Bishops and Deacons who lead them with as despotic a sway as the Italian tribes do their bears & monkies, and as for the independence of the mechanic, they are tyrannized over by their masters at pleasure.

What will the English Unionists say to the fact, had it happened in England, that as soon as the news reached President Jackson of the English & Irish Emigrants having struck for a rise of wages, who were employed upon the Canals, &c. up the country, he was so far from treating the matter with that forbearance the English Government is accustomed to do, that he instantly sent down sufficient troops & a company of artillery, as obliged them to submit passively to their employers? And republican America has thereby been the first to deny the principle, that a man has a right to fix the value of his own labour.

CHAPTER XV

No Vagrants Allowed—Punch Would Be Sent to Sing-Sing—No Relief out of the Poor-house—Nor Received therein for Less than 6 Months—Healthy Paupers Sent to Blackwell's Island to Work in Stone Quarries,—No Provision for Widows & Orphans—The Welch, Irish, & Scotch Have Established Charities for Their Own

I have noticed the fact in the preceding Chapter, that beggars are as plentiful in America as in England, though their appeals are made less openly. It is true, perhaps, that there are fewer vagrants generally, because no sort of streets exhibitions are allowed—no wandering Minstrels—and if *Punch* himself were to shew his face in New York, with his rubicund nose, he would as certainly be sent to Sing-Sing for his presumption, as he had a nose on his face—the only instance I heard of a street musician was that of *the wandering piper*, in which Jonathan, as in the case of the dog Tyke, was resolved to copy England, at all hazards.

A man reduced to such a state as to seek public relief, in New York, upon application to a Magistrate, if in ill-health, is sent to a Species of poor-house, where he must remain confined to the walls for a period of 6 months—imprisoned in fact. In the police report in the *Sun* American paper of the 16th of May, 1834, it is stated—"Janette Brown said she was sick, and had no home." The magistrate ordered her to be "sent to the Penitentiary for 6 months." The place, be it observed, to which *felons* are sent for moral improvement. No assistance is permitted out of the before-named poor-house. A man applying for relief, in health, is sent to Blackwell's Island to work in the Stone Quarries, where he must remain for a similar period, subject to labour of a character to which none but *convicts* are forced in England. And this is whether his necessitous condition is the offspring of misfortune or not. It is sufficient that he is in want of relief. This is the extent of provision made for the poor and unfortunate in America, and should the applicant have a family, they are left to the mercy of the world.

This *inhuman* policy, for I can give it no lighter epithet, no doubt has its origin in the natural selfishness of the American character, and a desire to force the emigrants to go up the country. But what, it may be asked, should 9 tenths of the Emigrants do up the country, clearing forests and bringing swamps into cultivation, who have no capital, constitutions unused to such employments, and no means of transporting their families? As there are no Poor Laws in America, of course there is no provision for the widow & orphan. The Welch, Irish, & Scotch, have, I learned, established Charitable Societies to aid the two latter classes of their own country folk, and at the time I left America, a paper published in New York, entitled *The Old Countryman* was calling upon the English Emigrants to follow their Example, and it was with pain I heard that the friends of several of these Charitable Societies had been swallowed up in the ruin brought about by the failure of some of the American Banks.

CHAPTER XVI

America Full of Care-worn Englishmen—State of Emigrants—Thousands Destitute without the Means of Returning—Surgeons & Farmers Begging in the Streets of New York—Swindling Misnamed Smartness—Difficulty of Getting Employment—Toilsome Character of Their Labour—Tricks of American Lawyers

I was told by an American gentleman (to whom I had letters of introduction) that "all I should see would be disappointed and care-worn Englishmen"—truly I saw a great many, and no wonder either. An Emigrant no sooner sets foot in America than he is surrounded by Jews & natives, who will never quit him whilst he has a pound left, if they can help it; and the tricks they play such as are tangible, would shock the most hardened. A young man who went in the same packet I did, unfortunately fell in with some of those *attached* American friends, who sold him the good will & fixtures of a grog-shop for all the money he had, 40 Sovereigns. He had scarcely taken possession when the Sheriff of New York entered & seized & sold every article, to which the Yankee, from whom he had bought them, had, it appeared, forfeited all claim. A friend then supposing there was an end of all further claim, lent him a like Sum, in his penniless state, to lay in a fresh store—these too were seized in a day or two by the same parties for debts his predecessor had contracted and I believe forgone, & his friend was obliged to hide himself lest he should be made a party. It is probable, that not knowing anything of either the Law or the customs of the country, he in his ignorance became liable: but be it remembered he was in a land where they profess to be above such knavery. After all, it was only a specimen of that *smartness* upon which an American prides himself.

It is the practice to relieve such Emigrants as were reduced to a state of destitution, with the *munificent* boon of a *basket of oranges* and the comfortable assurance *that they would keep them*. Nor is such meagre aid extended to them a 2nd time, but it is expected that you will consider it a species of stock in trade, to be replenished, from time to time, with the produce of its sale—the emigrant and his starving family, if he has any left him, being expected to live on the profits. I was assured by hundreds of wretched and reduced Emigrants, both English and

Irish, that the only reasons why they did not quit the country for their native soil was the impossibility they found of realizing the necessary means—indeed, thousands would return from all parts of America, were they not fixed by the same uncontrollable circumstance. But here I would remind them, if I am rightly informed, that there is a law in America by which all Emigrants in a destitute state can oblige the Captain of the vessel that brought them over to take them back: but from what I have seen of Captains of American packets, God help the poor wretch that shall attempt to enforce it.

Not only are the amenities of social life scarcely known amongst the people of America, but they seem to have shut their very hearts against that high-road to Heaven—Charity—They live not to dispense happiness, but to glean that which is corruptible. One effort was made to relieve the thousands of Starving Emigrants by the people of New York, and an American told me, with great satisfaction in his countenance that they had collected sufficient to give a sixpence relief (3 pence English) each to 700. But he stared credulously when I told him the fact, that in Aristocratic England, where there was no boast of all men being born equal, I had known more than £1000 to be collected in one day, in a small town, to relieve the distress of the poor.

On one occasion I relieved a destitute Irishman with a few cents in the streets of New York. He told me, and his manners bespoke him a man of education, that he was a graduate of Trinity College, Dublin, and a Surgeon by profession; but he could get no employment. I saw him the next day actually *Sawing wood in the streets*. I confess the sight cut me to the heart, and the bitterness of my feelings were not diminished when he lifted up his care-worn face and recognizing his humble benefactor, cried—"God bless you," as I passed him. I say it without any intention to wound their feelings, but if possible to *sting* them to a better spirit, that an American would have laughed both at the man and his speech.

Another young man, an Englishman, who had come over in a packet with a relation of mine, and was a regularly bred Surgeon, from London, but had yielded to the persuasion of others to try his fortune in America, having expended his all in his outfit & voyage, was driven to the greatest of necessity. I saw him, in a Species of livery, acting in the office of check-taker, at a low exhibition, in New York. It is an undeniable fact, too, that those who emigrate early in life, such is the baneful influence of the climate upon the constitutions of the English in particular, such the effect of the incessant course of labour which they are called upon to yield for a bare livelihood, such the state of exhaustion to which their bodies are reduced, aided by intemperance from the plenteousness and cheapness of ardent spirits, that not one in 50 live to see the *medium* of the years of a man's life, much less old age.

One respectable tradesman told me, that his life was one of never-ending toil; that had he used the same degree of industry in England, he should doubtless have amassed a fortune; but that all he could do in America, and that with difficulty, was to keep the little he had. All business in America, he said, was conducted upon principles that in England would be called *swindling*, but in America it had been dignified with the appellation of *Smartness*. "What," they exclaim, "you found the Yankey too smart for you." I can assure any who may have in view a voyage to America "to better their condition," that breaking stones for a Scanty parish pittance in England, is absolute pleasure compared to the life of eternal toil to which the majority are condemned in America, should they be fortunate enough to obtain employment; which, though Mr. Cobbett declares any industrious Englishman may do, I say it is by no means certain; and I must here add, that he, and such as he, are the vehicles of falsehoods, when they utter such language.

One poor old man accosted me in the street, and seeing I was an Englishman, begged a trifle. I gave him a few cents. He told me that he had emigrated from Suffolk with his wife & family, where he had once been an English Farmer, "well to do." "Now," he continued, "I sell milk, but have not had a cent this week: & Sometimes," he added, with tears in his eyes, "I have no food for days—all my little property is gone—I have lost my wife, my children—but," he exclaimed with energy, the tears rolling down his furrowed and care-worn face, "I durst not dwell upon it—I cannot trust myself to say more!"

Another English Emigrant, whom I met begging in the streets of New York, told me he had reached that city with a sum of £1500; & having purchased a farm 700 or 800 miles up the country, he hastened to his location. On reaching it, he found he had been shamefully imposed upon; or, as they say in America, "Jonathan had proved *too smart* for him." Instead of the land being tillable, it was covered with rocks & stones and the Stumps of large trees. He tried in vain to make it productive. He could not make a bare subsistence from it, and after expending his all, he was obliged to abandon it, and with difficulty made his way back to New York, where I saw him a man of broken health and spirits, and a beggar. But this is only one case out of a thousand. He was one of the many who had been duped by the multitude of shirtless vagabonds, Americans, Save the mark, who are employed by the lawyers in New York to prowl about the streets with more the air of subjects for Botany Bay, than the people of a *free* State, to catch the unsuspecting English Emigrant, and trick him into the purchase of land for which he may think himself lucky if he finds it worth a cent in the pound of what he pays for it in sterling English gold.

The most I could ever get from an emigrant was, he "could live." I never met with one who confessed he had realized any thing by his *toil*, for such is nearly every species of employment in America. The only English emigrants who have realized anything are those who having caught a spice of *Yankey Smartness*, have abandoned honest employments for tricking speculations and monopolies—and amongst these are generally included runaway bankrupts and other fraudulent characters. It is a singular fact, that hundreds of Native Americans are Emigrating at the present time from the United States to the British American Colonies. Several Emigrated for England in the Ship in which I returned; and many more are likely to follow.

Englishmen, who contemplate Emigrating, should also be told, that should they be lucky enough to gain a subsistence & a settlement, they would by no means be those freeborn republicans that their imaginations picture—as, if they do not declare themselves citizens, in case of any dispute between this country & America, they would be obliged to take up arms, or abandon their callings and retire into the dreary back-settlements; or, if they do forego their allegiance to England & become naturalized, they must become *firemen* for a period of 7 years (which is no sinecure, as they are liable to be hourly called out to serve their engines & I have seen, in New York, 7 fires blazing at once). Or, should they prefer it, they must enter the militia for the above period, and be liable to be constantly called out, and occasionally to be paraded under the orders of a Captain, probably some capricious Yankey *cartman*, or petty tradesman, who will take care to inform you, that he is *a freeborn American*. It is a common thing for the Americans to pride themselves upon that circumstance, and, in consequence, to look down upon their *betters* with contempt. I say betters, if education & manners constitute the distinction between man & man, in a civilized community—for I assert, without fear of disproof, that English Emigrants rise immeasurably above the Americans in both these respects.

CHAPTER XVII

MORE WORDS ON THE MISERIES OF EMIGRATION—MELANCHOLY STORY OF THE FAMILY OF A WATERLOO HERO—DEATHS OF EMIGRANTS BY SEA—AMERICA NO PLACE FOR ENGLISHMEN TO BETTER THEIR CONDITION IN—FACTS TO PROVE IT—SHAMEFUL DELUSIONS IN COBBETT'S *EMIGRANT'S GUIDE AND CHAMBERS'S EDINBURGH JOURNAL* ON THE SUBJECT OF EMIGRATION

NO idea can be found of the thousand & one melancholy episodes with which I could fill these pages, of the distressing situations into which persons & family are frequently thrown by emigrating to America. Colonel Crockett, of *Cowhide* notoriety, says in his autobiography, that he has witnessed the most heart-rending scenes amongst those who have emigrated up the country. The finest fellows, brought to a premature grave after having spent their all in unprofitable Speculations, have sunk down in the most horrid despair. And Suicides are very common, he might have added, amongst disappointed & heart-broken Emigrants in Boston and its neighbourhood. The New York paper, the *Morning Courier* of the 10th of June, 1834, says, "We are sorry, the Bostonians do not appear to have gotten over their Suicidal propensities." The poor factory girl recently supposed to have been murdered by Avery, the dissenting minister, says in a letter to her mother written in the most artless strains, that suicides were so frequent where she laboured, that she was resolved to quit the place. One young man shot himself before her face, and she seldom rose without finding that some had destroyed themselves in the night. But after all, we aught scarcely to be surprised at the constant recurrence of these fearful scenes, when we recollect the fact, that America is the great theatre wherein scenes of Atheism, Drunkenness, & Fanaticism, are studied universally.

The following is a recent and literally true story. A British Dragoon, who had by his valor alone risen from the ranks to the post of captain in the British army, during the late wars in Spain & Portugal, was killed at the head of his troop in the progress of the battle of Waterloo, leaving a wife, two daughters, & a Son but ill-provided for. The latter had been bred a Surgeon, and had emigrated to Utica, in the United States of America, where by his skill and assiduity he made a comfortable subsistence. This tempted him to write to his mother & sisters, begging they would come over to him and share his prosperity. They accordingly took their passages for New York, but the fatigues of a Sea-voyage was too much for the delicate frame of the mother, she died by the way and was consigned to the great deep with the customary solemnities on Shipboard, and those who never witnessed the awful & sudden Splash, as the body, sewn in a hammock or blanket, is consigned to the great deep, when the person officiating in the place of a Chaplain comes to the passage, "Ashes to ashes," can have no conceptions of the Solemnity of a burial at sea. The daughters reached New York, and, with their hearts swelling with affection at the prospect of meeting an only brother, almost their only relative in the world, with barely resources to meet their necessary expences in a strange land, they at once set off for Utica. This was at a time when the Cholera was raging fearfully in the United States, but they reached their destination without being arrested by the malignant visitant. But Alas! the brother had died of the disease the day previously. It is needless to describe their sorrow. Mother & brother, both snatched from them—In a foreign land without money or friends—the poor girls must have perished but for the humane interference of the English Settlers, who raised a small subscription to save them from Starvation & enable them to embark for their native village, to which their hearts naturally turned as their only place of rest. They were on their way to their native soil, when I was in America, and the melancholy recital of their story threw a gloom over the whole circle of English Emigrants in New York.

Perhaps they too may have perished. Many emigrants not only die on their way to America, from the deprivations they undergo and the diseases engendered on Shipboard, but others, after continuing in America for a few years, become victims to fevers & agues which quickly reduce them to the most lamentable state of debility, render them a prey to *Consumption* (a very prevalent disease in the United States). In this state they are often seized with an unconquerable desire to visit the scenes of their birth & childhood—& many pine out their remaining days without the most distant hope of ever gratifying that strongest of all desires, for want of means.

One poor fellow, in the last stage of consumption, took his passage in the same ship in which I came to England—the scene of his sufferings, his lamentations lest he should die before he once again saw happy England, were most heart-rending—He died about midway in crossing the Atlantic, and I saw him consigned to the deep—even now the solemn splash of his corpse, as it was shot from the plank, and the plank after it to deceive the sharks, hisses in my ears. The whole scene, from his embarkation till his burial, was one that ought to deter others from abandoning the humblest home in England, for the most tempting rewards that America can afford them.

But alas! rewards are the lot of few indeed. I have talked with hundreds of tradesmen & mechanics, Emigrants of all sorts, but never could meet with one that had *bettered* his condition. Yet, strange enough, so strong in hope is the breast of an Englishman, those half-ruined seemed insensible to their situation. I one day fell in with one of the latter class, who declared he was doing well. I went through his profits and losses with him, and proved he would in all likelihood have made more money in England. "Ah," he exclaimed, "but you forget the English taxes!" We then took an estimate of them, and set it against the high rents and high prices of nearly all Necessaries in America. Again the balance was in favour of England. Still, so strong is political prejudice he was not convinced. "How much money did you bring with you to America?" I asked. "£2000," he replied. "How much are you now worth?" "£500," was his answer. This comparison of the state of his finances was the only thing that raised in him a suspicion he might have done better. He was, indeed, one of that industrious class which in England never fail to realize an independence. But in America, with an application that thousands of Englishmen would shrink at, he had only saved a wreck of his stock in trade. But he was fortunate. Thousands have not done that.

The extraordinary thing is that those bent upon emigrating do not betake themselves to the Canadas, for notwithstanding the declaration of such men as Hume, it is notorious in the United States, that in the British settlements *taxes are lower, food cheaper, and labour more plentiful* than in the United States. This I had from a gentleman of high rank, great experience, and undoubted veracity. And, indeed, the Americans are themselves beginning to believe & act upon it. Six persons took their departure for Canada from one house in which I lodged in New York, and I was acquainted with one of the *turbulent French Canadians, who had transferred himself to the soil of independence & plenty*, as he had been taught to consider the United States, who found himself so completely deceived in the change, that he was about to retrace his steps when I left New York, disgusted with American institutions and manners.

A respectable tradesman in Norfolk in England, had a son living in New York, who had emigrated several years previously to the time I left for America. This young man wrote to his parents to say his circumstances *were in the most thriving condition*, that with 3 days labour he could live with ease, a fourth day's work was all profit, and that if his father had 3 or 4 hundred pounds he wanted to put out, he had only to send it to him and he could afford to allow him ten or 15 *per cent* interest for it. The father commissioned me to call upon his son on my arrival at New York, and send him the true state of the case. When I did so, so far was the statement of the young man from being the truth, that I found him in the most abject state of poverty, frequently without food either for himself or family, unable to get constant employment, and in the winter, I was told, but for the assistance of some friends, who had still a trifle left of the little property they had brought from England, he & his family must have perished in the inclement season.

Another English family, from the same part of Norfolk, the head of which had written to his friends to say he had got a valuable situation as clerk of an establishment where 300 persons were employed, I found in a subordinate post in a crockery store, receiving wages barely sufficient for his own support. His family were half starved, and in the winter were obliged to beg wood to keep them from perishing with the extreme cold. I knew a case of one English Emigrant's writing home to his brother, saying, "Come over. I can keep you for a year, if necessary, when you arrive in New York. Plenty of work, plenty to eat & drink." Thus tempted, the poor fellow sold his little all and contrived to reach his brother's residence in the United States, pennyless, it is true, but this he thought was a matter of no consideration. He was soon undeceived. He found his brother living in a state of poverty far more degrading than what he had quitted in England. He was just in time to share a scanty supper, and no sooner did he sit down to as scanty a breakfast next day, than his brother began, in the low phraseology common in America, "Come, Bob, you must go ahead! We can give you a meal or two, but no more, I guess!" The poor fellow told me he let fall his cup & saucer on hearing this declaration, as if he had been shot—exclaiming, "What, is this the twelvemonths' keeping you promised you could give me?" "Ah! Well," was the reply, "every one must look out for themselves here, *I guess*!" and so the poor fellow found it. Every renegade becomes Americanized in his language, before he has been a month in the country.

I can assure my readers that hundreds upon hundreds of unhappy creatures have been *tempted* from their comfortable English fire-sides, across the Atlantic, in the most *wicked & wanton* manner, by the misrepresentations of their disappointed friends, from the most selfish feelings, and crowds of them reach the Shores of America, as the above young man did, to experience the most unfeeling treatment and to deplore, too late, the rashness of relying upon the scandalous reports of friends. I asked many "Why they did not return," who had a little means left at command. The answer was, invariably, "They thought if they went home their friends & acquaintances would *laugh at them*." Hundreds are now *pining* in misery from no better motive.

And here I feel myself bound to say, that Cobbett's *Emigrants' Guide* is full of the most barefaced misrepresentations throughout, in fact it is a *mere romance*; as are the works of nearly all the writers who favour Emigration; and the accounts which have appeared are *a disgrace to the Proprietors & a fraud upon the public*. I have no doubt that many are at this moment preparing to quit *happy* England through them, in 9 cases out of 10, to pine away into an Early grave, in a strange land, the victims of delusion.

When I first set my foot upon American ground, I was accosted by two emigrants with "Did you come in that packet, Sir?" and seeing the nearly 200 poor creatures that were landing, they exclaimed, "My God, they will repent it in less than a month!" I told the two men, one of whom I found was a Plumber & Glazier, the other a Shoemaker, that they had better not dishearten any of the poor creatures, adding, that perhaps they had themselves not been long enough in America to try the country? "Oh, yes, Sir," was the reply, with a shake of the head, "we have been here 6 years, and know they must half starve!" I staid long enough to learn that they did not utter a delusion. Such is emigration, and such the prospects that await those who shall make the trial.

CHAPTER XVIII

AMERICAN PACKETS AND THEIR COMMANDS—SHAMEFUL TREATMENT OF STEERAGE PASSENGERS—NEGLECT OF SHIP—FALSE-SWEARING—DANGER FROM TAKING SICK PASSENGERS—ENGLISH PACKETS MAKE THE VOYAGE IN LESS TIME THAN AMERICAN PACKETS—SEVEN DEATHS DURING ONE VOYAGE ON BOARD AN AMERICAN LINE PACKET

I should feel I had not completed my self-imposed task, did I not appropriate a chapter to a description of "*The American Guinea-Traps*," as a Gentleman, a friend of mine, very appropriately designated the *Line Accommodation Packets*, trading between New York and the Ports of Great Britain. Never was there a more Scandalous species of Speculation carried on than this Emigration one. It is a common thing for the Americans to say,—in fact I had it *flung in my teeth* by them hundreds of times, that the British Government were constantly sending over their Paupers for them to provide for. "But how is it," was my inquiry, "that you Americans have built such a number of fine vessels, for the express purpose of trading in the conveyance of these same paupers, the profits arising from which have long been a source of wealth to the United States? & what is more, you have agents in England, who, by advertising & other means, are constantly alluring these same *paupers*, save the mark, to transport themselves to your Shores? Is there nothing to be made of them?" These were questions your money-loving American was ill-prepared to answer, and upon such occasions I was generally *too smart* for Jonathan.

The truth is the Americans not only find these paupers a source of profit to them, but they are so sensible of the fact, that they had a meeting in New York for the purpose of making it a rule, that none but Americans should command their Packets. And I have myself been an eye and ear witness to the fact that their agents in London are constantly in the habit of earwigging persons wishing to emigrate, and telling them, that *English* Packets are not to be depended upon in their sailing and other aspects—I say again, that this I have heard & seen.

But these objections to English Vessels are so far from being the truth, that several respectable persons assured me, who had sailed in both, that not only were the English packets to be preferred, but the conduct of English Commanders was infinitely above that of the American Commanders, both as to Seamanship & humanity to their passengers. One American Packet which arrived in the Bay of New York, when I was there, commanded by an American Captain, no sooner landed her passengers, than they one & all declared the Captain to be a perfect Monster, and united in publishing a letter descriptive of his treatment & brutality, which letter I read in the *Sun* American paper, and the Editor observed upon it, "this is as it ought to be. If a fellow who has a parcel of poor creatures under his protection so treat them, he not only ought thus to be shewn up, but to be made an example of at the public tribunals of the country."

These American Captains should also recollect that they are the hired servants of the passengers for the time being, and neither by law or usage are authorized to act towards the poorer class in the *brutal* manner they do. They not only crowd their vessels with passengers in the Steerage till they have room neither to breathe nor stir, but take in cargo to such a shameful extent, that their vessels are in constant danger of foundering at sea, in consequence. The Packet in which I took my passage, *The President*, had 100 tons more cargo on board, I speak on the authority of the mate, than she ought to have carried. And at Portsmouth the Captain, as these *Packet-Bashaws* are called, took in more passengers, mostly the poorer sort of Irish, upon the most mercenary principles, for they had neither proper food nor bedding, & several of them did not take off their clothes the whole voyage—it was, in consequence, one continued Scene of filth. Nor were any of them provided with berths. The vessel was no sooner out at sea, than the consequence was, there was an uproar, as to where they should be crowded.

More scandalous still was the conduct of the Commander of the Packet in which I returned to England, which was not only heavily laden with a cargo of turpentine and Wool, the stench from which was most disgusting, but the steerage was so crowded with boxes & lumber, that the numerous passengers had not room to stir. But this was not all, the Captain took a sick man on board, to the endangering of the lives of all besides in the ship, which man died on the voyage, and the deck of the vessel was kept in such a crowded state, between live stock & lumber, that the steerage passengers had not a foot of room left clear to get a breath of air, or to straighten their legs upon. No sooner did they attempt to set a foot on the quarter-deck than they were driven off & insulted by the Captain, with the most disgusting language & brutal effrontery. When the Packet arrived off Portsmouth &

the quarantine officer came off to examine the Captain, on the state of the Ship, the same Captain *took his oath* to the Statement, in my hearing, that the *steerage was cleaned out 3 times a week* during the voyage. This was so far from the truth, that *it was never cleaned out once during the whole time*! and the deck was also kept in a greasy & filthy state. In truth it was never *swabbed* during the whole voyage, till we were nearly in sight of Portsmouth, and, no doubt, only then from a fear of the passengers complaining to the quarantine officer. One poor old woman was thrown down by its greasy state, and had her eye nearly cut out against the anchor. Would it not be a judicious & just proceeding for the quarantine officer to examine some of the *Steerage* passengers as well as the captain? I am certain that it would have the happiest effects.

Another captain of these *Line (videlicet Lying) Accommodation* Packets took on board a poor Irishman who had been working on the canals up the country, in such a state of disease, that the effluvium from his body scented the whole Ship. Yet this man was stowed away in a Steerage crowded with healthy passengers, men, women, & children, and what is more Shameful still, the poor creature *was not provided with a single blanket to cover his wretched body*. He, too, died by the way. In fact, the scandalous treatment which steerage passengers receive from these *American Captains*, the shameful manner in which they take their *oaths* when examined by the quarantine officers, is a subject that our authorities ought to inquire most seriously into. They ought to see that no vessel left an English port, crowded as they invariably are with passengers, with its deck occupied with live stock and other lumber. But that it was left clean for the use of the Steerage passengers; and having so little regard for an oath, they ought to be mulct in a heavy fine in such case.

Persons who engage their passage in these packets as they are seen in the docks at London, are wofully taken in. It is not till they arrive at Portsmouth that the nuisance really begins to be felt, where numbers of additional passengers are added without regard to health. The consequence is that sickness commences almost before they lose sight of shore, and, from the stench from the crowded state of the vessels & the impossibility of getting exercise from the lumbered state of the deck, it seldom ceases during the whole voyage. The Consequence is a ship rarely reaches port without one or two deaths, sometimes more. The Captain of one of these Line *Accommodation* Packets confessed to me, that the idea of their making the voyage better or in a shorter period than the English Packets do, was all "humbug," as he termed it. One Ship, from Bristol, actually made the port of New York 10 days less than did one of these Line Packets, and I was told that this was not an infrequent occurrence.

But setting aside the brutality of these Bashaws, if people had the most distant idea of the horrors of a voyage across the Atlantic, with a wife and young family especially, subject to the stenches, inconveniences, & privations that they must endure in a beastly packet, few, I imagine, would undertake to transport themselves to such a people & country as America is. One poor old English farmer, from the county of Surrey, who had been deluded into the Experiment by some of our English political demagogues, a man with a very comfortable means at his command, went out in the same packet with myself. His sufferings were so dreadful during the voyage, that when he arrived at New York (from whence, after having seen the farm he had purchased at Buffalo, he was to return to England to fetch his wife & family), he declared that he would sooner "rot in a prison than make such a voyage again." In consequence, he offered to pay the passage backwards & forwards of any respectable man who would undertake the task of protecting his family, and give him a handsome premium besides.

I am told, and I have every reason to believe it, that the next voyage the Packet in which I came out made from England was fitted with *double berths* down the centre in addition to berths round the steerage—and the ship proved so unhealthy, that 7 persons died & were consigned to the waves before She reached New York—deaths, I feel no hesitation in saying, scarcely a degree short of murders, from the mercenary & barbarous manner in which the passengers must have been crowded together.

Plate 16. Anticipations for Emigrants. By permission of the Syndics of Cambridge University Library.

CODA:

"ON THE PERILS OF OBLIVION"

What, then, are we to make of Richard Gooch? For some, he may represent the worst Tory excesses; for others, proof of the old adage that a Jack of all trades is master of none. To me, what fascinates is what he symbolizes, the oblivion that awaits every single one of us. Gooch, after all, had every chance of making some permanent mark on history. He was the son of an English gentleman at a time when such things really mattered; he was well educated; he was by the late 1820s a wealthy man. And although he subsequently lost his fortune supporting Tory causes in Parliament and in the provincial press, he nonetheless had powerful—if distant—acquaintances among the country's politicians, and was a published author with several books to his name.

Yet, there are vast areas of Gooch's life that would be unrecoverable even to the archivist, genealogist, or historian without an expenditure of time and effort out of all proportion to any possible recompense. Where exactly and when precisely was he born? How many times did he marry? Where is he buried? Why was his eldest son treated so differently from his siblings? What was the source of his wealth in the 1820s? Why did he decide to pursue neither his education (for the Church, apparently) nor his legal interests to their conclusion? What is the provenance of the group of Gooch manuscripts in Cambridge University Library? I have no doubt that useful documents do exist that could help to answer some of these questions: Ralph Thomas's manuscript diary, for instance, or Gooch's 1843 memorial. However, as the Acknowledgments page suggests, that so little is known about Gooch's life is not for the want of trying on my part; rather, so little is known because so little can now be known even though Gooch died less than 150 years ago, even less, that is, than the span of two lifetimes.

I find that, personally, tremendously sobering. The ego seems at times inexhaustible, seems often to flame forth with remarkable brightness, and yet it sputters out easily enough. Despite humanity's best efforts to achieve individual immortality—some through words, others through actions, most through procreation—the attempt for all but a minuscule few is a futile one. For me, Gooch symbolizes perfectly that sea of oblivion that awaits almost all of us. As D. H. Lawrence says in one of his last poems:

> Oh build your ship of death, oh build it!
> for you will need it.
> For the voyage of oblivion awaits you.
> ("The Ship of Death" 720)

NOTES

For the sake of brevity I have used four abbreviations in these notes:

DAB	*Dictionary of American Biography*. Ed. Dumas Malone. 10 vols. New York: Charles Scribner's Sons, 1927–1936.
DNB	*Dictionary of National Biography from the Earliest Times to 1900*. Ed. Sir Leslie Stephen and Sir Sidney Lee. 22 vols. Oxford: Oxford UP, 1921–1922.
OED	*Oxford English Dictionary*. Compact ed. 12 vols. in 2. Oxford: Oxford UP, 1971.
RG	Richard Gooch

Page 2

Embellished with 15 Engravings The ms. reads "12." However, the ms. is accompanied by 15 sketches, 14 of which are numbered and all of which have captions and placement instructions in RG's hand.

Page 3

Messrs Trollope & Hall Mrs. Frances Trollope (1780–1863), and Basil Hall (1788–1844). RG is thinking of Hall's travels in North America in 1827 and 1828, and Mrs. Trollope's visit to the United States between 1827 and 1830.

poursuivant RG seems to intend the word as an appositive noun: *poursuivant (d'armes)*. In English, the phrase is spelled *pursuivant*, and means "herald." See *OED*: *pursuivant*, sense 1.

Jonathan A generic term for an American. See Brewer 464 (col. 1) and Winifred Morgan's *American Icon* for further background.

like Jupiter's boy The allusion is to Dionysus in Aristophanes' play *The Frogs* (ca. 405 B.C.). Dionysus was the son of Jupiter by an odd sort of double birth: first from Prosperine and, thence, via trickery from Semele. See Tripp 203–211.

"as naturally as pigs squeak" The quotation is from Samuel Butler's mock heroic poem *Hudibras* (1663), Pt. 1, Canto 1, ll. 51–52.

"a child taking notes" RG slightly misquotes two lines from the first stanza of Robert Burns, "On the Late Captain Grose's Peregrinations thro' Scotland, collecting the Antiquities of that Kingdom" (1793):

> A chield's amang you taking notes,
> And, faith, he'll prent it.

See *The Poems and Songs of Robert Burns* 1: 494–496.

RG clearly saw himself as a second Captain Grose, for Burns wrote of the latter: "I have never seen a man of more original observation, anecdote and remark. . . . His delight is to steal thro' the country

almost unknown, both as most favorable to his humour and his business" (*The Poems and Songs of Robert Burns* 3: 1320).
"said log" The reference here appears to be to the legend of Jupiter giving a log as king to the frogs. The frogs, however, find the log too quiet. See *Fables of Aesop* No. 42, p. 44: "We Get the Rulers We Deserve."
Domestic Manners of the Americans. The title of Mrs. Trollope's immensely popular travelogue.
Covent Garden or Billingsgate The former was "the great fruit, vegetable, and herb market of London" which had been entirely redesigned by the Duke of Bedford in 1830 (Wheatley 1: 463–465). The latter has remained to this day "the great fish-market of London" (Wheatley 1: 181). The costumes for both sites would, of course, have looked outlandish since they were specifically designed for the execution of a trade.
Page 4
bantling The *OED* defines the noun as "a young or small child, a brat." Here, RG uses it figuratively to describe his book.
nous verrons The French phrase means "we will see."
the saying of the Grecian Sage The saying, which means "Know Thyself," was an inscription at the Delphic Oracle, and is quoted in Plutarch's *Moralia*. It was attributed in Classical times to (among others) Pythagoras, Socrates, and one or other or all of the Seven Sages of Greek Antiquity (ca. 650–590 B.C.). See Bartlett 62 (col. 1), and *Brewer's Dictionary of Phrase and Fable* 638 (col. 2).
Page 7
When Cobbett took Cobbett left the Unites States for the last time in the autumn of 1819. See the Introduction to Cobbett's *Year's Residence in the United States of America* 11.
his Emigrant's Guide The text referred to is Cobbett's *The Emigrant's Guide. . . .* (London: The Author, 1829). A new augmented edition was published in 1830.
I took my passage for America early in 1833 RG indicates on p. 170 that he took passage for the United States on the packet ship *The President*. He must then be referring to that packet's sailing of February 22, 1833 from London, for that packet was not to sail again from England until the middle of the year.
Page 8
the celebrated Robert Hall I have been unable to find RG's reference to Hall's comment about the Willows in Cambridgeshire. However, Robert Hall is listed in *DNB* 8:969 (col. 2)–971 (col. 1), where he is described as a baptist divine. RG would have termed him "celebrated" because of his oratorical powers. His *Works* were published in six volumes in 1832. In the ms. RG deleted the word "Dissenting" from his description of Hall as a minister.
Page 9
Shenstone's Verse William Shenstone (1714–1763) was a minor poet,

who, according to Walpole, "'labour[ed] all his life to write a perfect song, and, in my opinion at least, never once succeeded'" (*DNB* 18: 50).

The poem from which RG quotes, with almost complete accuracy, the fifth and final stanza is entitled "Written at an Inn at Henley" and was published in Shenstone's collection, *Levities; or, Pieces of Humour*. For a biographical sketch of Shenstone, see *DNB* 18: 48–50; for the poem itself, see *The Poetical Works of William Shenstone* 84–85.

Page 10

haut ton The phrase literally means "high tone"; figuratively, it means "refined."

nearly a dozen persons Fol. 104 in the ms. ends here. The verso of fol. 104 contains a false start: five lines written upside down in relation to the rest of the ms and struck through.

a young man by the name of Worthington *The Sun* printed this story in two separate issues of the newspaper, each time a little differently. RG quotes from the story as it appears in *The Sun* Apr. 9, 1834: 3 (col. 1), where it was reprinted from the *Liverpool* (PA) *Mercury* and was given the title "Another Warning." The story had also appeared in *The Sun* Mar. 15, 1834: 2 (col. 2) under the title "Diabolical Murder." RG remains faithful to the original, departing from his source only by misspelling Natchitoches (as Natchiotoches) and by underlining (for reasons of propaganda) the fact that the lodgers were all sleeping in one room.

Natchitoches At this time, Natchitoches, Louisiana was "a place of considerable importance" as it was "the extreme southwestern entrepot of the United States towards Texas" (*The Evening Post* Dec. 4, 1833: 2 [col. 5]). It was the county seat of Natchitoches County. See Kane 268.

Page 11

Hiders I have been unable to trace a precise meaning for this slang term, and RG himself seems a little uncertain about it. However, if RG's information is correct, it is not difficult to see *Hiders* as being derived, via a nominal transferred sense, from the verb *to hide* as defined by the *OED*, sense 2 of v^2: "To beat the hide or skin of, to flog, thrash." Since the first use of the verb in this way dates from 1825 and the last from 1875, such a term as *Hiders* could well have been current slang at the time of RG's "visit."

Another possibility is that RG miswrote *Hiders* for *Hookers* or *Housers*. As Ellis points out, the last two terms were sobriquets of Irish gangs in the Five Points district of New York City. These gangs committed acts of random violence similar to RG's *"Banditti"*: unprovoked bludgeoning; cracking someone's spine, and so on. See Ellis 230–246.

Mr. Booth, the tragedian. Junius Brutus Booth (1796–1853). He travelled to the United States in 1821 and fostered the American tradition of tragic acting. Gene Smith's *American Gothic* is the most recent biography of the Brutus family (Junius, Edwin, and John Wilkes); it

makes no mention of the incident referred to by RG.
Wall Street Hardie locates this street as leading "from Broadway, in front of the Trinity Church, to the East River" (217).
Prince Street Hardie locates this street as leading "from the Bowery to M'Dougal, where it meets Charlton–street" (215).
the English vocalist, Mr. Anderson RG is referring to Joshua R. Anderson. For a full discussion of the affair, see Haswell 260– 261, and Odell, "The Anderson Riots," in his *Annals of the New York Stage* 3: 548–550. The rioting and demonstrations against Anderson occurred October 13–17, 1831.
the New Yorkers would not permit In the ms., RG originally wrote "Americans" rather than "New Yorkers." Throughout the text, RG tends to conflate the two terms.
Page 12
cowhide licking! Mathews defines the verb "to cowhide" as "To flog or beat (a person) with a cowhide," and the noun "cowhide" as "a severe whip made of one or more thongs of cowhide, twisted or plaited, often painted" (1: 423 [col. 2]; 424 [col. 1]). RG discusses the term further in an anecdote in Volume I, Chapter X; see p. 49.
Page 14
Counsellor Emmet's Monument Thomas Addis Emmet headed a group of Irishmen in New York who met at Harmony Hall on November 25, 1817 to form a society for helping Irish immigrants. On December 8 of that year he was elected first president of the New-York Irish Emigrant Association. He died on November 14, 1827. One week later New Yorkers of Irish extraction resolved to erect a monument to his memory. The monument, designed by Ingham and completed early in 1833, was located in St. Paul's Churchyard on Broadway. Stokes (quoting *The New York Evening Post* for December 11, 1832) describes the monument: "It is an obelisk of white marble, thirty feet high, hewn out of an entire block. On the side next to Broadway the monument bears near the top a bar [*sic*] relief likeness of the deceased" (5: 1716 [col. 1]).
City Hall City Hall was 216' long, 100' wide, and 51' high. It was constructed of white marble and "brown free stone" (Hardie 331). Construction on the building was begun on September 26, 1803 and completed in 1812 at a cost of $500,000. Hardie considered City Hall (also known as the "Temple of Justice") as "the handsomest structure in the United States; perhaps (of its size) in the world" and a "chaste and beautiful edifice" "seen to considerable advantage from almost every quarter" (331).
Masonic Lodge Designed by Hugh Reinagle, Esq., this building was 50' wide by 125' long; its cornerstone was laid on June 24, 1826. Hardie terms it the "New Masonic Hall," locates it on "the east side of Broadway, nearly opposite the Hospital," and praises it as a "superb edifice" in a "purely *Gothic*" style (337).
City Hotel According to Stokes (who quotes from Goodrich's *Picture of New York*), the hotel "occupied the entire block on the west side of

Broadway between Thames and Cedar Sts., and was the 'loftiest' hotel in the city, containing 'more than one hundred large and small parlours and lodging-rooms, besides the City Assembly Room, chiefly used for Concerts and Balls'" (5: 1672 [col. 2]). The hotel had been partially destroyed by fire on April 24, 1833, and when it was rebuilt in July of that year another story was added.

Roman Catholic Cathedral St. Patrick's Cathedral was built in 1815 at the corner of Mott and Prince streets. It was the largest place of worship in the city at 9,600 square feet (80' wide and 120' long). Hardie simply terms it "spacious" (180).

Broadway Since earliest times, Broadway has been one of the most important streets in New York City; it has also always been associated with the theatre. Allen offers a fine description of the street as it was in RG's time:

> Broadway, once exclusively residential, was becoming the busiest and most opulent shopping street in America; its lower reaches, from Bowling Green to Trinity Church, had yielded completely to banks and countinghouses. Farther uptown, while the thoroughfare still boasted some of the finest mansions in town, these were increasingly being replaced by deluxe stores (for example A.T. Stewart's magnificent emporium at Chambers Street) and hotels, as homeowners pulled up stakes and relocated farther north. (135–136)

Irish Barrister of the same name Robert Emmet was hanged in 1803 for leading the July rebellion in Ireland. The Irish melody to which RG alludes was a lyric prominently featured in the first number of Thomas Moore's *Irish Melodies*. As the first line of the lyric strongly suggests ("Oh! breathe not his name; let it sleep in the shade"), Moore does not directly name Emmett as the inspiration for the poem; its language, however (as Stephen Gwynn has pointed out in *Thomas Moore* 12–13), deliberately echoes Emmet's last words at his trial. For the lyric from *Irish Melodies*, see *The Poetical Works of Thomas Moore* 336.

their principal promenade Presumably RG means Castle Garden, which began life in 1807 (Hemstreet gives a date of 1811 [4]) as Castle Clinton. Its name was changed to Castle Garden in 1824 (according to Hemstreet, 1822 [5]) after Rathbone & Fitch leased it from the Corporation of New York. It was attached to the Battery at the southern tip of Manhattan by a bridge. *The New York Gazette & General Advertiser* for July 3, 1824 offers this description of the promenade, which lay on the roof of the socializing and dining ares beneath:

> The circular walk on the top, covered with an awning, is upwards of 500 ft. in length, and 14 feet in width. On this platform or walk are on both sides benches extending the whole 500 feet, and across the ends. From this walk, the waters of our Bay,

> the Narrows, the Hudson, and interesting landscapes, &c. are in full view, with all the bustle of our floating commerce. . . . [T] Castle Garden must become the most fashionable and healthy resort in the country (quoted in Stokes 5: 1639 [col. 2]).

On June 12, 1833, the bridge connecting Castle Garden with the Battery collapsed shortly after President Jackson crossed it. In 1855, the Battery was fitted out as an immigrant depot.

Page 15

Lancastrian System This system was named after the educational theories of an Englishman, Joseph Lancaster. It involved the instructor teaching pupils to teach other pupils in lower grades. The major benefit of the system was economic. The first school in New York City—Public School No. 1 (which opened on April 28, 1807)—used this system. See Ellis 202, and Fearon 38.

Park & Bowery The Park Theatre opened September 1, 1821 and closed Dec. 18, 1847. The Second Bowery Theatre opened August 28 [20?], 1828 and burned down September 22, 1836.

Haymarket Theatre The original Haymarket Theatre was built in 1720 and remodeled in the 1770s. It was rebuilt by John Nash in 1820–21 and sported a six-columned Greek portico. See Weinreb and Hibbert 371, and Wheatley 2: 200–201.

two Museums, private property. According to Williams' *New York As It Is in 1834*, the two museums were the American Museum in the New-York Institution off St. Paul's Church, Broadway, and Peale's Museum and Gallery of the Fine Arts on Broadway opposite City Hall Park. The former was founded in 1810 by John Scudder and constituted "the greatest and most valuable collection in America" (Hardie 343). The latter was founded in 1825, contained four spacious rooms, and boasted "a valuable collection of Paintings by eminent artists, of all ages" (Hardie 344). Hardie also lists a third museum, the Chatham Museum in the New-York Spectaculum on Chatham Street, and describes it as "a collection of natural and artificial Curiosities, of every description" (344). All three contained one of the favorite exhibits of the day, a cosmorama.

Clinton Hall In RG's time, Clinton Hall was the site of the National Academy of Design, which exhibited paintings by artists such as Allston, Ingham, Morse, and West. It was located at the soutwest corner of Nassau and Beekman streets. Before 1854, the Hall was also the site of the Mercantile Library. See Wilson 3: 369, and Hemstreet 170.

the house that Washington occupied The house was most likely located at 180 Pearl Street. Washington occupied it from April 13, 1776 to the end of May of that year. Other sources suggest that the headquarters may have been at the Kennedy house at 1 Broadway, the Mortimer house, or in front of the "Oyster Battery." See Stokes 3: 924 (col. 2).

the Corporation of New York Known as the Common Council. On April 7, 1830 a bicameral Common Council was created by Charter

amendments, and the business of the Corporation was to be done by departments rather than committees. See Stokes 5: 1691 (col. 1).
the New York Advertiser For the full account from which RG quotes, see "ABATEMENT OF NUISANCES" in *The New-York Commercial Advertiser* May 31, 1834: 2 (col. 3). The original has "river" where RG writes "water."
Page 16
One of the greatest nuisances Dickens in his *American Notes* echoes RG: "They are the city scavengers, these pigs. Ugly brutes they are. . . . Every pig knows where he lives, much better than anybody could tell him" (87).
the Bowery According to *An Alphabetical List* p. 7, this street divided the 10th and 11th wards from the 6th, 14th, and 9th. Hardie provides a different means of orientation. According to him, the Bowery "leads from Chatham-square to the point, where the Bloomingdale and old Harlem roads separate, at the place which was formerly the UNITED STATES' ARSENAL; but now the HOUSE OF REFUGE" (208).
the pig nuisance as well as others RG toned his comment down. In the ms., he originally wrote "the pig nuisance as well as other filthy nuisances."
Page 17
the cholera raged Asiatic cholera first appeared in New York City in July 1832. According to Stokes, between July 7 and October 20 of that year about 3,500 people in the city died (3: 523). According to Ellis (who provides slightly different data), about 5.5 per cent of the city's population died in a period of four months (240). An epidemic of cholera again hit the city in June 1834 (see Stokes 5: 1727 [col. 2]).

Documentary sources concur with RG's criticism of the condition of New York's streets. Stokes terms the streets in 1833 "shamefully dirty" and remarks that throughout the early 1830s they were "notorious for their filthy condition" (3: 523, 529).
Potter's Field The almshouse burial ground and city cemetery, Potter's Field (also Pottersfield) was originally located on the site of the present Washington Square. It was moved in 1823 to the site of the present Bryant Park and the New York Public Library at Fifth Avenue and 40th to 42nd streets. As a result of the move it was increased in size from six-and-a-half acres to ten. See Stokes 6: 337 (col. 3), and Hemstreet 114–115.

RG exaggerates the greed of speculators in the city. The remains were not "scarcely cold"; Washington Square was opened in 1827, four years after Potter's Field was moved two miles or so to the north.
the worst parts of London—Saffron Hill included Saffron Hill, situated in EC1, is an area of London between Holborn and Clerkenwell. Weinreb and Hibbert remark that the area was "notorious" as a "rookery" where "[c]rime and vice" "flourished" (687 [col. 2]). Dickens immortalized the district in *Oliver Twist*, which was published only four years after RG wrote *America and the Americans*.

Page 20

I have seen 50 houses blazing away For the primitiveness and bustle associated with fire prevention in New York in the 1830s, see Stokes 3: 585–586 and Plate 96: "New York Fire Engine No. 34 [ca. 1830]," by J. W. Hill; Ginsberg; Calhoun; Costello; and Dana.

RG's complaints focus on the noisiness of the alarm systems and on the rowdiness of the runners who helped out the volunteer firemen. The existence of the latter problem was acknowledged by the Common Council in the fall of 1834 when it criticized the "assemblages of boys, young men and persons of idle and dissolute habits, in Engine Houses and their neighbourhoods" (quoted in Ginsberg 169).

RG exaggerates the mayhem of fire prevention at this time in the history of New York City, but it is certainly the case that because the force was wholly volunteer until 1865, because the cholera epidemic of 1832 had decimated the ranks of firemen, and because the city's water supply was chronically inadequate even for drinking, New York City was prone to devastating fires. During the period covered by RG's account, for example, one fire on May 1, 1833 destroyed 90–100 buildings, cost $150,000– $200,000, and left 300 families homeless (see Calhoun 351).

Page 21

I have elsewhere noticed RG, as I indicate in my note on the text, had problems with the organization of *America and the Americans*. He hasn't yet mentioned the seven-year rule for firemen, yet he thinks he has. He discusses it in Volume II, Chapter XVI. He also defines the rule in a rather confusing way. By being a New York City volunteer fireman for a period of seven years continuously, a man would gain permanent exemption from service in the militia and from jury duty. See Ginsberg 165, and Calhoun 112–148.

the *Sun* American paper RG quotes from a story entitled "The Fireman's Dog" in *The Sun* May 16, 1834: 4 (cols. 1–2). He adds (presumably in consideration of his audience) the phrase "in America."

Page 24

the arbitrary law Fearon remarks in his *Sketches*, published less than twenty years before RG's account: "Houses are seldom let on long leases in the cities of America, the usual period being one year, taking date from the 1st of May. Upon this day the removals are so numerous, that the streets have a very singular appearance" (14n).

much to the consternation of a decent housewife In the ms., RG wrote "consolation" rather than "consternation." As such, it was clearly a slip of the pen. I corrected it to the word which seemed to me RG's likeliest intent.

vi et armis The phrase literally means "by power and arms." It can best be translated as "with main strength" or "by brute force."

Page 25

bon-feu Bonfire. RG's use of *bon-feu* is mannered and shows a reliance on a false etymology derived from Samuel Johnson. The word

bonfire derives not from the French *bon feu* (good fire) but from the Scots *bone fire* (literally a fire of bones, a means of summarily disposing of corpses).
Shakespeare's ghost The allusion is to the ghost of Hamlet's father, the old King. See *Hamlet* I., v.9–13.
Page 26
"Jack Robinson" The origins of this familiar phrase are obscure, and its early spelling was inconsistent. Taylor and Whiting quote one spelling as "Robberson" and another as "Robison" (202).
Page 28
Chapter V The chapter's subheadings (on fol. 125) are pasted over an earlier list.
Euclid's axioms The term refers to the principles of Eucleides, a Greek mathematician, who taught at Alexandria in about 300 B.C. See Euclid's *The Thirteen Books of Euclid's ELEMENTS*.
Page 29
mauvais honte The phrase in French means "self-conscious." In the ms. RG incorrectly wrote "mauvais hônte."
There is none of the liveliness of the French woman In the ms., RG accidentally wrote "Frenchman woman."
à la drone RG is lapsing into Franglais here; the phrase may be "translated" as "with his snoring." In the ms. RG incorrectly wrote "à là drone."
Page 30
à la nature RG's sense is plain here, although his French is nonstandard. He means *au naturel* in the sense of "in the natural state."
Page 31
goût The word means "relish."
Page 32
gaieté de coeur The phrase means "sheer wantonness." RG seems to mean something more like "lighheartedness."
Page 34
Indecent Display of Their Persons In the ms., RG had originally written "Offensive" rather than "Indecent."
the lady's hat Mayer provides a useful gloss on RG's reference to the ridiculousness of ladies' hats. Throughout the early years of English pantomime there was a tradition of wearing outrageous costumes; indeed, "dandies" and "dandizettes" were used as pantomime characters to poke fun at the oddity of contemporary fashions. Mayer refers in particular to two pantomimes, *Harlequin in His Element* (1807) and *Harlequin and the Red Dwarf* (1812), that RG might have seen as a young man. In the former, Clown (Grimaldi) wears, according to the stage directions, "'a curious habit surmounted by a large hat bordered with fur, as a satire on the present mode of female fashion'" (sc. 2). In the latter, a fishwoman—to quote again from the stage directions—"'was in a moment fashionably equipped with a veil, a ridicule [*sic*], a parasol, and a bonnet from a fruit-basket, a cabbage-net, a horse-

mushroom, and a rush pannier'" (quoted in Mayer 184). RG clearly had just such pantomimes in mind.
an American paper I have been unable to trace this quotation.
Page 35
Abernethy John Abernethy (1764–1831), an eminent surgeon who practiced at St. Bartholomew's Hospital and was famous for his lectures. For a biographical sketch of Abernethy, see *DNB* 1: 49 (col. 2)–52 (col. 1). RG spells Abernethy "Abernathy" in the ms.
Nevertheless, it is impossible for an English eye In the ms., fol. 132 has been cut after the word "Nevertheless"; it appears some text and about one-quarter inch of the folio may be missing.
some second Tillotson or Rowland Hill John Tillotson (1630–1694) and Rowland Hill (1744–1833). The former was Archbishop of Canterbury from 1690 to 1694 and "perhaps the only primate who took first rank in his day as a preacher" (*DNB* 19: 878 [col. 1]); the latter was a preacher educated at RG's college in Cambridge, St. John's. From 1783 he preached at Surrey Chapel, where "his earnest, eloquent, eccentric preaching attracted large congregations" (*DNB* 9: 862 [col. 2]). See *DNB* 19: 872–878, and *DNB* 9: 862 for biographical sketches of the two men.
these *same pastors assist in scenes of debauchery* RG toned down the final version. He first wrote "very vagabonds" rather than "same pastors."
Blackhawk I have been unable to trace the anecdote to which RG refers. It does not appear in either Black Hawk's *Autobiography of Ma-Ka-Tai-Me-She-Kia-Kiak or Black Hawk . . .* (which was first published in 1833), or in *The Great Indian Chief of the West: or, Life and Adventures of Black Hawk*, anonymously written by Benjamin Drake. Black Hawk, leader of the Fox and Sauk Indians in the Black Hawk War of 1832, was at the height of his fame during the period covered by *America and the Americans*, and visited New York City in June 1833.
Page 36
the notorious Fanny Wright Fanny Wright (1795–1852) shocked many through a lecture tour of the Eastern United States from 1833–1836. In her lectures she attacked slavery and other social institutions such as the church and marriage. RG would have particularly detested her espousal of "free love." For a biographical sketch of Wright, see *Appleton's Cyclopaedia of American Biography* 6: 622.
black-stock *The Random House Dictionary of the English Language*, second ed., unabridged, defines "stock" as "a collar or a neckcloth fitting like a band around the neck" (sense 31). RG's incredulity is caused, presumably, by the stock's being black. Such a color would not show the dirt, but it would hardly—as a result—be "conducive to cleanliness."
warming-pan RG's outrageous comparison of the American doctor's rosette to a warming-pan was mirrored seven years later by Dickens in

The Old Curiosity Shop, Ch. XIV: "a nosegay resembling in shape and dimensions a full-sized warming-pan with the handle cut off" (123).
Page 37
The two principal Theatres At this time, the only other New York theatre of significance besides the Park and the Bowery was Niblo's Garden Theatre at Broadway and Prince Street, which opened on July 4, 1827, was rebuilt in 1829, and burned down on September 18, 1846.
The Kembles Charles (1775–1854) and Frances (Fanny) Anne Kemble (1809–1893). This father–and–daughter team toured the United States in 1832–34.
Mr. and Mrs Wood Joseph Wood (1801–1890) and Mary Ann (née Paton) Wood (1802–1864 [June 1863?]). The Woods toured the United States together three times: 1833–34; 1835–36; and 1840– 41.
The thinness of the audiences Precise information is available about how much money the Kembles made in the 1833–34 season at just two of the theatres in which they performed, and it suggests that RG's puzzlement is misplaced. At the Park, according to Ireland, they played forty–five nights at an average of $732.00 per night, while their eight benefits brought in more than $1,200.00 each (85n). At the Tremont Theatre, according to Clapp, total receipts (including premiums) for the Kembles' eighteen-night engagement were $11,671.75—this at a time when box tickets at the Tremont cost $1.00 (300).
Forrest Edwin Forrest (1806–1872) was, according to Hartnoll, "the acknowledged head of his profession for nearly 30 years" (292 [col. 1]). In the ms., RG refers to this actor as "Forrester."
Kean Edmund Kean (1787–1833) was an extraordinarily gifted actor, particularly in Renaissance tragedy.

RG's comparison of Forrest and Kean is, perhaps, a pointed one since Forrest's first engagement in New York (June 23, 1826) was at the Park, playing one of Kean's best roles, Othello. Forrest played Othello in New York at the Bowery on December 12, 1833—during, that is, the period covered by RG's account.
Mrs Drake Frances Ann (née Denny) Drake (1797–1875) was actually born in Schenectady, New York. She was, however, related by marriage to the renowned English-born actor-manager Samuel Drake.
our Miss O'Neill Eliza O'Neill, later Lady Eliza Becher (1791– 1872), was an Irish actress with a reputation based on an acting career in London, 1814–19. In the ms. RG spells her name "O'Neil."
Page 38
"Jim Crow" The name of a minstrel song-and–dance routine developed by Thomas Dartmouth ("Daddy") Rice (1808–1860). According to the New York diarist Philip Hone (in an entry dated August 4, 1837) the "Jump Jim Crow" song was so popular that its creator, Thomas D. Rice, "has eclipsed the fame of Kean, Kemble and Macready" (quoted in Spaeth 71).
on the *qui vive* RG intends this phrase metaphorically. It derives through French from the Italian phrase *Chi viva* (a corruption of *Chi*

vi, va) or "Who goes there?" used by soldiers on guard duty. RG simply means that the audience is all attention. See Jones 327.
during Mrs Wood's engagement RG may be referring to Mrs. Wood's role as Isabel in Lacy's adaptation of Meyerbeer's opera *Robert the Devil*. She played the role on April 7, 1834 (during the time, that is, covered by RG's account), and Ireland comments about the opera's lackluster reception: "It proved successful, but not to the same degree with most of the Woods' other operas" (80).
They are going to sing 'Jim Crow' Since RG refers to the performance of "Jim Crow" at the Park and Thomas D. Rice (the song's originator) played the role in New York only at the Bowery, he must be referring to a Rice imitator. The likeliest candidate is T. H. Blakeley, who acted at the Park from 1829 to 1836 and 1838 to 1841, and who "jumped Jim Crow" at the Park on at least two occasions in the 1833–34 season: December 25, 1833 (see *The Sun* for that date [3 (col. 2)]), and January 1, 1834 (Ireland 77).
***The Sun* American paper** RG quotes extensively from a story entitled "Boston Pride." He omits only one sentence at the end of the story: "Wish our New York grandees were as flush of their cash—guess people wouldn't be so likely to feel 'the pressure.'" See *The Sun* Apr. 15, 1834: 2 (col. 1). RG is less accurate about citing his source: in the ms. he indicates that the story appeared in *The Sun* in March 1834.

RG's discussion of price-gouging at popular performances by stars is borne out by information on the receipts taken in by Master Burke at the Tremont Theatre when he was at the height of his fame: a little less than $20,000.00 for a nineteen-night run in the 1830–31 season (Clapp 284).
The Tremont The Tremont Street Theatre opened Sept. 24, 1827 and closed June 22 [23?], 1843.
Master Burke Charles St. Thomas Burke (1822–1854) specialized in playing multiple parts either in quick succession or over a short theatrical run.
An English actress I have been unable to identify the "English actress & vocalist" RG alludes to. No calendar of performances at the Tremont exists, and although both Clapp and Durham do indirectly offer some possible names none represents a certainty.
Page 39
the Haymarket From RG's reference to the Haymarket Theatre, it is unclear whether he means the original Haymarket (built in 1720 and remodeled in the 1770s) or its replacement (constructed between 1820 and 1821 a little to the south of the original building and designed by Nash).
our admirable Liston John Liston (1776?–1846) specialized in clownish, country-bumpkin characters. Liston's "favorite characters" among the 55 he played at the Haymarket during his 25-year career there (1805–1829) included Sir Peter Pigwiggin in *Pigeons and Crows* (1818), Sam Swipes in *Exchange no Robbery* (1819), and Paul Pry in

the play of the same name (1825). The first of these was often identified with Liston; the second was "Liston's major hit" in 1819 (Jim Davis 41); the last, "one of the greatest theatrical hits of the age" (Jim Davis 56).

Page 41

The Kingston Spectator RG actually took this account of the dangers of sleighing from *The Sun* Apr. 15, 1834: 3, col. 1—where it is headlined "[From the Kingston Spectator.]"—and pasted it into the ms. at the bottom of fol. 141. He has deleted a couple of insignificant phrases from the clipping in order to make the quotation flow more smoothly. He is incorrect in calling *The Kingston Spectator* an American paper; it was Canadian.

Page 43

the well-being of a social & civilized community chiefly depends After "depends" RG first wrote and then deleted this phrase: "setting aside all other considerations, both religious & political."

Page 44

***left–handed* marriage** The *OED* defines this phrase as synonymous with morganatic marriage (see "Left–handed," *a.* sense 5).

Page 45

a proverbial saying I have been unable to validate the proverbiality of RG's comment about bigamy in the United States. Some of the oddness of RG's comment about New York and Brooklyn being in different states may arise from the latter being a separate village or city at this time rather than a borough. Williams' *New York As It Is in 1833* calls Brooklyn a village (20); on April 8, 1834 it was granted a city charter by the legislature. RG acknowledges this status for Brooklyn in a sentence deleted in the ms.

the *Sun*, a short time since I have been unable to trace RG's reference.

Page 46

According to a late number of the *Sun* I have been unable to trace RG's reference.

an American Judge has lately decided RG's comment is actually an unacknowledged quotation from an article entitled "*Look out 'Gentlemen!*" in *The Sun* May 3, 1834: 2 (col. 2).

Page 48

O'Connell & Spring–Rice Daniel O'Connell (1775–1847) and Thomas Spring-Rice (1790–1866). These two MPs represented political opposites: O'Connell was Catholic, Spring-Rice Protestant; O'Connell was a Tory, Spring-Rice a Whig. RG may have chosen these two MPs because of their debate over the Irish question in the House of Commons in April 1834. A motion by O'Connell was defeated by 523 to 38, but only after nine days of debate from both sides of the House. See *DNB* 14: 816 (col. 2)–834 (col. 1), and *DNB* 18: 835 (col. 2)–837 (col. 1).

"two of a trade can never agree" According to *Brewer's Dictionary*, the proverb is "Two of a trade did never agree" (1145). *Brewer's* terms it a “very old” proverb, and cites its occurrence in Hesiod’s *Works and Days* and Gay’s *Fables*. The form of its occurrence in the latter source almost exactly matches RG’s quotation; it may have been this source which RG was recalling. See “The Rat-catcher and the Cats” in *Fables by the Late Mr. Gay* (London: A. K. Newman, [1833?]).

Mr. Stuart, in his *Three Years in America* James Stuart’s account (actually entitled *Three Years in North America*) was published in two vols. in Edinburgh by R. Cadell in 1833. I have been unaable to find the quotations ascribed by RG to Stuart’s *Three Years*. Stuart’s agreement with Ferrall seems unlikely as he spends some space in *Three Years* criticizing Ferrall’s superficiality. It may also be that the *Free Enquirer* is exaggerating for effect the pro-American stance of Stuart.

Mr Ferrall’s work RG refers to S. A. Ferrall’s *A Ramble of Six Thousand Miles through the United States of America*, which was published in London by E. Wilson in 1832. RG incorrectly spells Ferrall “Ferrel” in the ms.

tact in turning the penny RG seems here to be altering the idiomatic phrase: “to turn an honest penny” (meaning, to earn money legitimately). He is doing so at Stuart’s expense: *tact* has hardly the same moral value as *honesty*.

Undeserved praise is satire in disguise RG slightly misquotes Broadhurst’s “To the Celebrated Beauties of the British Court” (ca. 1700). See Stevenson 1860 (col. 2).

to induce a *friend* to take a morning’s walk with them RG had originally written “induced” rather than “induce” but altered it. This whole anecdote displays a conflict in tenses; I have tried to resolve that conflict as simply as possible.

Page 49

a ride as far as Epping Forest The ride would have been considerable—from Westminster to what is now E17 in London. At the time RG was writing, the massive forest had shrunk through enclosures to about 9,000 acres. It was, however, one of the major open spaces for residents of East London. See Weinreb and Hibbert 261 (col. 2)–262.

Turpin’s Cave The notorious highwayman Dick Turpin (1705–1739) along with Tom King terrorized travelers in Epping Forest in the mid-1730s.

the autobiography of Colonel Crockett Davy Crockett (1786–1836) served two terms in the U.S. Congress (1827–31, and 1833–35) as a Tennessee representative. His autobiography was published in 1834 by the Philadelphia publishing house of E. L. Carey and A. Hart as *A Narrative of the Life of David Crockett, of the State of Tennessee. Written by Himself*. This text, however, RG’s comment notwithstanding, contains no account of politicians’ fighting. The incident to which RG refers actually appears in *Sketches and Eccentricities of Col. David Crockett of West Tenessee* 9 (col. 2)–10 (col. 1), a book which was not by Crockett although it was purported to be. The incident consisted of an altercation between Crockett and Mr. M ——. RG is incorrect, too, in suggesting that a whipping took place. In fact, according to the author of *Sketches and Eccentricities*, Crockett remarked: "the fellow [Mr. M ——] said he didn't mean any thing, and kept 'pologizing, till I got into a good humour" (10 [col. 1]).

Page 50

Thurtell-like RG refers here to the murder of William Weare by John Thurtell, Joseph Hunt, and—in all likelihood—William Probert on October 24, 1823. RG's audience will have understood the reference immediately, for the murder was notorious for a generation or more and was alluded to by such writers as William Cobbett, Charles Lamb, Washington Irving, Sir Walter Scott, and Robert Browning. For a mid-nineteenth century account, see *Celebrated Trials of All Countries, and Remarkable Cases of Criminal Jurisprudence*. The major study is a recent one by Borowitz.

which is generally suffered to grow a little above each eye In the ms., this phrase follows the prepositional phrase "between . . . thumb." Its placement there, however, makes nonsense of RG's meaning, so I have moved it to its present position.

The *Sun* American Paper, dated the 9th of April, 1834 The column RG refers to, entitled "POLICE OFFICE.", occupies almost all of col. 2 of p. 2.

Page 51

the Kentuckians have the credit RG may be correct in suggesting that the Kentuckians were skilled in the art of eye-gouging. However, Ellis credits the "refinement" to one gang leader called "Dandy Johnny Dolan," who "invented copper wedges, which he wore on his thumbs to make it easier to gouge out eyes" (233).

The husband then communicated his disgrace to her father Rather revealingly, RG first wrote "his daughter's disgrace."

a dead shot This phrase is now a cliché; however, in 1834 it was newly minted. Indeed, the *OED* incorrectly credits the first use of the phrase to 1852, eighteen years after RG wrote his ms.

Page 54

an American paper of the other day I have been unable to trace RG's reference.

through a mist For a further discussion of the ideas and language RG presents here, see the extract from *Audubon's Ornithological Biography* published in *Chambers' Edinburgh Journal* 1.18 (June 2, 1832): 144. The extract is entitled "Kentucky Sports."

Page 55

The poor wounded boy, whose name was Buckland I have been unable to trace RG's source for this story, although he may have initially read the accounts in *The Sun*: "*Accidents*" (Apr. 15, 1834: 3 [col. 1]) and "*Moses Elliot*" (Apr. 18, 1834: 2 [col. 1]). There was also a full account in *The Evening Star* entitled "*Terrible Warning against Keeping Bad Company*" (Apr. 11, 1834: 2 [col. 6]).

***The Man*, American paper, dated 13th of May, 1834** See the article entitled "EDUCATION" in *The Man* May 13, 1834: 288 (col. 1). RG's transcription contains minor, innocent errors. He was also confused about his source, writing *"The Sun"* rather than *"The Man"* in the ms.

Page 56

as Longinus has declared RG quotes loosely from the opening paragraph of the second section of *On the Sublime*. See *Classical Literary Criticism: Aristotle; Horace; Longinus* 101.

"The only Art to attain it is to be born to it." The material below this quotation is clearly an afterthought by RG since he deleted a concluding pair of short underlines beneath the quotation from Longinus. In addition, he had to crowd the quotation from the *Boston Transcript* into the bottom third of fol. 160 in order to make it fit.

the *Boston Transcript* of May, 1834 I have been unable to verify RG's quotation.

Page 58

"whilst her Parliament voted a Sum of £10,000 for In the ms., fol. 162 ends here. The verso of fol. 162 contains a deleted false start to the chapter. The text is inverted and indicates that RG obviously changed the contents of this chapter at a fairly late date.

A Narrative of a Pole RG transcribed this story not from *The New-England Galaxy* but from its reprinting in *The Sun* Apr. 9, 1834: 1, cols. 2–3. His transcription is extraordinarily faithful, even down to mimicking *The Sun*'s use of linear asterisks to indicate ellipses in the narrative. His only addition is to translate for his audience the French phrases in the "Narrative."

Page 59

hectic The word is meant in sense B. *sb* 1 of the *OED*: "(ellipt use of the adj.)—A hectic fever."

Page 60

the success which had thus far attended their armies RG mistranscribed the newspaper account at this point and wrote "her armies" rather than "their armies." In this way, he unintentionally turned God into a woman.

Page 63

the *New Orleans Bulletin*, American paper RG actually clipped the letter in its reprinted form from *The Sun* May 16, 1834: 3 (col. 1), where it has the headline "DESPERATE CONFLICT." He pasted it into his ms. unaltered except for the deletion of the headline and the addition of opening and closing quotation marks. There are no paragraph indentions in the original; I have added them to increase ease of reading.

Bexar

At this time Bexar was an important town, the capital of one of the three political departments in Texas. Later, San Antonio grew more important and became the major city in Bexar County. See Richardson 112, and Kane 59.

Page 65

***The New York Commercial Advertiser* of the 29th of May, 1834**

This quotation appears on p. 2, col. 4 of the day's issue. For some reason RG has made the last sentence of the newspaper's account—which is untitled—the first in his transcription; in other ways, too, he has been rather free with the original.
Etawah, Cherokee County, (Georgia) For background, see Kane 92, and Cooper 2: 110. Etawah is now spelt "Etowah."
Cassville A town on the Etowah River (see Cooper 3: 12).
Page 66
It was the same Indian Chief I have been unable to substantiate RG's assertion. It would be more accurate to say that imprisonment, rather than arrest, for debt was abolished in 1832 when President Jackson added his prestige to Colonel Richard M. Johnson's decade-long effort in the U.S. Senate "to abolish imprisonment as a punishment for complaints of debt in federal courts" (Schlesinger, *Age* 134–136).
His celebrated paper in the *Idler* RG is referring to Dr. Johnson's essay "Imprisonment of Debtors," which appeared in *The Idler* for September 16, 1758. See Johnson 69–71.
Another Indian chief I have been unable to trace the source for RG's anecdote.
Page 67
the British-American war, the half pay of which "war, the" is a conjectural addition. The words are lost because the bottom of fol. 171 in the ms. has crumbled.
"White man & Redman I have been unable to find the exact quotation RG uses here.
Page 68
The only idea of independence RG first defined his criticism more narrowly by writing "political independence" rather than simply "independence."
Page 70
the famous Mrs Macaulay Catherine Macaulay, afterward Graham (1731–1791). She was a Republican historian, famous principally for her *History of England* (1763–1783; 8 vols.). Dr. Johnson sparred with her over her radical views. See Drabble 598.
Dr Johnson was one day dining at her table RG spices up a little the version of this episode as it appears in Boswell 1: 447–448.
Page 73
Yet this same Thomas Jefferson RG is thinking of the affair Jefferson is alleged to have had with his mulatto slave Sally Hemings, an affair which supposedly produced several illegitimate light-skinned children. For recent scholarly discussion of the issue see Brodie's and Dabney's accounts. For a fictionalized version of the scandal, see Chase-Riboud. For a recent newspaper account, see Cohen.
one of the *largest slave-owners in America* RG is guilty of hyperbole here, although it is entirely true that Jackson was a slave owner.
Page 74
the *American Quarterly* RG's quotation comes from an article in *The*

Sun entitled "*Slavery*" (Apr. 9, 1834): 4 (col. 1). In the ms. RG mistakenly wrote "American" where the original read "Mexican."
as Cowper so beautifully expresses it The quotation is from *The Task*, Bk. 2: *The Time-Piece* 40–42. RG misquotes Cowper, although he does retain the sense of the original. See *Cowper: Verse and Letters* 418–419.
a New York paper of April, 1834 I have been unable to trace RG's source. *The Sun* for April 2, 1834, however, includes an untitled account—reprinted from the "U.S. Gaz."—of what sounds like the same incident (3 [col. 1]).
at a Coffee-House Slip This slip was located at the foot of Wall Street between Pearl Street and Front Street. It was bracketed by Piers 14 and 15. See Stokes 5: 1595 (col. 2), and "A New Map of the City of New York" in Hardie.
the *New York Standard*, of the 29th of June, 1833 The article RG refers to has the title "NULLIFICATION AMONG THE BLACKS," and appears in *The New-York Standard* June 29, 1833: 1 (col. 7). RG omits a couple of paragraphs from the version in the *Standard*, and in addition makes numerous minor changes; the meaning of the extract remains unaffected.
Page 75
observed the Editor of the New York *Sun* paper I have been unable trace the account to which RG refers.
Page 76
their new Colony *of Liberia* Liberia is the oldest republic on the African continent. It was founded on the site of land bought by the American Colonization Society in 1822. See *Dictionary of Afro-American Slavery* 400–402.
Page 79
as Mr Stuart would say RG is referring to Stuart's *Three Years*. I haven't located the citation, although RG is most likely reacting to Stuart's treatment of his own text as an improvement on the work of Ferrall, Hall, and Trollope. RG would also have found Stuart's even-handed, sympathetic portrait of the Americans irksome.
Page 80
"But," said the poor old man, The text on fol. 185 in the ms. ends with "man,". The verso of f. 185 contains five-and-a-half lines of a false start. The text is inverted and heavily scored through; it seems to be an earlier version of an idea expressed towards the beginning of this chapter.
Page 81
his American fellow-workmen RG first wrote "white" rather than "American."
Page 82
Washington* died a *Slave–Owner RG is correct here, although Washington's Will makes clear that he would have granted his slaves their freedom long before and certainly at his death had it been practi-

cal to do so. This, at least, is Harwell's conclusion (741).
Page 85
New Year's Day For a much more favorable view of the New Year's Day celebrations, see "New Year in New York" in *The New-York Gazette & General Advertiser* Jan. 7, 1834: 2 (cols. 3–4).
young Corydon As the *OED* puts it, Corydon was the "generic proper name in pastoral poetry for a rustic."
Page 86
to make a single effort on my own account The final two sentences of this chapter were originally written—in a slightly altered form—after this phrase. RG deleted them heavily and added the brief anecdote that follows. It's worth noting here that RG's comment is out of character: he was probably married at this time; at least, he had certainly fathered a child four or five years before.
Saturnalia According to the *OED*: "A period of unrestrained licence and revelry."
No wonder there are so many divorces This is an odd point for RG to make at this juncture. He may have been picking up on contemporary newspaper accounts about the high rate of divorce in Ohio; see, for example, *McDowall's Journal* 2.10 (Oct. 1834): 76 (col. 1).
Page 87
But it will be allowed that your money-loving American RG first wrote "Jonathan" instead of "money-loving American." He apparently decided to heighten his description.
"Hard is my fate" RG is probably referring to the song with that title which has the first line, "Hard is the fate of the man that lacks content" (see Havlice 126 [col. 2]). The song is collected in Taylor and Dyk. It's possible that RG could be thinking of "The New Song of the Broom of Cowden Knows," which has a first line: "Hard fate that I should banisht be" (see Chappell 2: 783).
"My Lodging is on the cold ground" Sears lists three songs with this title. It seems likely that the composer of the music was Matthew Lock (or Locke), that there were some traditional words to go with the tune, and that variations on the original lyrics were provided by Gay and by Rochester. RG will have known that his readership would be very familiar with the song to which he refers, for as Chappell points out "My Lodging Is on the Cold Ground" "may be traced in constant favour in England from the time of Charles II down to the present day" (2: 785).
"given the bag" Taylor and Whiting define the term as the equivalent of "jilting" someone. Brewer connects the term via substitution with the earlier phrase "to get the sack" (776 [col. 2]). Farmer suggests that the phrase in its early uses may also have implied "chicanery and cheating" (1: 96).
Apollo RG invokes him here as god of music and poetry.
an anecdote told of our divine Gainsborough I have been unable to find the anecdote to which RG refers. There is, however, a similar tale

testifying to Gainsborough's passion for music in Edwards 133–134, and the *DNB* comments "music at this time [ca. 1750], as afterwards, was the principal amusement of his leisure hours" (7: 803 [col. 1]). For a summary of Gainsborough's life, see *DNB* 7: 801 (col. 2)–807 (col. 1).

Page 89

"Lost is my quiet" RG is almost certainly referring here to the song, "Lost, lost, lost is my quiet forever." It was printed in Dale's *Collection of English Songs* (1780) 1:157, although the song dates from much earlier than that and may originally have been Scots. See Chappell 2: 794–795.

As for RG's familiarity with popular tunes, it is worth remembering the fondness for music implied by his authorship of *The Masonic Melodist*.

a lily . . . elsewhere (end of paragraph) RG wrote this section on fol. 12 of the ms., a torn quarter-leaf.

upon "change" The context here makes it fairly clear that RG means the sense defined in *OED* sb. 3: "A place where merchants meet for the transaction of business, an exchange."

a story of the celebrated English controversial Divines RG only provides an abbreviated version of the anecdote, although he does not distort Nichols' story. RG's use of italics with the phrase "reclining upon his bosom" is his own. For the full anecdote see Nichols 4: 720.

Doctors Samuel Clarke & Arthur Ashley Sykes Clarke (1675–1729) "was generally regarded as the first of English metaphysicians" in the first two or three decades of the eighteenth century (*DNB* 4: 443 [col. 2]). He became involved in the Arian controversy. See *DNB* 4: 443–446 for a biographical sketch. Sykes (1684?–1756) was a latitudinarian divine who spent most of his career at the rectory of Rayleigh in Essex. He was a "voluminous controversial writer of the school of Hoadly" (256 [col. 1]) who became involved in a number of doctrinal disputes. See *DNB* 19: 255 (col. 2)–256 (col. 1) for a biographical sketch.

Rothschild Nathan Meyer, Baron de Rothschild (1777–1836), English banker, father of Lionel Nathan, Baron de Rothschild (1809–1879), English banker and the first Jewish MP. It's not clear whether RG means father, son, or a generic composite.

Cornhill A major commercial center in London between the Poultry and Leadenhall Street. See Wheatley 1: 457–459, and Price.

Page 90

an excellent ballad The ballad is entitled "A Shake by the Hand" and appears in Plumptre's *A Collection of Songs* 1: 281–282 (with the author's name spelled "Plumtre" on the title page). The song is one of the most unintentionally funny compositions I've read. Its first verse goes as follows:

When my hand thus I proffer, your own O deny not,
Nor offer it cold, nor a finger extend;
It freezes my blood when I find a man shy on't.

'Tis delightful when shook with the warmth of a friend

The chorus reads thus:

For the hand of the heart is the index declaring
If well or if ill, how its master will stand;
I heed not the tongue of its friendship that's swearing,
I judge of a friend by the shake of his hand.

Dr. Charles Hague Dr. Charles Hague (1769–1821); see *DNB* 8: 883.
the late Theo^{n} James Plumptre James Plumptre (1770–1832) is described by the *DNB* as a "dramatist and divine" (15: 1324 [col. 2]). See *DNB* 15: 1324–1325 for a biographical sketch. RG spells his last name "Plumptree" in the ms.
Page 91
An article extracted from the *New York Gazette* The article RG cites (which is entitled "EXCESSIVE HEAT IN AMERICA") appeared in *The Times* (London) Aug. 16, 1834: 5 (col. 3). RG quotes the entire piece, doing so with very minor changes only.
Page 92
a showy store headed "Ready Made Coffins" See Hamilton's *Men and Manners in America* for a similar comment:

> As we passed, many of the signs exhibited by the different shops struck me as similar . . . . "COFFIN WAREHOUSE," however, was sufficiently explanatory of the nature of the commerce carried on within.

Page 93
***The New York Standard* of 1833** I have been unable to trace RG's reference.
Page 94
***The Petersburg Intelligencer*, a Virginia paper** RG actually took this quotation from the article's reprinting, under the headline "DESTRUCTIVE TORNADO," in *The Man* 1.71 (May 13, 1834): 286 (col. 2). There are some changes in spelling and words. *The Petersburg Intelligencer* (which *The Man* gives as its source and which RG spells "Presburgh Intelligencer") is presumably *The Intelligencer and Petersburg Commercial Advertiser*, which was published between 1786 and 1860.
the county of Lunenburg Lunenburgh, VA. The extract from *The Man* spells the name "Lunenburg"; RG spells it "Lunenburgh." See Kane 234.
Notaway Courthouse Presumably Nottoway, county seat of Nottoway County, VA. See Kane 273.
Page 95
***The New York Advertiser* of the 2$^{\underline{nd}}$ of June, 1834** See *The New-York Commercial Advertiser* June 2, 1834: 1 (col. 5).
Florence, Alabama County seat of Lauderdale County. See Kane 220.

Pulaski, Tennessee County seat of Giles County. See Kane 155.
The same paper of the previous 29th of May See *The New-York Commercial Advertiser* May 29, 1834: 2 (col. 4).
Spartanburgh & Greenville, S.C. Spartanburg, SC, county seat of Spartanburg County; and Greenville, SC, county seat of Greenville County. See Kane 336 and 164.
Page 97
Monsieur Chabert *Longworth's American Almanac, New-York Register, and City Directory* includes the following entry:

> Chabert J. Xavier botanic physician 322 Broadway.

This may be the same Chabert as the one mentioned in Haswell 279. See also the testimonial to Dr. Chabert with which RG concludes this chapter.
a lady physician in Delancy Street *Longworth's American Almanac* includes the following entry:

> Bird widow Esther, doctoress 39 Delancey (125)

Blue-pill *Webster's Third New International Dictionary* defines "blue pill" as "*n. 1*: a pill of prepared mercury used esp. as an aperient *2:* BLUE MASS (where BLUE MASS is defined as *n. pharmacy*: a pillular preparation containing finely divided mercury—called also *blue pill, mass of mercury.*"
calomel See *The New-York Gazette & General Advertiser* July 2, 1834, which includes an advertisement entitled: "GUMS, DRUGS AND CHEMICALS, 115 maiden-lane." This lists (among other things for sale): "30 do [cases] Colomel [*sic*]" (1 [col. 5]).
ad libitum at one's pleasure.
Page 98
Morison's pills. The *Biographical Sketch of James Morison, the Hygeist . . .* bears out RG's comment about the popularity of Morison's pills. According to this self-serving source, 828,000,000 had been consumed by January 1849, with a further 1,500,000 being taken in the form of "family packets" (6).
Page 99
The following admirable specimen This "communication" (part of an advertisement) appeared in *The Sun* Apr. 15, 1834: 3 (col. 2). RG clipped it out of the paper and pasted it into the ms.
The Hygeist School A regimen of health founded on the supposed value of frequent vegetable purgation in purifying the blood and the entire system. T. Moat claims that such a regimen can cure depression, sciatica, eruptions, measles, wasting, asthma, cholera, fits, dropsy, toothache, and general debility. See his *Practical Proofs* (45) for an explanation of the philosophy behind the Hygeists. The Hygeists were governed by the British College of Health, with James Morison as president and Thomas Moat as vice president.
Page 100

They are eternally talking of their peaches Hedrick seems to support RG's skepticism about American fruit, at least in New York state (see 383, 389, 391). By contrast, Fearon's *Sketches* comments "The quality of provisions I think is, in general, very good" (44).
***The New York Advertiser* of the 3rd of June, 1834** RG quotes from a short article entitled "EARLY FRUIT" in *The New-York Commercial Advertiser* June 3, 1834: 2 (col. 5). RG omits only an unimportant clause from the item.
one of the Royal Horticultural establishments RG is probably referring to the Royal Horticultural Society's garden at Chiswick (1821–1861). The garden was 33 acres in size; it should not be confused with the three-hundred-acre Royal Botanic Gradens at Kew. See Wheatley 2: 234–235, and Weinreb and Hibbert 674.
especially in Harrow Harrow-on-the-Hill in Middlesex.
Captain's biscuit The *OED* defines this food as a "hard variety of fancy biscuit."
for the bakers to ruin the most delicious matter with it In the ms. RG wrote "deliterious." It is hard to know what word RG intended here. "Deleterious" is close in spelling but far away in meaning; "delicious" is farther away in spelling, but closer in meaning. I have adopted the latter reading, albeit speculatively.
Page 102
the philosopher's stone *Brewer's Dictionary* defines this stone as "The hypothetical substance which, according to the alchemists, would convert all baser metals into gold; by many it was thought to be compounded of the purest sulphur and mercury" (858 [col. 2]).
Page 105
As politicians they are perfect babies RG wrote "they are either perfect" and then deleted material after this sentence, part of which probably included the correlative "or." Logic demands eliminating "either."
Well might the editor of the *Cosmopolite* I have been unable to locate this comment.
Page 106
vox et praeterea nihil This phrase means "a voice and nothing more." For its first use, see Plutarch's *Apophthegmata Laconica* 233a (cited in *Brewer's Dictionary* 1169 [col.2]).
Yet a member of the American Congress It is difficult to know to what event precisely RG is referring, since as foreign secretary Canning was responsible for commercial treaties with a number of South American countries in the mid-1820s, among them Rio de la Plata, Colombia, and Brazil. See Parry Vols. 74 (1823–1824), 75 (1824–1825), and 77 (1826–1827) *passim*.
Mr. Canning George Canning (1770–1827): Foreign secretary (1807–1809; 1822–1827); prime minister (Apr.–Aug. 1827). See *DNB* 3: 872–883 (col. 1), and Treasure 246–254.
the President of which people For the assault on Jackson, see "Brutal

Assault upon the President of the United States," in *The Evening Post* May 8, 1833: 2 (col. 4). The assault was not, however, carried out by a member of Congress but, rather, by a Mr. Randolph, who had been recently discharged from the Navy. The story is continued in *The Evening Post* on May 13, 15, and 17.

as the *Montreal Herald* did lately to the French Canadians RG gets these quotations from *The Sun* Apr. 9, 1834: 4 (col. 1). His transition also appropriates some wording from the same brief article. The article was reprinted from the *New England Galaxy* and given the title "*Liberty.*"

Papineau Louis Joseph Papineau (1786–1871) He was a politician and lawyer, and Speaker of the House of Assembly for Lower Canada from 1815 to 1837. In 1834 he encouraged the Canadians to seek greater self-determination and independence from Britain. See the *Cambridge Biographical Dictionary*.

Page 107

"It is not generally known," RG's source for this article (entitled "Jewing") is *The Sun* Apr. 9, 1834: 2 (col. 3). RG quotes the entire article except for the final sentence; there are only minor changes from the original.

the present quarrel The quarrel between Jackson and the U.S. Bank dated from 1820 and Jackson's opposition to the Tennessee relief-system. It was exacerbated by Jackson's belief that banking interests had funded his opponents during the 1828 election. It peaked on July 10, 1832 with Jackson's veto of the bill renewing the charter of the Second U.S. Bank. Thereafter, with the help of Roger B. Taney, Jackson weakened the U.S. Bank by depositing government funds in eighty-nine reliable state banks. By 1836, the power of the U.S. Bank had been broken; however, the economic insecurity that resulted caused in part the severe depression of the late 1830s. Jackson's dislike of the U.S. Bank was based on principle and on his support for the idea of "hard money." For general discussions of this complex quarrel, see Faulkner 244–246, and Schlesinger's *Political and Social History* 40–47. For more detailed accounts, see Schlesinger's *Age* Chs. 7–10, and Catterall. For the effect of the Bank crisis on New York (RG's focus), see Benson Ch. 3.

"no wonder the times are hard" Quoted from *The Sun* May 16, 1834: 2 (col. 3).

Mordecai Noah Mordecai Manuel Noah (1785–1851) was a lawyer, playwright, and journalist of Portuguese-Jewish ancestry. His contribution to journalism in New York included editing the *National Advocate* in 1817, establishing *The New York Enquirer* in 1826, and *The Evening Star* in 1833. RG's dislike of Noah was probably both political and religious. See *DAB* 7: 534–535 (col. 1).

his notorious project Noah's project was to move a number of the world's 7,000,000 Jews to his refuge of the City of Ararat on Grand Island on the Niagara River in Erie County, New York (or, as RG disparagingly terms it, "Mud Island"). The idea was conceived of in 1820, and promoted in September 1825 through a Manifesto to the Jews. Although he had purchased 2,555 acres for the city and erected a monument to the enterprise, the project was quickly abandoned when it received no Jewish support. See French 290–291, 291n1, and *The Jewish Encyclopedia* 2: 74–75 (col. 1); 9: 323–324.

Page 109

"When Greek meets Greek, then comes the tug of war" RG slightly misquotes from Nathaniel Lee's play *The Rival Queens; or, the Death of Alexander the Great* IV.i.421.

Nathaniel Lee (ca. 1650–1692) was a minor Restoration dramatist, and *The Rival Queens* his best-known play. The line RG quotes is, according to Stroup and Cooke, "usually misquoted" and "probably the most famous in all Lee's works" (Lee 1: 472).

But "The President," says *The Man* These two quotations come from the lead column of *The Man* 1.71 (May 13, 1834): 285. The column takes up the whole of the front page of the issue, and is entitled "GOOD NEWS!!" RG makes some minor changes.

Page 110

***The Sun* American paper of the 9th of April, 1834** RG's quotation comes from an article entitled "*The Election*" in *The Sun* Apr. 9, 1834: 2 (col. 1). RG extracts only paragraphs three and four from the article, which is five paragraphs in length. He has made only minor changes to the portion of the original he quotes.

the Elections of May, 1834 Does RG mean the New York mayoral elections of April 1834? the Brooklyn Charter election of May 5, 1834? or even, possibly, the Virginia election of May 1834?

Page 111

Major Jack Downing This pseudonym was used by two writers in 1834, Charles Augustus Davis and Seba Smith. The former produced *Letters of J. Downing, Major Downingville Militia, Second Brigade . . .*; the latter, *The Select Letters of Major Jack Downing of the Downingville Militia. . . .* For an example of Downing's anti–Jackson, pro–Bank stance, see his letter in *The New-York Commercial Advertiser* December 3, 1833: 2 (col. 4). In the ms. RG incorrectly spells his name "Dowling."

"Before I conclude," I have been unable to trace RG's quotation, presumably from *The Sun*.

Page 112

Whilst I am upon the subject of English Democrats RG began a false start here: "Emigr." He apparently intended to write "Emigrants" and substituted "Democrats."

In the *Crisis* American paper I have been unable to trace RG's quotation from the article "Republican Young Men" in *The Crisis*. *The Crisis* was a tri-weekly newspaper, first published, probably, on March 20, 1834. *American Newspapers 1821–1936* gives no date for when the newspaper was last published. The Library of Congress possesses only one issue (for March 27, 1834). *The Crisis* was clearly a very short-

lived newspaper.
Page 113
The following is a List of the Salaries RG has pasted this lengthy extract (greatly abbreviated here)—actually newspaper clippings from *The Crisis*—into the ms. RG has deleted some short sentences from the clippings, but since no copy of *The Crisis* for this date exists, it is impossible to tell what words RG struck through.
Page 115
An American cannot keep or drive a common cart Williams' *New York As It Is in 1834* supports RG's assertion by listing the fee for licensing as $2.00 when first licensed, and 12¢ annually when renewed (173).
Page 117
Nor could any honest man entertain RG is unfair about the election for mayor of New York in April 1834. He is correct about the violence at the election, but neglects to point out (or, he may not have known) that this was the first occasion since the election of Peter Delanoy in October 1689 that the people of New York were allowed to elect a mayor by popular vote. The state constitution was amended on November 4–6, 1833 to permit such a vote, and the city charter was similarly altered on March 3, 1834 (see Stokes 5: 1726 [col. 2]).

The two mayoral candidates were Cornelius W. Lawrence (the Jackson, anti-Bank, and Tammany candidate) and Gulian C. Verplanck (the Bank candidate). On April 10, 1834, Lawrence won by 179 votes (203 according to Haswell [287]). On May 13, 1834, he was inducted into office. As Haswell comments, the election produced such fervor "as never was witnessed before or since" (287).
Page 118
"Never before," says the *Sun* American paper I have been unable to trace RG's reference.
the Elections of 1833 Does RG mean the Ward elections for Charter officers, held between April 9 and April 11, 1833? See the advertisements in, for example, *The New-York Commercial Advertiser* Apr. 2, 1833: 3 (col. 1). For the intensity of election fever, see "CHARTER ELECTION" in *The New-York Commercial Advertiser* Apr. 6, 1833: 2 (col. 1).
"It is worthy of remark I have been unable to trace this quotation by RG.
Governor Marcy William Learned Marcy (1786–1857) was the eleventh governor of New York (1833–1839). He held various state and national offices before becoming a three-time governor of New York. See *New York Biographical Dictionary* . . . 348–349, and the *Biographical Directory of the Governors of the United States 1789–1978* 3: 1076–1077. In the ms. RG spells Marcy "Mercy."
Page 120
"O! Shades of Washington, &c. RG is inaccurate about *The Sun* here. The exclamation is inserted *not* in a leader but in the "POLICE

OFFICE.—(Yesterday)" column. RG also misquotes the exclamation slightly and wrongly indicates that the newspaper says the Irishman was attacked by "6000 Americans." The copy actually reads: "One Irishman . . . drove before him more than 2000 men." The article appeared in *The Sun* Apr. 12, 1834: 2 (col. 2), and describes an event which took place on April 10, 1834.

One American paper, the *Evening Star* RG originally wrote a prepositional phrase after the newspaper's name: "in the interest of the Bank," but deleted it. I have been unable to trace RG's quotation.

One fellow RG extracts this quotation from a piece entitled "*Good!*" in *The Sun* Apr. 9, 1834: 2 (col. 3). In the ms. he has his dates wrong: the date of the episode was April 8; he wrote April 10.

the Fourth Ward According to Williams' *New York As It Is in 1834*, the Fourth Ward ran "from Spruce and Ferry streets, and Peck-slip, east, to Catherine-street" and was "bounded on the north by Chatham-street, south, by the East River" (192).

after the fashion of London Omnibuses According to DeVoe, *The New-York Gazette and General Advertiser* of August 20, 1833 describes an "Omnibus Line called 'Red Rover' from Wall, Chatham, Bowery, Fourth to Military Hall 6th Av" (2: 303). See also DeVoe 2: 303, 306.

Page 121

and another marked "Mayor." RG wrote "backed." That is surely an error; I have emended it to the closest likely word.

the Bank Candidate, Verplanck Gulian Crommelin Verplanck (1786–1870) served in a number of elected offices at both the state and national levels before and after running unsuccessfully for the office of the Mayor of New York. See *DAB* 10: 253–254.

as regards *forged* or *spoiled* Tickets What RG talks of here was noted by the press at the time. See, for example, an article entitled "TICKETS, TICKETS!" in *The Evening Star* Apr. 8, 1834: 2 (col. 4). The article warns voters to look out for fraudulent Verplanck ballots (missing the "k" or "c").

Page 122

Each master . . . truth RG wrote this section on a torn, unnumbered half-leaf in the ms. between fol. 38 and fol. 39.

Page 123

the New York petition See Stokes 5: 1723 (col. 2); McMaster, *History of the People of the United States* 6: 202; and Haswell 286. For the results of separate petitions by merchants and mechanics to the president, see *Courier and Enquirer* Feb. 7, 17, and 25, 1834.

***The Crisis*, American paper** I have been unable to verify RG's quotation.

***The Man* American paper, in a letter** The letter, which was published in *The Man* 1.71 (May 13, 1834): 286 (col. 1) in its "*Correspondence of 'The Man'*" column, was transcribed by RG with only minor changes. One of the changes, however, makes nonsense of the extract

by implying that the name of the man was "*Crockery*"; in fact, as the letter makes clear, he was a "*Crockery* merchant."
Pages 123–24
the expatriated Poles For a discussion of these expatriates, see *The New-York Gazette and General Advertiser* May 15 and June 5, 1834 (cited in DeVoe 2: 307).
Page 124
'our quiet Ballot-box' The source for this quotation is likely to be the *Journal of Commerce*, because in an article entitled "THE RIOTS" in *The Evening Star* Apr. 11, 1834: 2 (col. 2), the editor refers to extracting (i.e. paraphrasing) "an account of the riots of yesterday from the Journal of Commerce," and continues: "Well, we have had quite *a peaceable appeal to the ballot boxes. . . .*"
the editor of the Evening Star RG's opinion of Mordecai Noah is supported by the editor of *The Evening Post*, who remarks—in an article on *The Evening Star*:

> When the editor of that print puts his pen to paper, no matter what the theme he is going to write, it is ten to one that the first ten lines will contain a positive and wilful falsehood. (Dec. 30, 1833: 2 [col. 4])

in the pages of a contemporary paper I have been unable to verify RG's quotation.
Page 125
a book appeared, by a Methodist Preacher RG is almost certainly referring to Calvin Colton's *Church and State in America. Part II. Review of the Bishop of London's Reply*. The book was mentioned in an article entitled "Ministers in the United States" in *The Sun* Apr. 29, 1834: 2 (col. 1).
Girard's *Sketch of All Religions* I have been unable to trace RG's reference.
"The number of sects The article RG transcribes appeared under the headline "RELIGION IN AMERICA" in *The Times* (London) July 28, 1834: 3 (col. 2). It was reprinted from the *Subaltern's Furlough*.
Girard's College *The Evening Star* Apr. 22, 1834: 2 (col. 2) has an article entitled "*Girard College*." It concerns the construction of Girard College in Philadelphia, which began in Spring 1834.
Page 126
a *Taylor* or a *Carlile* Robert Taylor (1784–1844) was a deistical writer educated at St. John's College, Cambridge. RG would have thought of him not simply because he went to the same college at Cambridge, but also because he became notorious after being found guilty once in 1828 and again in 1831 of blasphemous discourse. He was a friend of Carlile. See *DNB* 19: 461–463.

Richard Carlile was a freethinker who was fined often during the 1820s and 1830s for publishing seditious journals and pamphlets. RG would have thought of him because of his celebrated trial in the 1830s arising out of the liberty of speech promoted at the Rotunda on Blackfriars Road in London. See *DNB* 3: 1009–1012. In the ms., RG misspells Carlile "Carlisle."

Alexander Keilden I have been unable to trace this reference.

I happened to be one day I have been unable to trace which case RG might be referring to.

One of their pastors RG may have taken this story from *The Sun* Mar. 15, 1834: 2 (col. 2), where it is headlined "*Tragical Event*." It is said to have come from the editor of the *Independent Messenger*. The event apparently took place in the western part of New York State.

Page 127

One of the most singular persecutions I have been unable to trace the article (*Persecution*) which RG has clipped and pasted into the ms. It may possibly be a reprinting of an article entitled "The Disturbances in Jackson County" written by Isaac McCoy. It was originally published in the *Western Monitor*, but was reprinted in the *Missouri Republican* on December 20, 1833. RG himself seems uncertain of his source, for in the ms. he has struck through the the words "*St. Louis Inquirer*" before settling on the far more general "an American paper." RG has only made a few alterations to the clipping, such as deleting proper names. His intent in so doing seems to have been simply to enable the text to flow more smoothly.

The best recent discussion of RG's topic is Richard L. Bushman's "Mormon Persecutions in Missouri."

Page 131

***The Sun* American Paper of May, 1834** I have been unable to trace RG's quotation.

the Society for the *promotion of the Seventh Commandment* With regard to the Society's owing its existence to *McDowall's Journal*, see Timothy Dwight's "Seventh Commandment—Lewdness" in *McDowall's Journal* 1.10 (Oct. 1833): 73–75 (col. 2). For the Constitution and membership of the society, as well as the history of its organization, see the article entitled "Moral Reform" in *McDowall's Journal* 2.1 (Jan. 1834): 6 (col. 2)–7.

In the ms. RG spelled "McDowall's," "McDowell's."

Page 132

This society probably owes its existence RG is correct in his assertion about the connection between the American Society for Promoting the Observance of the Seventh Commandment and *McDowall's Journal*. *McDowall's Journal*, which was edited by the Reverend J. R. McDowall, was the mouthpiece for the society. The journal ceased publication with Vol. 2.12 (Dec. 1834).

The grand jury criticized *McDowall's Journal* as "a 'public nuisance,' calculated to increase the very evil it professes to prevent, and inviting the young to the gratification of criminal passions" (quoted in the "COURT OF SESSIONS—(Yesterday)" column in *The Sun* Mar. 15, 1834: 2 [col. 2]).

The same authority RG quotes here from a story entitled "*Kissing with an appetite*" in *The Sun* Apr. 9, 1834: 3 (col. 1). His alterations are very minor.
the county of Surry This could be either Surry, NC or Surry, VA (see Kane 344–345).
the writings of Mrs Trollope, and to the more recent publication of Mr Ferrall For Mrs. Trollope's discussion of camp-meetings, see Ch. 15 (167–175) of her *Domestic Manners of the Americans*. For Ferrall's discussion of camp-meetings, see *A Ramble of Six Thousand Miles through the United States of America* 71–78. See also Stuart's *Three Years* 2: 554–555.
Page 133
One man, now a popular preacher I have been unable to identify RG's reference, although the contents headnote for this chapter includes a reference to a "Parson Frey," who is not otherwise named by RG. This may, then, be the name of the "popular preacher."
a popular preacher at Brooklyn I have been unable to identify RG's reference. RG's comment about Brooklyn having recently achieved the status of a city is correct: it received its city charter on April 8, 1834.
the Revd E.K. Avery Ephraim Kingsbury Avery was born in Coventry, CT, the son of a farmer. After trying various pursuits, he finally decided to become a minister of the Methodist Church. In 1827 he became an elder. He was found not guilty of Cornell's murder on June 3, 1833; he died on October 23, 1869. For a recent discussion of the entire Avery-Cornell case, see Kasserman.

RG could hardly have failed to notice the case: it was given a great deal of newspaper and small-press coverage at the time. See, for example, *The New-York Commercial Advertiser* for May 25, 30, June 1, 3, 4, 5, 6, 8, 11, 17, July 10, 15, August 20, and September 7, 1833, and *The New-York Gazette and General Advertiser* for May 21, 22, 31, June 1, 3, 5, 6, 14, 18, and December 30, 1833 (cited in DeVoe 2: 300–302). Public opinion was overwhelmingly against Avery.
Sarah Maria Cornell Born May 3, 1802 in Rupert, VT. As an adolescent, she converted to Congregationalism. By the early 1820s she had earned a reputation as a thief. She converted to Methodism in 1825, and underwent a church trial, possibly for lewdness, in 1826. She was re–admitted to the Methodist Church in 1827, and worked briefly as a domestic servant in Avery's household in Lowell, MA. She died on December 20, 1832.
Moloch *Brewer's Dictionary* defines this term as "Any influence which demands from us the sacrifice of what we hold most dear" (748 [col. 1]).
Page 134
enceinte The highly euphemistic term for "pregnant." In French, it literally means "girdled."
Doctor Wilbur Dr. Thomas Wilbur, Cornell's physician.
oil of Tansy Also known as Sodium Taurocholate and Taurocholic

Acid, tansy oil is, according to *Webster's Third New International Dictionary*, "a yellow poisonous essential oil obtained from the leaves and tops of the common tansy."
Page 136
Amongst other instances I have been unable to trace RG's quotation.
the camp meeting at Thompson This meeting occurred in late August 1832 in Thompson, CT.
Fall River Fall River, MA. See Fowler's *An Historical Sketch of Fall River*.
Mrs Bidwell also, wife of the Rev$^{\underline{d}}$ Ira M. Bidwell Mrs. Nancy Bidwell and the Reverend Bidwell, a Methodist minister from Fall River.
Page 137
M$^{\underline{rs}}$ Mayo Betsy Mayo—she had known Cornell in Lowell and befriended her.
for which he was tried & convicted. Those RG began another train of thought between these two sentences, part of which is decipherable: "Up the country the power of these pastors." He deleted the incomplete idea.
Page 138
the whole account forming a large volume RG is referring to one of several books on the case. Indeed, there were no less than fourteen different books about the case published in the United States in 1833 and 1834, one of which—by Richard Hildreth—apparently went through three editions in one year (1833). The case was notorious enough to be written about as late as 1876 in *The Terrible Hay-Stack Murder*.
a Hume, a Cobbett David Hume (1711–1776) was one of the major philosophers of the eighteenth century. RG's dislike would have been based on three factors: Hume's repect for polytheism, his attack upon the mercantile system, and his political pragmatism. RG did, however, respect Hume's ideas enough apparently to read them: he owned a copy of his *Essays and Treatises* (1825; 2 vols.) (see Puttick and Simpson lot no. 641). See Drabble 482 (col. 2)– 483 (col. 1), and Stapleton 428–429.

William Cobbett (1762–1835) was one of the major radical thinkers in England at the end of the eighteenth century. It is hard to isolate one text that RG may be objecting to here; it is more likely that RG vilifies Cobbett as a radical and a threatening authority on American culture. See Drabble 208, and Stapleton 176 (col. 2)–177.
Page 140
Chapter X Above the title RG wrote "Sunday" and then deleted it.
Sir Andrew Agnew's Sabbath Observance Bill Sir Andrew Agnew (1793–1849) actually introduced a Sabbath Observance Bill four times between 1832 and 1837. The first three times it was defeated; the fourth time it was carried by 110 to 66, but was never enacted into law since Parliament was dissolved after the death of William IV. See *DNB* 1: 178.
Drunken Barnaby's Puritan The reference is to Richard Brathwait's

Drunken Barnaby's Four Journeys to the North of England (1805) 5. For a discussion of the printing history of this text and the history of its author, see Black's *Richard Brathwait: An Account of His Life and Works*, especially pp. 105–114.
with the exception of the English portion at their Church RG is referring to the Central Presbyterian Church (or Centre Church), which was built in 1821. Broome Street ran from "the East River to Greenwich at Canal-street, crossing the Bowery and Broadway" (Hardie 208).
Page 141
which we might expect them to observe in a degree After this phrase, the ms. appears to continue on; the folio (59) has, however, only been crudely cut.
our Hyde Park drive Hyde Park, as a public park, dates from the early sixteenth century. Until as late as 1825, the west end of the park was gated and constituted one of the major entrances into London. See Wheatley 2: 249–256, and Weinreb and Hibbert 400 (col. 2)–403 (col. 2).
Page 142
pigtail The *OED* defines "pigtail" (under sense 1) as "Tobacco twisted into a thin rope or roll."
I was one day in a New York Court I have been unable to trace the case to which RG refers.
One case I heard I have been unable to trace the case to which RG refers.
Page 143
the notorious Sheriff Perkins *The Evening Post* for December 12, 1833: 2 (cols. 6–7) has a story (which originally appeared in *The New-York Standard*) entitled "SHERIFF PARKINS," which concerns a suit against Sheriff Parkins brought before the Marine Court on December 11 by the sculptor H. J. Brower. This may be the "Perkins" to whom RG refers.
tailor's goose Brewer defines this object as "A tailor's smoothing-iron, so called because its handle resembles the neck of a goose" (355 [col. 2]).
One case happened during 1833, of a man named Wilson RG may be referring to the case of George Wilson, an Englishman who was found guilty of Grand Larceny and sentenced to five years imprisonment. *The Sun* May 9, 1834: 2 (col. 2) highlights Wilson's nationality in an article entitled "*Trollopism*." Four days later, *The Sun* notes: "George Wilson, attempt to commit Grand Larceny, State Prison 2 years 6 months" (May 13, 1834: 2 [col. 2]). If this is the case RG is referring to then he is inaccurate as to date and length of sentence.
Sing-Sing The New York State prison at Ossining, built in 1825 (see Ellis 245).
Page 144
And the *New York Advertiser* of the 31st of May RG quotes from a

piece entitled "CIRCUIT COURT, AND OYER AND TERMINER" in *The New-York Commercial Advertiser* May 31, 1834: 2 (col. 4).

I was witness to a case of the latter kind For a contemporary newspaper account of the case, see *"The Unfortunate Negress"* in *The Sun* Apr. 21, 1834: 2 (col. 3)–3 (col. 1). *The Sun*'s account only gives Wright's name as "J——W——."

Staten Island In RG's time, Staten Island formed the county of Richmond, New York (see Williams' *New York As It Is in 1834* 221).

the watchman For New York City's use of watchmen at this time, see Williams' *New York As It Is in 1834* 37.

Page 145

Another instance of the way I have been unable to trace RG's story.

The following is a Specimen RG pasted this clipping, from the "POLICE OFFICE—(Yesterday Morning) column," into his ms. from *The Sun* May 16, 1834: 2 (col. 3). He deleted one two-line item from the clipping (the case of Janette Brown), which appeared between those of Mary Dehilton and Robert Kidd. He did so in order to use the story elsewhere; see Vol. II, Ch. XV (p. 155). RG also made some editing marks on the clipping that suggest he *may* not have meant the whole to be typeset; interpreting the marks with any certainty is, however, impossible.

Page 146

"the good old Bridwell" Since at least 1593, "Bridewell" has—according to the *OED*—generically denoted a prison. Here, however, the judge refers to a specific prison in New York City. Williams' *New York As It Is in 1833* locates the prison at Bellevue in the Sixth Ward. It housed those convicted of petty larceny and those remanded for trial. According to Hemstreet, the prison was torn down in 1838 (35). An indication of the speed with which New York City was changing at this time is that another source, this one from the late 1820s, describes Bridewell very differently (see Hardie 188–189, 191, 205).

"black and secret midnight hag" *The Sun* misquotes Shakespeare's *Macbeth* IV.i.48.

Page 147

Labour Scarce . . . Climate The chapter subheadings have been pasted over some text underneath.

the *Sun* American paper of March, 1834 observes I have been unable to trace RG's quotation. There's a possibility that RG was himself uncertain of the date. He deleted "the 15th of" before "March" in the ms.

Page 148

the English *truck-system* *Brewer's Dictionary* defines this as a system where employees where paid—completely or partly—with good or vouchers rather than with money. These vouchers would be redeemable only at employer-owned or -operated stores (also known as Tommy shops). Acts of Parliament in England in 1831, 1881, and 1896 almost entirely eradicated the practice (see 1140 [col. 1]).

Page 149

the British Museum Established in 1753 with a Foundation Act that purchased the collection of Sir Hans Sloane, the British Museum first opened to the public on January 15, 1759. Many of its present buildings date from RG's time (the 1820s and 1830s). See Weinreb and Hibbert 89 (col. 2)–91 (col. 1), and Wheatley 1: 251–276.
The *painters' cholic* Quain defines this illness as a form of intestinal colic associated with lead poisoning. Its effect was what Quain terms a "retracted abdomen" (1351 [col. 1]).
Page 150
"Sawdy Wood" I have been unable to find a citation for this slang term; however, it is not difficult to see how the phrase would have been formed: by abbreviation of the phrase RG mentions, "any Wood to be sawed today, Sir?" Fearon's *Sketches*, from earlier in the nineteenth century, observes a similar scene: "Most of the streeets are dirty: in many of them sawyers are preparing wood for sale, and all are infested with pigs,—. . ." (11).
sub juge The phrase means "under the yoke."
Page 152
"an American carries his whole wardrobe on his back" I have been unable to find a reference source listing this saying.
Blackwell's Island When RG wrote his account, Blackwell's Island was a very new prison, less than six years old in fact. See Stokes 6: 319 (col. 3), and Williams' *New York As It Is in 1833* 37. In his ms. RG spells the prison's name "Blackwall Island."
Mendicity Society The *OED* sense 3 of "Mendicity" gives a quotation from Theodore E. Hook's *Sayings and Doings* Series 1 (1824) which defines the Society as "an institution which proposes to check beggary by the novel method of giving nothing to the poor" (3: 329). Hook is being ironic and probably accurate; RG is being serious and probably disingenuous.
Page 153
"with poverty there is always pride" I have been unable to locate this quotation, although the conjunction of poverty and pride occurs as early as John Wilmot, Earl of Rochester's "Like a Great Family": "oppressed with pride and poverty" (see Bartlett 315 [col. 2]). Alliteration makes such a conjunction natural.
St Paul's St Paul's Cathedral was designed by Sir Christopher Wren and built under the supervision of Thomas Strong between 1675 and 1710. It is acknowledged as an architectural masterpiece. See Weinreb and Hibbert 756 (col. 2)–760, and Wheatley 3: 45–52.
their *city*-Hall Hardie is in disagreement with RG. He considered New York's City Hall (also known as the Temple of Justice) "the handsomest structure in the United States; perhaps (of its size) in the world" (331).
London University Coincidentally in *The Evening Star* for April 12, 1834, there is an engraving of the University of London with captions praising the central façade's "portico" and "ten Corinthian columns." This building later became University College. London University is

not to be confused with the University of London, which was founded in 1836 by the government of Lord Melbourne. See Weinreb and Hibbert 903.

Page 154

but his hand is up to his hat RG wrote:"but his hat is up to his hand." That doesn't make sense, and so I have corrected it.

Page 155

Punch For the origins of Punch (and the Punch and Judy show), see *Brewer's Dictionary* 904 (col. 2).

the wandering piper RG takes his reference from an article entitled "*The wandering Piper*" in *The Sun* May 10, 1834: 3 (col. 1). The article, which originally appeared in the *Reading Chronicle*, describes a street musician in Pennsylvania who gives his earnings to the poor.

as in the case of the dog Tyke See the annotation to p. 21.

In the police report in the *Sun* American paper See the "POLICE OFFICE—(Yesterday Morning)" column in *The Sun* May 16, 1834: 2 (col. 3).

Blackwell's Island See the annotation to p. 152.

they are left to the mercy of the world RG followed this clause with a further sentence: "I could not learn that any provision was made for them: nor indeed that there was anything in the shape of poor laws independent of this barbarous provision." He subsequently deleted it, presumably because he didn't have evidence for his assertion.

Page 156

The Old Countryman *American Newspapers 1821–1836* (474) gives the full title of this newspaper as *Old Countryman: and English, Irish, Scotch, Welsh, and Colonial Mirror*. It was published between 1829 and 1835.

Page 157

He had . . . claim RG clearly botched a revision here. The original reads: "He had scarcely taken possession when the Sheriff of New York entered & seized & sold every article, which the Yankee, it appeared, had forfeited all claim to, of whom he had bought them." I have emended the text as conservatively as possible in order to restore sense to the sentence.

for debts his predecessor had contracted and I believe forgone RG committed a solecism here by writing "forwent." Even my correction slightly misuses the verb "forgo"; it does, however, make the sense clearer.

Page 159

"Jonathan had proved too *smart* for him." The word "Jonathan" finishes fol. 82. On that folio's verso, RG struck through a false start to this chapter.

Page 160

Save the mark According to *Brewer's Dictionary*, this phrase is used either to apologize for mentioning something disagreeable or to ward off evil. The "mark" may be the sign of the cross (712 [col. 2]). The

closest equivalent today is perhaps "God forbid!"
Botany Bay Located just south of Sydney, Australia, the bay was—from 1788—the disembarkation point for English convicts transported to Australia. The penal colony itself was located at Port Jackson. See *Brewer's Dictionary* 140 (col. 1).
they must become *firemen* for a period of 7 years See the annotation to p. 21.
probably some capricious Yankey *cartman* RG clearly dislikes New York City's cartmen. For a more sympathetic view, see the letter from "A NATIVE" in *The New-York Gazette & General Advertiser* Jan. 30, 1834: 2 (cols. 3–4).
to look down upon their *betters* with contempt In the ms. RG follows this sentence with another: "Yet a writer in one of their own Newspapers, (*The Cosmopolite*), declared that *the Americans are only republicans by birth, Englishmen* ***by principle.***" RG used this remark earlier, in Volume I Chapter I. On that occasion, too, he struck it out.
Page 162
Chapter XVII Above the chapter title is a deleted version of the chapter's subheadings. The chapter title and subheadings are written on a one-third size, numbered folio (85) which obscures the folio underneath (86).
Cobbett's *Emigrant's Guide* See the annotation to p. 7.
Chambers's *Edinburgh Journal* on the Subject of Emigration *Chambers's Edinburgh Journal* was published from 1832 to 1843 and edited by William and Robert Chambers. The discussion of emigration appeared quite frequently in 1832 and 1834 in a column of that name in the journal, with most of the early material extracted from Ferguson's "Notes Made during a Visit to the United States and Canada, in 1831" (originally published in the *Agricultural Journal*).

RG may have been objecting to the general tenor of the discussion of emigration, which praised life in the United States. Three articles in particular, however, will have infuriated him: "Emigration—New York" (1.11 [Apr. 14, 1832]: 88 [cols. 1–2]); "Emigration" (2.102 [Jan. 11, 1834]: 395–396 [col. 1]); and "A Word to Intending Emigrants" (3.112 [Mar. 22, 1834]: 63 [col. 3]–64 [col. 2]). The first praises New York as "a fine commercial city" (col. 1); the second comments that farmers "for little more than the annual rent of a farm here [in Britain], may purchase the freehold of one almost equally good" in the United States (395 [col. 1]); the third states that emigration to the United States will give anyone "a large and liberal return for the degree of exertion he puts forth" (col. 3).
Colonel Crockett, of *Cowhide* notoriety Crockett's autobiography, which was published in 1834 by the Philadelphia publishing house of E. L. Carey and A. Hart as *A Narrative of the Life of David Crockett, of the State of Tennessee. Written by Himself*, contains no references to having witnessed any "heart-rending scenes amongst those who have

emigrated up the country." The references which RG is thinking of actually appear in *Sketches and Eccentricities of Col. David Crockett of West Tennessee* 10 (col. 2)–11 (col. 1), a book which was not by Crockett although it was purported to be. *Sketches and Eccentricities* does catalogue the misfortunes and poverty of many in America, but does so in a clearly mock-heroic, self-deprecating way. RG also stretches the meaning of "up the country," since the book discusses the American West rather than the East.

RG's reference to "Cowhide notoriety" puzzles me—it may be a faulty allusion to Crockett's 'coon skin hat. He may, however, be thinking of a contemporary newspaper comment with which I am unfamilar.

The New York paper, the *Morning Courier* of the 10th of June 1834 See *Morning Courier and New–York Enquirer* June 10, 1834: 2 (col. 3).

The poor factory girl Sarah Maria Cornell. RG's reference to a letter by Cornell suggests he may have looked at David Melvill's *Fac-simile of the Letters Produced at the Trial of the Rev. Ephraim K. Avery*. . . . See the annotation to p. 000. RG devotes much of Chapter IX of Volume II to the famous murder case.

Utica Utica City was incorporated on April 7, 1817 and received its city charter on February 13, 1832. Gordon terms it "a point whence direct roads and commodious stages run to many interesting parts of the state" (571).

Page 166

and the accounts which have appeared are *a disgrace* For some reason, RG has deleted from the ms. an underscored reference here to "*Chambers' Edinburgh Journal*," yet has retained it on the chapter's contents page. He may have intended to strike both as too inflammatory or libelous, but have forgotten one of them.

Page 167

Line Accommodation Packets The Workers of the Writers Program point out that the term "packet" is a confusing one (143–144). It defined a function (the carrying of passengers as opposed solely to freight) rather than a particular design of ship. RG appears to mean by the phrase the regular passenger-carrying transatlantic sailing ships which predated the custom-designed clipper ships. Regular passenger service between New York and Liverpool began in 1818 (with the Black Ball Line), between New York and London in 1823. It took at least 18 days to travel from New York City to Liverpool and averaged 22. It took about 40 days to return.

earwigging Hotten's definition of this word as indicating a private rebuke is clearly wrong in this context (128). Farmer seems closer with "to influence by covert statements; to whisper insinuations" (2: 351).

Page 168

which letter I read in the *Sun* American paper I have been unable to trace RG's reference.

The packet in which I took my passage, *The President* *The President* was probably the ship of that name built in 1823 (see the Workers of the Writers Program 149). It was owned by John Griswold of the London Line, and captained by George Moore. It is probably the same ship as that mentioned by Haswell as having sunk in March 1841 on a trip from New York City to England (274). We know from Chapter I of Volume I that RG sailed for America "early in 1833" (7). The voyage to which he refers then was the one in which *The President* left London on February 22, 1833, stopped at Portsmouth on February 27, and arrived in New York on April 1.

See *The New-York Gazette & General Advertiser* of Jan. 20, 1834: 4 (col. 6) for an advertisement describing the "London Line of Packets." See another advertisement entitled "London Line of Packets" in *The New-York Commercial Advertiser* of Feb. 26, 1833: 1 (col. 1) for information about the scheduled departure of *The President*. See "ARRIVED SINCE OUR LAST" in *The New-York Commercial Advertiser* of Apr. 1, 1833: 1 (col. 4) for *The President*'s manifest and a description of its troubled transatlantic voyage. Finally, see the same issue of *The New–York Commercial Advertiser*: 2 (col. 5) for a partial passenger list of those on board *The President* (a list on which RG's name does not appear).

the Packet in which I returned to England RG does not give the name of the vessel on which he sailed back to Britain.

But this was not all, the Captain RG first wrote "mercenary commander," but subsequently deleted it.

Page 169

videlicet This word means "namely" or "that is to say." It is the full word for the abbreviation "viz."

Page 170

in which the passengers must have been crowded together The text to the volume (incorrectly numbered I in the ms.) concludes here, at the bottom of fol. 97. Fol. 98 is a blank, numbered folio. In the ms., Volume II (in this edition correctly numbered I) begins on fol. 99.

BIBLIOGRAPHIES

ANGLO–AMERICAN TRAVEL WRITING BY GOOCH'S CONTEMPORARIES[1]

This bibliography lists the 26 British travelers' accounts written or published during the two years (1833–1834) covered by Gooch's account.

Abdy, Edward Strutt. *Journal of a Residence and Tour in the United States of North America from April, 1833, to October, 1834*. 3 vols. London: J. Murray, 1835.

Alexander, J. E. *Transatlantic Sketches, Comprising Visits to the Most Interesting Scenes in North and South America, and the West Indies. With Notes on Negro Slavery and Canadian Emigration*. 2 vols. London: R. Bentley, 1833.

Boardman, James. *America and the Americans, by a Citizen of the World*. London: Longman, Rees, Orme, Brown, & Longman, 1833.

[Burlend, Rebecca]. *A True Picture of Emigration; or Fourteen Years in the Interior of North America; Being a Full and Impartial Account of the Various Difficulties and Ultimate Success of an English Family Who Emigrated from Berwick-in-Elmer, near Leeds, in the Year 1831*. London: G. Berger, 1848. [1831–1845]

Butler, Frances Anne. *Journal*. 2 vols. London: J. Murray, 1835. [Aug. 1832–July 17, 1833]

Caswall, Henry. *America and the American Church*. 2nd ed. London: J. and C. Mozley, 1851. [1828–1842]

Coke, E. T. *A Subaltern's Furlough Descriptive of Scenes in Various Parts of the United States, Upper and Lower Canada, New Brunswick, and Nova Scotia, During the Summer and Autumn of 1832*. 2 vols. London: Saunders and Otley, 1833.

Davis, Stephen. *Notes of a Tour in America, in 1832 and 1833*. Edinburgh: Waugh & Innes, 1833.

Duhring, Henry. *Remarks on the United States of America, with Regard to the Actual State of Europe*. London: W. Simpkin and R. Marshall, 1833.

Eyre, John. *The Christian Spectator*. Albany: Printed by J. Munsell, 1838. [1832–1833]

——. *The European Stranger in America*. New York: Sold at

Folsom's Book Store, 1839. [1834–1838]

Featherstonaugh, G. W. *Excursion through the Slave States, from Washington on the Potomac to the Frontier of Mexico; with Sketches of Popular Manners and Geological Notices*. 2 vols. London: J. Murray, 1844. [1834–1835]

Fidler, Isaac. *Observations on Professions, Literature, Manners, and Emigration in the United States and Canada, Made During a Residence there in 1832*. London: Whittaker, Treacher, 1833.

Finch, I [John]. *Travels in the United States of America and Canada, Containing Some Account of Their Scientific Institutions and a Few Notices of the Geology and Mineralogy of Those Countries. To Which is Added an Essay on the Natural Boundaries of Empires*. London: Longman, Rees, Orme, Brown, Green, and Longman, 1833.

Hamilton, Thomas. *Men and Manners in America*. 3 vols. Edinburgh: W. Blackwood, 1833.

Latrobe, Charles Joseph. *The Rambler in North America: MDCCCXXXII–MDCCCXXXIII*. 2 vols. London: R. B. Seeley and W. Burnside, 1835.

Mackenzie, William Lyon. *Sketches of Canada and the United States*. London: E. Wilson, 1833.

Martineau, Harriet. *Retrospect of Western Travel*. London: Saunders and Otley, 1838. [1834–1836]

—. *Society in America*. 2 vols. London: Saunders and Otley, 1837. [1834–1836]

Murray, Charles Augustus. *Travels in North America During the Years 1834, 1835, & 1836 Including a Summer Residence with the Pawnee Tribe of Indians in the Remote Prairies of the Missouri and a Visit to Cuba and the Azore Islands*. 2 vols. London: R. Bentley, 1839.

Power, Tyrone. *Impressions of America; During the Years 1833, 1834, and 1835*. 2 vols. London: Bentley, 1836.

Stuart, James. *Refutation of Aspersions on "Stuart's Three Years in North America."* London: Whittaker, 1834.

—. *Three Years in North America*. 2 vols. Edinburgh: Printed for R. Cadell, 1833.

Todd, Henry Cook (*pseud.* A Traveller). *Notes upon Canada and the United States from 1832 to 1840. Much in a Small Space, or a Great Deal in a Little Book*. 2nd ed.

Toronto: Rogers and Thompson, 1840. [1832–1840]
Tudor, Henry. *Narrative of a Tour in North America; Comprising Mexico, the Mines of Real del Monte, the United States, and the British Colonies: with an Excursion to the Island of Cuba. In a Series of Letters, Written in the Years 1831–2*. 2 vols. London: J. Duncan, 1834.
Weston, Richard. *A Visit to the United States and Canada in 1833; with the View of Settling in America. Including a Voyage to and from New York*. Edinburgh: R. Weston and Sons, 1836.

THE PUBLISHED WORKS AND MANUSCRIPTS OF RICHARD GOOCH[2]

"Ambition, or the Retreat from Moscow." Add. Ms. 2616 Pt. 8. In fols. 112–199: Assorted poems (and stories). Cambridge University Library.[3]
"America and the Americans—in 1833–4. By an Emigrant." Add Ms. 2616 Pt. 4. Cambridge University Library.
"America and the Americans in 1833–4. By an Emigrant. Chapter I: New Year's Day in New York. Chapter II: Serenading in America." Add. Ms. 2616 Pt. 5. Fols. 140–147. Cambridge University Library.[4]
"Banquet with Alluring Spring. A Melody." Add. Ms. 2616 Pt. 8. In fols. 112–199: Assorted poems (and stories). Cambridge University Library.
"The Bereft. Sonnet VIII." Add. Ms. 2616 Pt. 8. In fols. 112–199: Assorted poems (and stories). Cambridge University Library.[5]
The Book of the Reformed Parliament; Being a Synopsis of the Votes of the Members of the Reformed House of Commons upon All Important Questions, etc. London: A. H. Baily, 1834.[6]
"The Boon-Rose." Add. Ms. 2616 Pt. 8. In fols. 112–199: Assorted poems (and stories). Cambridge University Library.
"The Bouquet of Humour: or, Choice Anecdotes, Original and Select. The Medley of Humour. Choice Morsels of Wit Original and Select." Add. Ms. 2616 Pt. 6. Fols. 1–66. Cambridge University Library.
"The British Eccentric Biographer: or—Ready Antidote to Blue-Devils and Ennui." Add. Ms. 2616 Pt. 7. Fols.

220–252. Cambridge University Library.
"The British Youths' Familiar History of, and Popular Guide to, the Town & University of Cambridge." 2 vols. Vol. 1: fols. 1–106 of Add. Ms. 2616 Pt. 3. Vol. 2: fols. 107–223. Cambridge University Library.[7]
"The British Youths' Familiar History of, and Stranger's Guide to, the University and Town of Cambridge." Add. Ms. 2616 Pt. 5. Fols. 218–249.[8]
The Cambridge Tart: Epigrammatic and Satiric Poetical Effusions, &c., &c.; Dainty Morsels Served up by Cantabs on Various Occasions. Dedicated to the Members of the University of Cambridge by Socius [pseud.]. London: J. Smith and J. Anderson, 1823.[9]
"Cantabrigia." Add. Ms. 2616 Pt. 5. Fols. 1–63. Cambridge University Library.
"Charity. A Sonnet." In *Juvenile Forget-Me-Not*. London: F. Westley, 1830. 54.[10] Also published in his *Redemption; The Song of the Spirit of Hiram; and Other Poems*. 130.
"The Churchyard." Add. Ms. 2616 Pt. 8. In fols. 112–199: Assorted poems (and stories). Cambridge University Library.
"The Confessions of a Cantab." *Blackwood's Edinburgh Magazine* 16.93 (Oct. 1824): 459–467.
"The Confessions of a Cantab. No. II." *Blackwood's Edinburgh Magazine* 16.94 (Nov. 1824): 571–579.
Confessions of the Faculty. A Collection of Curious and Important Facts, Deeply Interesting to Heads of Families and Invalids, by Socius [pseud.], 1848. St. Neots, Camb.: J. Topham, [1848].[11]
"Crude Notions on the Advantages of a Property-Tax." Add. Ms. 2616 Pt. 5. Fols. 250–285. Cambridge University Library.[12]
"Disappointment. Sonnet XI." Add. Ms. 2616 Pt. 8. In fols. 112–199: Assorted poems (and stories). Cambridge University Library.
"Elegiac Stanzas: Addressed to Lady Heathcote, on the Sudden Death of Her Beloved Son, Lieutenant Tho[s] Heathcote, at Bombay." Add. Ms. 2616 Pt. 8. In fols. 112–199: Assorted poems (and stories). Cambridge University Library. Published as "Elegaic Stanzas on the Death of Lieutenant Heathcote." In his *Redemption; The Song of the Spirit of Hiram; and*

Other Poems. 137.
"Evening. A Poem Written for the Chancellor's Medal, Given at the University of Camb., A.D. 1821—R.G." Add. Ms. 2616 Pt. 8. In fols. 112–199: Assorted poems (and stories). Cambridge University Library.[13]
Facetiae Cantabrigiensis. Dedicated to the Students of Lincoln's Inn by Socius [pseud.]. 1st ed. London: W. Cole, 1825.
Facetiae Cantabrigiensis. Dedicated to the Students of Lincoln's Inn by Socius [pseud.]. 3rd. ed., considerably enlarged. London: C. Mason, 1836.[14]
"The Fair Suicide." Add. Ms. 2616 Pt. 8. In fols. 112–199: Assorted poems (and stories). Cambridge University Library.
"Friendship. Written at the Request of J. Fitzgerald. M.D. On His Departure for the East Indies." Add. Ms. 2616 Pt. 8. In fols. 112–199: Assorted poems (and stories). Cambridge University Library.
The Georgian Era: Memoirs of the Most Eminent Persons Who Have Flourished in Great Britain from the Accession of George the First to the Demise of George the Fourth. 4 vols. London: Vizetelly, Branston, 1832–1834.[15]
"The Georgian Slave. Sonnet X." Add. Ms. 2616 Pt. 8. In fols. 112–199: Assorted poems (and stories). Cambridge University Library.
"Hint to a Scolding Fair. An Epigram." Add. Ms. 2616 Pt. 8. In fols. 112–199: Assorted poems (and stories). Cambridge University Library.
The Illiberal! (To Be Continued Occasionally). A Drama in Verse, not Prose, from the North. Add. Ms. 2616 Pt. 8. Fols. 7– 15. Cambridge University Library.[16]
"Imprecatory—On the Murder of Amy Robsart, Countess of Leicester." Add. Ms. 2616 Pt. 8. In fols. 112–199: Assorted poems (and stories). Cambridge University Library.
"Introduction to Arithmetic." Add. Ms. 2616 Pt. 8. Fols. 200–214. Cambridge University Library.
Key to the Pledges of the New Parliament of 1835. [London]: Ridgway, Mar. 1835.
Last Will and Testament. September 3, 1849. Prob 11/2110. Public Record Office.
"The Law of Debtor and Creditor, Morally Considered." Add. Ms.

2616 Pt. 5. Fols. 64–137. Cambridge University Library.
Letter, with Memorial and Testimonials, to Sir Robert Peel. Add. Ms. 40594. Fols. 225–245. British Library.
"Letters from Cambridge. Letter I.—Water Parties." *The Brighton Magazine* 1.4 (Apr. 1822): 403–411.[17]
"Letters from Cambridge. Letter II. Breakfast Parties." *The Brighton Magazine* 2.8 (Aug. 1822): 144–153.
"Liber Cantabrigiensis: or, Memoirs, Traits, Records, and Remains, of the Chancellors, High-Stewards, Vice-Chancellors, Representatives in Parliament, Professors, Tutors, University Officers, Scholars, Prizemen, and Others, the Most Celebrated Divines, Statesmen, Authors, and Men of Science, Who Have Studied In, or Graduated at, the University of Cambridge. By Richard Gooch, Esqre of St. John's College, Cambridge, and of the Middle Temple. One of the Compilers of "The Georgian Era," &c., &c., &c." 2 vols. Vol. 1: fols. 1–194 of Add. Ms. 2616 Pt. 1. Vol. 2: fols. 195–419 of Add. Ms. 2616. Cambridge University Library.[18]
"Light Let the Strain Be." Add. Ms. 2616 Pt. 8. In fols. 112–199: Assorted poems (and stories). Cambridge University Library.
"Love. An Irregular Ode." Add. Ms. 2616 Pt. 8. In fols. 112–199: Assorted poems (and stories). Cambridge University Library.
The Masonic Melodist. Bolton: W. Holcroft, 1836.
"Melancholy. Sonnet XIII." Add. Ms. 2616 Pt. 8. In fols. 112–199: Assorted poems (and stories). Cambridge University Library.
"Memoirs Miscellaneous." Add. Ms. 2616 Pt. 7. Fols. 1–219; 253– 398. Cambridge University Library.
"Memoirs of the Christian Advocates." Add. Ms. 2616 Pt. 2. Fols. 87–224. Cambridge University Library.
"Memoirs of the Members' Prizemen." Add. Ms. 2616 Pt. 2. Fols. 225–409. Cambridge University Library.
"Memoirs of the Norrisian Prize-men." Add. Ms. 2616 Pt. 2. Fols. 1–86. Cambridge University Library.
"Moscow." Add. Ms. 2616 Pt. 8. In fols. 112–199: Assorted poems (and stories). Cambridge University Library.[19]
"The Neglected Rose." Add. Ms. 2616 Pt. 8. In fols. 112–199: Assorted poems (and stories). Cambridge University Library.

Nuts to Crack: or, Quips, Quirks, Anecdotes and Facete of Oxford and Cambridge Scholars. London: A. H. Baily, 1834; Philadelphia: E. L. Carey & A. Hart, 1835.[20]

"The Office of Friendship. Sacred to X X X X." Add. Ms. 2616 Pt. 8. In fols. 112–199: Assorted poems (and stories). Cambridge University Library.

"On the Death of General Desaix. Sonnet IX." Add. Ms. 2616 Pt. 8. In fols. 112–199: Assorted poems (and stories). Cambridge University Library.

Oxford and Cambridge Nuts to Crack, or Quips, Quirks, Anecdotes, and Facetiae of Oxford and Cambridge Scholars. By the Author of *Facetiae Cantabrigiensis*, etc. 2nd ed. London: A. H. Baily, 1835.[21]

"The Pious Man's Communion with His Maker; or, Family Devotional. Containing a Brief and Devout Exposition of the Lord's Prayer, and the Apostle's Creed; Also Original and Select Prayers, Suited to All Occasions, for the Use of Families. By Mr. Richard Gooch, B.A. of St. John's College, Cambridge." Add. Ms. 2616 Pt. 5. Fols. 192–208.[22]

"A Popular Sketch of All the Governments of the World." Add. Ms. 2616 Pt. 5. Fols. 153–190. Cambridge University Library.

Redemption; the Song of the Spirit of Hiram; and Other Poems. London: J. Hearne, 1832.

"The Soldier's Orphan." Add. Ms. 2616 Pt. 8. In fols. 112–199: Assorted poems (and stories). Cambridge University Library.

"Stanzas Addressed to Miss Georgiana Jemima Heathcote, with a Bouquet of Lilies of the Valley." Add. Ms. 2616 Pt. 8. In fols. 112–199: Assorted poems (and stories). Cambridge University Library.

"Story." Add. Ms. 2616 Pt. 8. In fols. 112–199: Assorted poems (and stories). Cambridge University Library.[23]

"The Tears of Virgil. Sonnet VIII." Add. Ms. 2616 Pt. 8. In fols. 112–199: Assorted poems (and stories). Cambridge University Library.[24]

"The Tears of Virgil." In *Amulet* (London) 5 (1830): 51.[25]

"To ________." Add. Ms. 2616 Pt. 8. In fols. 112–199: Assorted poems (and stories). Cambridge University Library.

"The Triumph of Moscow." Add. Ms. 2616 Pt. 8. Fols. 117–128. Cambridge University Library.

"Tulips and Roses: An Epigram." Add. Ms. 2616 Pt. 8. In fols. 112–199: Assorted poems (and stories). Cambridge University Library.

"The War-Song of the Chief of the Isles." Add. Ms. 2616 Pt. 8. In fols. 112–199: Assorted poems (and stories). Cambridge University Library.

"The Weary Plaint. Sonnet XIV." Add. Ms. 2616 Pt. 8. In fols. 112–199: Assorted poems (and stories). Cambridge University Library.

"The Witchery of Beauty. Composed after Viewing the Statue of the Medicean Venus." Add. Ms. 2616 Pt. 8. In fols. 112– 199: Assorted poems (and stories). Cambridge University Library.

Works Cited by the Editor

This bibliography includes all citations except those presented in two lists earlier in this text: the bibliography of British travelers' accounts written or published during the two years (1833–1834) covered by Gooch's account (see pp. 213–215), and the bibliography of Gooch's published works and manuscripts (see pp. 215–220).

"Abatement of Nuisances." *The New–York Commercial Advertiser* May 31, 1834: 2 (col. 3).

"Accidents." *The Sun* Apr. 15, 1834: 3 (col. 1).

Allen, Oliver E. *New York, New York. A History of the World's Most Exhilirating and Challenging City*. New York: Atheneum, 1990.

An Alphabetical List of the Public Buildings, Institutions, Streets, Places, &c. in the City of New York, with References to the Annexed Plan, Forming a Complete Key for the Use of Strangers and Citizens. New York: A. T. Goodrich, 1830.

American Newspapers 1821–1836. A Union List of Files Available in the United States and Canada. Ed. Winifred Gregory. New York: Bibliographical Society of America, 1937; rpt. New York: Kraus Reprint, 1967.

"Another Warning." *The Sun* Apr. 9, 1834: 3 (col. 1).

Appleton's Cyclopaedia of American Biography. Ed. James Grant Wilson and John Fiske. 6 vols. New York: D. Appleton, 1888–1889.

Aristophanes. *The Frogs*. In his *The Wasps; The Poet and the Women; The Frogs*. Trans. with an Introd. David

Barrett. Harmondsworth, Middx., Eng.: Penguin Books, 1964. 147–212.

"Arrived Since Our Last." *The New-York Commercial Advertiser* Apr. 1, 1833: 1 (col. 4).

Bartlett, John. *Familiar Quotations: A Collection of Passages, Phrases and Proverbs Traced to Their Sources in Ancient and Modern Literature*. Ed. Emily Morison Beck. Fifteenth and 125th anniversary ed., rev. and enlarged. Boston: Little, Brown, 1980.

Benson, Lee. *The Concept of Jacksonian Democracy: New York As a Test Case*. Princeton: Princeton UP, 1961.

Berger, Max. *The British Traveller in America, 1836–1860*. New York: Columbia UP, 1943.

Biographical Directory of the Governors of the United States 1789–1978. Ed. Robert Sobel and John Raimo. 4 vols. Westport, CT: Meckler Books, 1978.

Biographical Sketch of James Morison, the Hygeist. . . . London: Lofts, Printer, [1849?].

Black, Matthew Wilson. *Richard Brathwait: An Account of His Life and Works. . . .* Philadelphia, n.p., 1928.

Black Hawk. *Autobiography of Ma–Ka–Tai–Me–She–Kia–Kiak, or Black Hawk. . . .* St. Louis: P of Continental Printing, 1882.

Boase, Frederic. "Gooch, Richard Stephen St. George Heathcote." In his *Modern English Biography*. 6 vols. 1912; rpt. New York: Barnes & Noble, 1965. 5: 437 (col. 1).

Borowitz, Albert. *The Thurtell-Hunt Murder Case: Dark Mirror to Regency England*. Baton Rouge: Louisiana State UP, 1987.

"Boston Pride." *The Sun* Apr. 15, 1834: 2 (col. 1).

Boswell, James. *Boswell's* Life of Johnson *together with Boswell's* Journal of a Tour to the Hebrides *and Johnson's* Diary of a Journey into North Wales. Ed. George Birkbeck Hill; rev. and enlarged ed. by L. F. Powell. 6 vols. Oxford: Clarendon P, 1971.

Brathwait, Richard. *Drunken Barnaby's Four Journeys to the North of England*. London: Printed for J. Harding, 1805.

Brewer, E. Cobham. *Dictionary of Phrase and Fable, Giving the Derivation, Source, or Origin of Common Phrases, Allusions, and Words That Have a Tale to Tell*. 2nd ed. Philadelphia: Claxton, Remsen, &

Haffelfinger, 1870.
Brewer's Dictionary of Phrase and Fable. Ed. Ivor H. Evans. Centenary ed. New York: Harper & Row, 1981.
Brodie, Fawn M. *Thomas Jefferson: An Intimate History*. New York: W. W. Norton, 1974.
"Brutal Assault upon the President of the United States." *The Evening Post* May 8, 1833: 2 (col. 4).
Burns, Robert. *The Poems and Songs of Robert Burns*. Ed. James Kinsley. 3 vols. Oxford: Clarendon P, 1968.
Bushman, Richard L. "Mormon Persecutions in Missouri." *Brigham Young University Studies* 3.1 (Autumn 1960): 11–20.
Butler, Samuel. *Hudibras*. Ed. with an Introd. and Commentary by John Wilders. Oxford: Clarendon P, 1967.
Byatt, A. S. *Possession: A Romance*. New York: Random House, 1990.
Calhoun, Richard B. "From Community to Metropolis: Fire Protection in New York City, 1790–1875." Diss. Columbia U, 1973.
Cambridge Biographical Dictionary. Ed. Magnus Magnusson. Cambridge: Cambridge UP, 1990.
Cann, Kathleen. Letter to the author. Dec. 16, 1991.
Catterall, Ralph Charles Henry. *The Second Bank of the United States*. Chicago: The U of Chicago P, 1902.
Celebrated Trials of All Countries, and Remarkable Cases of Criminal Jurisprudence. Sel. by a Member of the Philadelphia Bar. Philadelphia: E. L. Carey & A. Hart, 1837.
Chappell, William. *The Ballad Literature and Popular Music of the Olden Time. . . .* 2 vols. London: Chappell, 1859; rpt., with a new Introd. by Frederick W. Sternfeld, New York: Dover Publications, 1965.
"Charter Election." *The New-York Commercial Advertiser* Apr. 6, 1833: 2 (col. 1).
Chase-Riboud, Barbara. *Sally Hemings*. New York: The Viking Press, 1979.
"Circuit Court, and Oyer and Terminer." *The New-York Commercial Advertiser* May 31, 1834: 2 (col. 4).
Clapp, William W., Jr. *A Record of the Boston Stage*. Boston: James Monroe; rpt. New York: Greenwood P, 1969.
Classical Literary Criticism: Aristotle; Horace; Longinus. Trans. with an Introd. by T. S. Dorsch.

Harmondsworth, Middx., Eng.: Penguin Books, 1965. 97–158.
Cobbett, William. *The Emigrant's Guide; in Ten Letters, Addressed to the Tax–Payers of England. . . .* London: The Author, 1829. New ed. London: The Author, 1830.
———. *A Year's Residence in the United States of America.* Introd. by J. E. Morpurgo. Carbondale: Southern Illinois UP, 1964.
Cohen, Roger. "Judge Says Copyright Covers Writer's Ideas of a Jefferson Affair." *The New York Times* Aug. 15, 1991: C13, 17.
Collins, S. H. *The Emigrant's Guide to the United States of America. . . .* New and enlarged ed. Hull, Eng.: J. Noble, 1829.
Colton, C. *Tour of the American Lakes and among the Indians of the North-West Territory in 1830; Disclosing the Character and Prospects of the Indian Race.* London: F. Westley and A. H. Davis, 1833.
Colton, Calvin. *Church and State in America. Part II. Review of the Bishop of London's Reply.* London: Westley & Davis, 1834.
"Communication." *The Sun* Apr. 15, 1834: 3 (col. 2).
Conrad, Peter. *Imagining America.* New York: Oxford UP, 1980.
Cooper, Walter G. *The Story of Georgia.* 3 vols. New York: The American Historical Society, 1938.
"Correspondence of 'The Man.'" *The Man* 1.71 (May 13, 1834): 286 (col. 1).
Costello, Augustine E. *Our Firemen. A History of the New York Fire Departments, Volunteer and Paid.* New York: Augustine E. Costello, 1887.
"Court of Sessions"—(Yesterday)." *The Sun* Mar. 15, 1834: 2 (col. 2).
Cowper, William. *Cowper: Verse and Letters.* Sel. Brian Spiller. Cambridge: Harvard UP, 1968.
Crane, Stephen. *Red Badge of Courage.* Restoration and Introd. Henry Binder. New York: W. W. Norton, 1982.
Crockett, David. *A Narrative of the Life of David Crockett, of the State of Tennessee. Written by Himself.* 5th ed. Philadelphia: E. L. Carey and A. Hart, 1834.
Dabney, Virginius. *The Jefferson Scandals: A Rebuttal.* New York: Dodd, Mead, 1981.
Dana, David D. *The Firemen: The Fire Departments of the*

United States. . . . Boston: James French, 1858.
Date, Christopher. Letter to the author. Jan. 30, 1992.
Davis, Charles Augustus. *Letters of J. Downing, Major Downingville Militia, Second Brigade. . . .* New York: Harper & Brothers, 1834.
Davis, Jim. *John Liston, Comedian.* London: The Society for Theatre Research, 1985.
Davis, Kenneth C. *Don't Know Much about History: Everything You Needed to Know about American History but Never Learned.* New York: Avon Books, 1990.
"Desperate Conflict." *The Sun* May 16, 1834: 3 (col. 1).
"Destructive Tornado." *The Man* 1.71 (May 13, 1834): 286 (col. 2).
DeVoe, Thomas Farrington. "Historical Incidents from Newspapers, 1800–1850." 2 vols. Ms. in the New York Historical Society, New York.
"Diabolical Murder." *The Sun* Mar. 15, 1834: 2 (col. 2).
Dickens, Charles. American Notes *[1842] and* Pictures from Italy. London: Oxford UP, 1966.
—. *The Old Curiosity Shop.* 1841; London: Oxford UP, 1983.
—. *Oliver Twist.* 1838; London: Oxford UP, 1983.
Dictionary of Afro-American Slavery. Ed. Randall M. Miller and John David Smith. New York: Greenwood P, 1988.
Dictionary of American Biography. Ed. Dumas Malone. 10 vols. New York: Charles Scribner's Sons, 1927–1936.
Dictionary of National Biography from the Earliest Times to 1900. Ed. Sir Leslie Stephen and Sir Sidney Lee. 22 vols. Oxford: Oxford UP, 1921–1922.
Drabble, Margaret, ed. *The Oxford Companion to English Literature.* 5th ed. Oxford: Oxford UP, 1985.
[Drake, Benjamin]. *The Great Indian Chief of the West: or, Life and Adventures of Black Hawk.* Cincinnati: Applegate, 1854.
Durham, Weldon B., ed. *American Theatre Companies, 1749–1887.* New York: Greenwood P, 1986.
Dwight, Timothy. "Seventh Commandment__Lewdness." *McDowall's Journal* 1.10 (Oct. 1833): 73–75 (col. 2).
"Early Fruit." *The New-York Commercial Advertiser* June 3, 1834: 2 (col. 5).
"Education." *The Man* May 13, 1834: 288 (col. 1).
Edwards, Edward. *Anecdotes of Painters Who Have Resided or Been Born in England; with Critical Remarks on*

Their Productions. London: Luke Hansard & Sons for Leigh and Sotheby, W. J. and J. Richardson, R. Faulder, T. Payne, and J. White, 1808.

Ekirch, Arthur Alphonse, Jr. *The Idea of Progress in America, 1815–1860*. New York: Columbia UP, 1944; rpt. New York: Peter Smith, 1951.

"The Election." *The Sun* Apr. 9, 1834: 2 (col. 1).

Ellis, Edward Robb. *The Epic of New York City*. New York: Coward-McCann, 1966.

"Emigration." *Chambers's Edinburgh Journal* 2.102 (Jan. 11, 1834): 395–396 (col. 1).

"Emigration—New York." *Chambers's Edinburgh Journal* 1.11 (Apr. 14, 1832): 88 (cols. 1–2).

The English Catalogue of Books (Including the Original "London" Catalogue) . . . 1801–1836. Ed. and comp. Robert Alexander Peddie and Quintin Waddington. London: The Publishers' Circular, n.d.; New York: Kraus Reprint, 1963.

The English Catalogue of Books Published from January, 1835, to January, 1863. Comp. Sampson Low. London: Publishers' Circular, 1864; rpt. New York: Kraus Reprint, 1963.

Euclid. *The Thirteen Books of Euclid's* Elements. Trans. Sir Thomas Heath. Chicago: Encyclopaedia Britannica, 1952.

"Excessive Heat in America." *The Times* (London) Aug. 16, 1834: 5 (col. 3).

Fables of Aesop. A New Trans. by S. A. Handford. London: Penguin Books, 1954.

Farmer, John S., comp. and ed. *Slang and Its Analogues Past and Present. . . .* 7 vols. London: Printed for Subscribers Only, 1890–1904.

Faulkner, Harold Underwood. *American Political & Social History*. 7th ed. New York: Appleton-Century-Crofts, 1957.

Fearon, Henry Bradshaw. *Sketches of America. A Narrative of a Journey of Five Thousand Miles through the Eastern and Western States of America. . . .* London: Longman, Hurst, Rees, Orme, and Brown, 1818; rpt. New York: Benjamin Blom, 1969.

Ferrall, S. A. *A Ramble of Six Thousand Miles through the United States of America*. London: E. Wilson, 1832.

"The Fireman's Dog." *The Sun* May 16, 1834: 4 (cols. 1–2).

Flanders, Robert Bruce. *Nauvoo: Kingdom on the Mississippi*. Urbana: U of Illinois P, 1965.

Fowler, Orin. *An Historical Sketch of Fall River, from 1620 to the Present*. Fall River, MA: Benjamin Earl, 1841.

French, J. H. *Gazetteer of the State of New York*. . . . 1860; rpt. Port Washington: Ira J. Friedman, 1969.

"[From the Kingston Spectator]." *The Sun* Apr. 15, 1834: 3 (col. 1).

Gay, John. "The Rat-catcher and the Cats." In *Fables by the Late Mr. Gay*. London: A. K. Newman, [1833?]. 40–41.

Gibbens, Lilian. Letter to the author. Oct. 8, 1991.

Ginsberg, Stephen F. "Above the Law: Volunteer Firemen in New York City, 1836–1837." *New York History* Apr. 1969: 165–186.

"Girard College." *The Evening Star* Apr. 22, 1834: 2 (col. 2).

"Good!" *The Sun* Apr. 9, 1834: 2 (col. 3).

"Good News!!" *The Man* 1.71 (May 13, 1834): 285.

Gordon, Thomas F. *Gazetteer of the State of New York*. . . . Philadelphia: Printed for the Author, 1836.

Green, Jim. Telephone conversation with the author. June 21, 1991.

Grene, Asa. *Travels in America. By George Fibbleton, Esq., Ex– barber to His Majesty, the King of Great Britain*. New York: W. Pearson, P. Hill, and others, 1833.

"Gums, Drugs and Chemicals, 115 maiden-lane." *The New-York Gazette & General Advertiser* July 2, 1834: 1 (col. 5).

Gwynn, Stephen. *Thomas Moore*. New York: Macmillan, 1905.

Hall, Captain Basil. *Fragments of Voyages and Travels, Including Anecdotes of a Naval Life*. . . . 3 vols. Edinburgh: R. Cadell, 1832.

—. *Travels in North America in the Years 1827 and 1828*. 3 vols. Edinburgh: Cadell; London: Simpkin and Marshall, 1829.

Hardie, James. *The Description of the City of New-York*. . . . New York: Samuel Marks, 1827.

Hardyment, Christina. *Home Comfort: A History of Domestic Arrangements*. Chicago: Academy Chicago Publishers in assoc. with the National Trust, 1992.

Hartnoll, Phyllis, ed. *The Oxford Companion to the Theatre*. 4th ed. Oxford: OUP, 1983.

Harwell, Richard. *Washington*. An abridgment in one vol. of the seven-vol. *George Washington*, by Douglas

Southall Freeman. New York: Charles Scribner's Sons, 1968.

Haswell, Chas. H. *Reminiscences of New York by an Octogenarian (1816 to 1860)*. New York: Harper & Brothers, 1896.

Havlice, Patricia Pate. *Popular Song Index: Second Supplement*. Metuchen, NJ: The Scarerow P, 1984.

Hedrick, Ulysses Prentiss. *A History of Agriculture in the State of New York*. Albany: New York State Agricultural Society, 1933.

Hemstreet, Charles. *Nooks & Corners of Old New York*. New York: Charles Scribner's Sons, 1899.

Hibbert, Christopher. *London: The Biography of a City*. New York: William Morrow, 1969.

Hildreth, Richard. *A Report of the Trial of the Rev. Ephraim K. Avery, before the Supreme Judicial Court of Rhode Island, on an Indictment for the Murder of Sarah Maria Cornell. . . .* Boston: Russell, Odiorne, D. H. Ela., 1833.

[Hotten, John Camden]. *The Slang Dictionary; or, the Vulgar Words, Street Phrases, and "Fast" Expressions of High and Low Society. . . .* London: John Camden Hotten, 1865.

Ireland, Joseph N. *Records of the New York Stage, from 1750 to 1860*. 2 vols. New York: T. H. Morrell, 1866–1867. Vol. 2.

"Jewing." *The Sun* Apr. 9, 1834: 2 (col. 3).

The Jewish Encyclopedia. A Descriptive Record of the History, Religion, Literature, and Customs of the Jewish People from the Earliest Times to the Present Day. Ed. Isidore Singer. 12 vols. New York: Funk and Wagnall, 1901–1906.

Johnson, Samuel. *The Idler and The Adventurer.* Ed. W. J. Bate, John M. Bullitt, and L. F. Powell. Vol. 2 of The Yale Edition of the Works of Samuel Johnson. New Haven, CT: Yale UP, 1963. 69–71.

Jones, Hugh Percy. *Dictionary of Foreign Phrases and Classical Quotations. . . .* New and rev. ed. N.p.: n.p., n.d.; Edinburgh: John Grant Booksellers, 1958.

Kane, Joseph Nathan. *The American Counties. Origins of Names, Dates of Creation and Organization, Area, Population, Historical Data, and Published Sources*. 3rd ed. Metuchen, NJ: The Scarecrow P, 1972.

Kasserman, David Richard. *Fall River Outrage: Life, Murder, and Justice in Early Industrial New England*. Philadelphia: U of Pennsylvania P, 1986.

"Kentucky Sports." *Chambers' Edinburgh Journal* 1.18 (June 2, 1832): 144.

"Kissing with an appetite." *The Sun* Apr. 9, 1834: 3 (col. 1).

Lawrence, D. H. "The Ship of Death." In *The Complete Poems of D. H. Lawrence*. Coll. and ed. with an Introd. and Notes by Vivian de Sola Pinto and Warren Roberts. 2 vols. New York: The Viking Press, 1964. 2: 716–720.

Lee, Nathaniel. *The Rival Queens; or, the Death of Alexander the Great*. In *The Works of Nathaniel Lee*. Ed. with an Introd. and Notes by Thomas B. Stroup and Arthur L. Cooke. 2 vols. 1954; rpt. Metuchen, NJ: Scarecrow Reprint, 1968. 1: 211– 283.

Lewis, Samuel. *A Topographical Dictionary of England*. 4th ed. 4 vols. London: S. Lewis, 1840.

"Liberty." *The Sun* Apr. 9, 1834: 4 (col. 1).

"London Line of Packets." *The New-York Commercial Advertiser* Feb. 26, 1833: 1 (col. 1).

"London Line of Packets." *The New-York Gazette & General Advertiser* Jan. 20, 1834: 4 (col. 6).

Longworth's American Almanac, New-York Register, and City Directory for the Fifty-Eighth Year, of American Independence. . . . New York: Thomas Longworth, 1833.

"Look out Gentlemen!" *The Sun* May 3, 1834: 2 (col. 2).

Mathews, Mitford M., ed. *A Dictionary of Americanisms on Historical Principles*. 2 vols. Chicago: The U of Chicago P, 1951.

Mayer, David. *Harlequin in His Element: The English Pantomime, 1806–1836*. Cambridge: Harvard UP, 1969.

McCord, Norman. *British History 1815–1906*. Oxford: Oxford UP, 1991.

McGann, Jerome J. *A Critique of Modern Textual Criticism*. Chicago: The U of Chicago P, 1983.

McMaster, John Bach. *History of the People of the United States from the Revolution to the Civil War*. 8 vols. New York: D. Appleton, 1883–1913.

McNeill, Miss E. Letter to the editor. January 17, 1986.

Melvill, David. *A Fac-simile of the Letters Produced at the*

Trial of the Rev. Ephraim K. Avery. . . . [Boston: Pendelton's Lithography], 1833.
Mesick, Jane Louise. *The English Traveller in America 1785–1835*. New York: Columbia UP, 1922; rpt. Westport, CT: Greenwood P, 1970.
Mineka, Francis E. *The Dissidence of Dissent*: The Monthly Repository, *1806–1838 under the Editorship of Robert Aspland, W.J. Fox, R.H. Horne, & Leigh Hunt, with a Chapter on Religious Periodicals, 1700–1825*. Chapel Hill: The U of North Carolina P, 1944.
"Ministers in the United States." *The Sun* Apr. 29, 1834: 2 (col. 1).
Moat, T. *The Practical Proofs of the Soundness of the Hygeian System of Physiology, Selected from the Appendix of "Morisoniana:". . . .* Brooklyn, NY: Printed for H. Shepheard Moat, 1831.
Moore, Thomas. *The Poetical Works of Thomas Moore*. Ed. William Michael Rossetti. London: E. Moxon, n.d.
"Moral Reform." *McDowall's Journal* 2.1 (Jan. 1834): 6 (col. 2)– 7.
Morgan, Winifred. *American Icon: Brother Jonathan and American Identity*. Cranbury, NJ: U of Delaware P/Associated UP, 1988.
Morison, Samuel Eliot. *The Oxford History of the American People*. New York: Oxford UP, 1965.
"Moses Elliot." *The Sun* Apr. 18, 1834: 2 (col. 1).
Mulvey, Christopher. *Anglo-American Landscapes: A Study of Nineteenth-Century Anglo-American Travel Literature*. Cambridge: Cambridge UP, 1983.
"A Narrative of a Pole." *The Sun* Apr. 9, 1834: 1 (cols. 2–3).
National Archives and Records Administration, General Reference Branch (Washington, DC). "The Index to New York Arrivals 1820–1846."
——. "Ship Passenger Arrival Records": *The President* (Apr. 1, 1834).
Nevins, Allan, comp. and ed. *American Social History As Recorded by British Travellers*. New York: Henry Holt, 1923. Rev. and enlarged ed. *America through British Eyes*. New York: Oxford UP, 1948.
Nevins, Allan, and Henry Steele Commager. *A Pocket History of the United States*. Ninth rev. ed. New York: Pocket Books, 1992.
"New Year in New York." *The New-York Gazette & General*

Advertiser Jan. 7, 1834: 2 (cols. 3–4).
New York Biographical Dictionary: People of All Times and All Places Who Have Been Important to the History and Life of the State. Wilmington, DE: American Historical Publications, 1986.
Nichols, John. *Literary Anecdotes of the Eighteenth Century; Comprizing* [sic] *Biographical Memoirs of William Bowyer, Printer, F.S.A. and Many of His Learned Friends. . . .* 9 vols. London: Printed for the Author, 1812–1816.
The Nineteenth Century Short Title Catalogue, Series I Phase I (1801–1815). 5 vols. Newcastle-upon_Tyne, Eng.: Avero, 1984.
"Nullification Among The Blacks." *The New-York Standard* June 29, 1833: 1 (col. 7).
Odell, George C. D. *Annals of the New York Stage*. 9 vols. New York: Columbia UP, 1927–1937.
Owen, Dorothy. Letter to the author. January 15, 1986.
Oxford English Dictionary. Compact ed. 12 vols. in 2. Oxford: Oxford UP, 1971.
Parry, Clive, ed. and annotated. *The Consolidated Treaty Series*. 231 vols. Dobbs Ferry, NY: Oceana Publications, 1969–1981.
Patterson, Jerry E. *The City of New York: A History Illustrated from the Collections of the Museum of the City of New York*. New York: Harry N. Abrams, 1978.
Plumptre, Rev. James, sel. and rev. *A Collection of Songs, Moral, Sentimental, Instructive, and Amusing*. 3 vols. London: F. C. and J. Rivington, 1824.
"Police Office." *The Sun* Apr. 9, 1834: 2 (col. 2).
"Police Office.—(Yesterday)." *The Sun* Apr. 12, 1834: 2 (col. 2).
"Police Office—(Yesterday Morning)." *The Sun* May 16, 1834: 2 (col. 3).
Pool, Daniel. *What Jane Austen Ate and Charles Dickens Knew: From Fox Hunting to Whist—The Facts of Daily Life in Nineteenth-Century England*. New York: Simon & Schuster, 1993.
Price, Hilton. "Cornhill and Its Vicinity." *Journal of the Institute of Bankers* 8.4 (Mar. 1887): 181–202.
Public Record Office (Kew. Eng.). *Naval Stores Diary 1822–1880*. ADM 7/807.
—. *Treasury Board Papers 1843, Alphabetical, No. 1: Public*

Offices A–M. T2/182.
——. *Treasury Board Papers 1843 Numerical*. T2/185.
Puttick and Simpson. *Catalogue of a Collection of Books. . . .* 2591 d.3: *Catalogues 1–20 (July 20, 1846 to April 1, 1847)*. Bodleian Library, Oxford.
Quain, Richard. *A Dictionary of Medicine*. 9th ed. New York: D. Appleton, 1885.
The Random House Dictionary of the English Language. 2nd ed., unabridged. New York: Random House, 1987.
"Religion in America." *The Times* (London) July 28, 1834: 3 (col. 2).
"Republican Young Men." *The Crisis* March 22, 1834 [?].
Rich, Obadiah. *A General View of the United States of America. With an Appendix Containing the Constitution, the Tariff of Duties, the Laws of Patents and Copyrights* &c. London: O. Rich, 1833.
Richardson, Rupert Norval. *Texas: The Lone Star State*. New York: Prentice-Hall, 1943.
Riegel, Robert E. *Young America 1830–1840*. Norman: U of Oklahoma P, 1949; rpt. Westport, CT: Greenwood P, 1973.
"The Riots." *The Evening Star* Apr. 11, 1834: 2 (col. 2).
Robbins, Keith. *Nineteenth-Century Britain: Integration and Diversity*. Oxford: Clarendon P, 1988.
Schlesinger, Arthur M., Jr. *The Age of Jackson*. Boston: Little, Brown, 1945.
Schlesinger, Arthur M., Sr. *Political and Social History of the United States 1829–1845*. New York: Macmillan, 1927.
Scholes, Jas. C. *Bolton Bibliography, and Jottings of Book-Lore; with Notes on Local Authors and Printers*. Manchester, Eng.: Henry Gray, 1886.
Scott, Sir Robert Forsyth. Manuscript notes. Library of St. John's College, Cambridge.
——. *St. John's College Cambridge*. London: J. M. Dent; New York: E. P. Dutton, 1907.
Sears, Minnie Earl, ed. *Song Index: An Index to More Than 12,000 Songs in 177 Song Collections Comprising 262 Volumes, and Supplement, 1934*. 2 vols. in 1. [New York]: H. W. Wilson, 1926; rpt. n.p.: The Shoe String P, 1966.
Sexton, Linda Gray. "A Daughter's Story: I Knew Her Best." *The New York Times Book Review* Aug. 18, 1991: 20.
Shakespeare, William. *Hamlet*. Ed. Harold Jenkins. The Arden

Ed. of the Works of William Shakespeare. London: Methuen, 1982.

—. *Macbeth*. Ed. Kenneth Muir. The Arden Ed. of the Works of William Shakespeare. London: Methuen, 1983.

Shenstone, William. *The Poetical Works of William Shenstone*. With Life, Critical Dissertation, and Explanatory Notes, by the Rev. George Gilfillan. Edinburgh: James Nichol, 1854; rpt. St Clair Shores, MI: Scholarly P, 1973.

"Sheriff Parkins." *The Evening Post* Dec. 12, 1833: 2 (cols. 6–7).

Shirreff, Patrick. *A Tour through North America; together with a Comprehensive View of the Canadas and United States. Adapted for Agricultural Emigration*. Edinburgh: Oliver & Boyd, 1835.

Sketches and Eccentricities of Col. David Crockett, of West Tennessee. New ed. London: J. Limbird, 1834.

Slack, Ellen. Letter to the author. May 16, 1991.

"Slavery." *The Sun* Apr. 9, 1834: 4 (col. 1).

Smith, Seba. *The Select Letters of Major Jack Downing of the Downingville Militia. . . .* Philadelphia: Printed for the publisher, 1834.

Smith, Gene. *American Gothic: The Story of America's Legendary Theatrical Family— Junius, Edwin, and John Wilkes Booth*. New York: Simon & Schuster, 1992.

Spaeth, Sigmund. *A History of Popular Music in America*. New York: Random House, 1948.

Spann, Edward K. *The New Metropolis: New York City, 1840–1857*. New York: Columbia UP, 1981.

Sparke, Archibald. *Bibliographia Boltoniensis: Being a Bibliography, with Biographical Details of Bolton Authors, and the Books Written by Them from 1550 to 1912; Books about Bolton; and Those Printed and Published in the Town from 1785 to Date*. Manchester, Eng.: Manchester UP, 1913.

Stapleton, Michael. *The Cambridge Guide to English Literature*. Cambridge: Cambridge UP; Feltham, Middx., Eng.: Newnes Books, 1983.

Steadman, R. "Vox Populi: The Norfolk Newspaper Press, 1760– 1900." FLA Thesis, 1971.

Stevenson, Burton. *The Home Book of Proverbs, Maxims and Familiar Phrases*. New York: Macmillan, 1948.

Stokes, I. N. Phelps. *The Iconography of Manhattan Island 1498– 1909*. . . . 6 vols. New York: Robert H. Dodd, 1926–1928; rpt. New York: Arno P, 1967.

Tanselle, G. Thomas. "The Editing of Historical Documents." In his *Selected Studies in Bibliography*. Charlottesville: UP of Virginia for the Bibliographical Society of the U of Virginia, 1979. 451–506.

——. "External Fact as an Editorial Problem." In his *Selected Studies in Bibliography*. Charlottesville: UP of Virginia for the Bibliographical Society of the U of Virginia, 1979. 355–401.

---. "Some Principles for Editorial Apparatus." In his *Selected Studies in Bibliography*. Charlottesville: UP of Virginia for the Bibliographical Society of the U of Virginia, 1979. 403–450.

Taylor, Archer, and Bartlett Jere Whiting. *A Dictionary of Proverbs and Proverbial Phrases, 1820–1880*. Cambridge: Harvard UP, 1958.

Taylor, Mary Catherine, and Carol Dyk. *The Book of Rounds*. New York: E. P. Dutton, 1977.

The Terrible Hay-Stack Murder. Life and Trial of the Rev. Ephraim K. Avery. . . . Philadelphia: Barclay, 1876.

"Terrible Warning against Keeping Bad Company." *The Evening Star* Apr. 11, 1834: 2 (col. 6).

Thomas, Ralph. "Richard Gooch." *Notes and Queries: A Medium of Intercommunication for Literary Men, General Readers, etc.* 8th ser. 12 (July-Dec. 1897): 3 (col. 2)–4 (col. 1).

"Tickets, Tickets!" *The Evening Star* Apr. 8, 1834: 2 (col. 4).

Timbs, John. *Clubs and Club Life in London. With Anecdotes of Its Famous Coffee–Houses, Hostelries, and Taverns, from the Seventeenth Century to the Present Time*. London: Chatto and Windus, [1872]; rpt. Detroit: Gale Research, 1967.

"Tragical Event." *The Sun* Mar. 15, 1834: 2 (col. 2).

Treasure, G. R. R. *England 1789–1837*. Vol. 5 of *Who's Who in History*. 5 vols. Oxford: Basil Blackwell, 1960–1974.

Tripp, Edward. *The Meridian Handbook of Classical Mythology*. New York: New American Library, 1970.

Trollope, Frances. *Domestic Manners of the Americans*. Ed., with a History of Mrs. Trollope's Adventures in America, by Donald Smalley. Gloucester, MA: Peter Smith, 1974.

"Trollopism." *The Sun* May 9, 1834: 2 (col. 2).

Tuckerman, Henry. *America and Her Commentators. With a Critical Sketch of Travel in the United States*. 1864; rpt. New York: Antiquarian P, 1961.

"The Unfortunate Negress." *The Sun* Apr. 21, 1834: 2 (col. 3)–3 (col. 1).

Van Deusen, Glyndon G. *The Jacksonian Era 1828–1848*. New York: Harper & Brothers, 1959.

Venn, John and J. A., comp. "Gooch, Richard." In their *Alumni Cantabrigiensis, Part 2: 1752–1900*. 6 vols. Cambridge: Cambridge UP, 1947. 3: 78 (col. 2).

Vizetelly, Henry. *Glances Back through Seventy Years*. 2 vols. London: Kegan Paul, Trench, Trübner, 1893.

"The Wandering Piper." *The Sun* May 10, 1834: 3 (col. 1).

Webster's Third New International Dictionary of the English Dictionary, Unabridged. Springfield, MA: Merriam-Webster, 1986.

Weinreb, Ben, and Christopher Hibbert, ed. *The London Encyclopedia*. London: Macmillan, 1983; rpt. Bethesda, MD: Adler & Adler, 1986.

Wheatley, Henry B. *London Past and Present. A Dictionary of Its History, Associations, and Traditions Based upon* The Handbook of London *by the Late Peter Cunningham*. 3 vols. London: John Murray, 1891; rpt. Detroit: Singing Tree P, 1968.

Whitman, Walt. "Song of Myself." In his *Leaves of Grass*." Ed. Sculley Bradley and Harold W. Blodgett. New York: W. W. Norton, 1973. 28–89.

Williams, Edwin, ed. *New York As It Is in 1834*. . . . New-York: J. Disturnell, 1834.

—. *New York As It Is in 1833*. . . . New-York: J. Disturnell, 1833.

Wilson, James Grant, ed. *The Memorial History of the City of New-York, from Its First Settlement to the Year 1892*. 4 vols. New York: New-York History, 1892–1893.

"A Word to Intending Emigrants." *Chambers's Edinburgh Journal* 3.112 (Mar. 22, 1834): 63 (col. 3)–64 (col. 2).

Workers of the Writers Program of the Work Projects Administration for the City of New York, comp. *A Maritime History of New York*. Garden City, NY: Doubleday, Doran, 1941.

NOTES

1. Bibliographies of Anglo-American travel literature sometimes mistakenly include three texts from the years 1833 and 1834 in the list of British travelers' accounts: Grene's *Travels in America . . .* ; C. Colton's *Tour of the American Lakes and among the Indians of the North-West Territory in 1830 . . .* ; and Rich's *A General View of the United States of America. . . .* The first two of these texts were, however, written by Americans, and the third is a tourist and emigrant guidebook rather than a travel account.

The dates of the writer's visit are given in square brackets after the citation when the book itself was published significantly later than the years that are the focus of discussion: 1833 and 1834.

2. Excluded from this list are the following parts of Add. Ms. 2616 in the Cambridge University Library:

Pt. 5. Fols. 138–139. "The People's Book of the Church. By a Layman, etc."

Pt. 5. Fols. 250–285. RG's university lecture notes, annotations on Horace's *Ars Poetica*, and a lengthy essay on tragedy.

Pt. 5. Fols. 266–276. "Copies of College Exami^{n} Papers. Richard Gooch St. John's Coll. Camb. 1823."

Pt. 5. Fols. 277–286. Lecture notes on theology.

Pt. 8. Fols. 1–6; 16–20. A notebook of work-in-progress.

Pt. 8. Fols. 22–95. A loose collection of anecdotes about Oxbridge.

Pt. 8. Fols. 96–111. Early work on *The Cambridge Tart* and some scraps of poetry.

I have excluded this material because it is too ephemeral or fragmentary. Otherwise, the bibliography is exhaustive.

3. With the exception of the long poem "The Triumph of Moscow," I have not cited the individual folios for the poems (and story outline) in Add. Ms. 2616 Pt. 8: fols. 112–199. The sequence of folios seems to be haphazard, and I did not wish to impose the appearance of order where there was none.

4. This ms. appears to be a second draft of two chapters from *America and the Americans*, possibly transcribed for periodical publication.

5. RG appears confused with this sonnet and "The Tears of Virgil." He labels both of them "Sonnet VIII."

6. This work (which is catalogued in the Cambridge University Library as Bbb. 25. 41^{4}) is bound as Chapter 4 of a book entitled *The People or the Peerage?*, introd. by Edward Lytton Bulwer, Esq. (London: Edward Churton, 1835).

7. The titles of the individual volumes differ from each other as well as from the group title. The title of Volume 1 reads: "The British Youth's and Undergraduates' Familiar History of, and

Stranger's Guide to, the University and Town of Cambridge. Descriptive of Their Origin, Antiquities, Colleges, and Public Buildings, and the Peculiar Manners, Customs and Costume of the Former: With Some Useful Hints for Those Who Contemplate Pursuing Their Studies at the University of Cambridge. The Whole Being Brought down to 1833; and Embellished with Drawings, in Lithographs, of the Most Interesting Scenes, Including the New Buildings and Most Recent Improvements." The title to Volume 2 reads: "The British Youths' Familiar History of and Popular Guide to the Town and University of Cambridge: With Many Useful Hints for Those Who Contemplate Pursuing Their Studies thereat."

8. This work appears to be an earlier version of Add. Ms. 2616 Pt. 3.

9. For the early work on this text, see Add. Ms. 2616 Pt. 8: fols. 96–111.

10. Among the books in RG's library sold by Puttick and Simpson, February 5–10, 1847 was Lot no. 870: "Magnet (The)—Juvenile Forget-Me-Not; and 2 others."

11. This work (which is catalogued in the Cambridge University Library as VII. 29. 21^{15}) is bound as part of a volume entitled *Pamphlets & Tracts Medical*, with the only additional information being that it was "bound by Armstrong 12/58."

12. This work is an editorial. It is dated Oxford, Nov. 1834, and was apparently intended for the *Monthly Repository*. There is no indication, however, that it was published by that journal. Mineka's *The Dissidence of Dissent* 400–424 (Appendix: Identification of Authorship, Second Series: 1827–1837) includes no attribution to RG.

13. The title of the poem has been subsequently altered, in a hand that looks like RG's, to read: "An Unsuccessful Poem"! Based on length alone (the poem is 322 lines long), RG obviously worked hard to win the Chancellor's Medal.

14. Part of the ms. of *Facetiae Cantabrigiensis* is contained in Add. Ms. 2616 Pt. 5: fols. 1–63 ("Cantabrigia").

15. RG was "principal compiler" of this work. See his comment in his letter to Sir Robert Peel fols. 232, 234.

16. This work is fragment of a verse play. Its main interest lies in its satiric dedication: "To My Lord Byron in the South!!" Despite the fragment's optimistic title, it does not seem to have been continued.

17. RG published this Letter and the later one under the pseudonym T____.

18. The second volume of this work is entitled "Memoirs of the Professors."

19. "Ambition, or the Retreat from Moscow" is an extract from—or much shortened version of— this poem.

20. How RG came to publish this work in the U.S. is something

of a mystery. Although The Historical Society of Pennsylvania has an extensive and well-catalogued collection of material concerning the publishing house of Carey & Hart, according to Ellen Slack, the Society's Manuscripts and Archives Librarian, no record of correspondence about *Nuts to Crack* has survived. Jim Green, the Curator of Printed Books at the Library Company of Philadelphia, has suggested that as one of the largest publishing companies in the United States at this time, Carey & Hart may simply have offered RG a small sum to reprint *Nuts to Crack*, and have hoped that the interest in all things English would yield them a profit. RG was, of course, apparently in the United States in 1833 and 1834, and may have visited Philadelphia at that time to arrange the deal.

21. This second edition of *Nuts to Crack* is virtually identical to the first. There is now a frontispiece, a slightly altered title, new title-page typography, and nine pages of additional anecdotal material unlisted on the Contents page.

22. Since RG never graduated from Cambridge University and, according to Dorothy Owen, Keeper of the University Archives, "there is no sign that he ever even contemplated graduation" (Letter to the editor), this degree seems more for show than anything else.

23. This work is an outline for a novel on the Fall of Moscow.

24. This is the ms. of the published poem with the same title.

25. Among the books in RG's library sold by Puttick and Simpson, February 5–10, 1847 was Lot no. 856: "Amulet (The), 1829–31; and 1 other."